# THE LEGENDARY
# ST. GEORGE
# AND THE DRAGON

FR. JOSEPH LOJACONO, IVE

# THE LEGENDARY
# ST. GEORGE
# AND THE DRAGON

**IVE Press**
Maryland – 2015

Cover Design
    Leo Winstead
    © IVE Press

*Text*

    © IVE Press, Maryland
        Institute of the Incarnate Word, Inc.
        All rights reserved

Manufactured in the United States of America

IVE Press
    5706 Sargent Road
    Chillum, Maryland 20782


    www.ivepress.com

ISBN: 1-939018-38-2
ISBN-13: 978-1-939018-38-0


Printed in the United States of America

## Acknowledgments

I would like to give thanks to our Lord Jesus Christ, who I came to know through the intercession of the Blessed Virgin Mary, and St. George who in his heroic battle to live virtuously inspired this story. I must also thank those who heroically witnessed to the gospel of life as they stood on the frontlines in the battle for Blessed John Paul II's "culture of life." These heroic witnesses helped inspire this story. In particular, I remember the memory of my sister Kathleen Werner, who was a great example of a wife and mother, who stood for life and emptied herself out for her last child, Micah.

I must also give thanks to those who gave advice to me about the manuscript and helped to edit it. In particular, I want to thank my brother religious in the Institute of the Incarnate Word, Christopher McGlone, David Wiltgen, Sylvia Villarreal, my sister Lara Galbreath, and the Minor seminarians at the Blessed Jose Sanchez Del Rio Minor Seminary in Mankato, Minnesota. Thank you all!

# THE LEGENDARY ST. GEORGE AND THE DRAGON

# Chapter 1

# *A Warrior rises to the challenge*

*O*ur story began in an age long ago when monsters still roamed
the earth, wizards and witches were common, and heroes
fought beast and man with sword and shield…

Rome had sent a legion out from its army to put down barbarians
who were harassing a peaceful village. The praetorian legate, whom
we might call a general today, assembled his officer corp to explain
the situation as they perused a map. "Our scouts inform me that the
barbarian tribe has entrenched itself in this small valley here enclosed
by the river to the North, and the two hills to the West, and the East
and this forest to the South. They have chosen their camp well; our
scouts tell us the river is deep and difficult to ford anywhere in the
valley. To the west and east steep cliffs rise enclosing them more
securely than any fort. They also have archers on its peaks that have
a clear view of the whole valley. Only this forest to the south offers
an unhindered approach for an assault. Apparently, these barbarians
believe the tales of demons in this forest will prevent any possible
assault through the thick forest, for they left it nearly undefended.

The officer corp, made up of prefects, tribunes and centurions,
looked uncomfortable as he spoke about an assault through the
haunted forest. The legate noticed how his officer's eyes turned away
from his sight and noticed them shuffling their feet back and forth.
"I see my officers look disturbed by my plan."

He thus, confronted the head of the cavalry sternly, "Why does
my head of cavalry turn so pale when I ask him to make a simple
charge through a forest?"

"Well, sir. My cavalry have heard the stories of this haunted
forest. They are simple-minded you see. Many of them have been

stationed in this area for a long time and the locals have told them all the tales about this forest. They are a superstitious lot. They don't want to rile up any demons, you see. You have to understand, they carry charms and amulets to protect them from demons and other spirits under their cloaks. They fear the forest too."

"Stories, so what are these stories that puts fear into legionnaires?"

"Well, the locals say that this forest was inhabited by a fierce demon in centuries past. But some visiting chieftain killed him in a great battle. Then the stories go on to detail how the demon's mother tried to avenge her son, but the chieftain killed her.[1] Eventually this chieftain then came back to this same land here and became their King. He died long ago, but ever since then this tribe has reigned over this kingdom."

"What then is the problem? These fleshy demons are dead right?"

"Well, the locals believe that this tribe summoned its own demons when they laid claim to the land and invited them to inhabit the forest here to protect them from invading tribes. They have some god called Mirkaesir who directs these demons. They say anyone who dares enter into this forest without the chieftain's permission is said to be cursed and the demons surely will devour them. None of the locals dare venture into the forest for fear of these demons. Even the chieftain only goes in there once year flanked by a whole core of priests to offer sacrifice to Mirkaesir."

"Enough of these blasted stories! Just drunken tales anyway. Surely, a tribune can lead by example. Just go out there and drive these men right into the forest. Show them the Roman way that fears neither man nor demon."

"Well, sir, I don't want to want to disturb the divine order. I mean we are far from Apollo's realm. Are we so sure our gods will protect us? We might bring down the curse of another god. They say there is a dragon in this area also."

"A dragon, Tribune?"

"Well, yes. They said it mortally wounded the chieftain who killed the demons. They do say that one of his men killed it, but one never knows whether such a beast is really dead."

"So, Tribune, you believe in all of these demons and dragons, also? Ah, the blasted superstition of plebeians! I think our wise Roman philosophers have put the lie to such superstitions as believing in haunted forests or immoral gods. I don't believe any of these fairytales. It is the Roman might and ingenuity that made us great; we should not fear any so called haunted forest. Who will rid us of this unreasoning belief in wandering spirits?

"Tribune, go back and find some hole to hide in. Get out of my sight!"

He then turned to the Tribune of the infantry stating, "You there. Tell me my chief of infantry is not such a scared rabbit. Tell me that my infantry will not cower in fear of superstitious tales. I thought I could trust the mounted cavalry who fears no men of foot; I see now my trust was misplaced. Tell me you will lead the charge into this blasted forest showing the whimpering cavalry who are the real stalwart men in our army?"

"Well sir, the peditatus fear the forest also. I have noticed that many of them keep idols of the local gods under their armor for protection such as Artemis, Fauna and some add Thor. They even have a name for this forest. I must say I don't blame them; the forest is thick and nearly impenetrable. I don't know how one could wield a spear in it. Demons or no demons I think my infantry would draw back in fear."

Sarcastically the Legate said, "Well, you better run and hide too and run fast because I tell you Orcus, that god of cowardly soldiers may be in hot pursuit."

The legate then in exasperation at the cowardice of his officers raced out of tent and called out to all the assembled soldiers, "Hear me good men. I need everyone's attention. My officers have failed me. Therefore, I need a leader who will take up a charge, someone courageous, who will not shrink from our duty as Roman legionaries.

*I have been told* that there are many cowards amongst us. *I have been told* that a few tales about demons, curses and a dragon are putting fear into a mighty Roman legion. I, however, do not believe that such tales could scare any Roman army. In all my years, I have never seen a Roman legion balk at a battle with any barbarian tribe. Now I ask for a leader, someone who does not fear any supposed demon or barbarian sword. Who amongst you will lead us through this forest showing the world the Roman army fears no army, demon or even a dragon if it should appear?"

There was silence for a moment. Then a courageous young man from the ranks of the cavalry trotted out. He was stout in appearance, but a bit fair-faced, a young looking soul. "I will Legate. I will lead the charge into this forest. I am not afraid of any demons, curses, or dragon. Let us be at it and we will show those barbarians oppressing those poor people that Rome is not made of cowards."

The Legate looked him over. He looked to be a fair-looking young man about six foot tall, well built, a man who held himself well looking of confidence. Yet, the Legate wanted to test him. "Who do you think you are rushing forward so quickly? Are you looking for glory on some fool-hardy adventure?"

"No sir, I am just responding to your call to duty. Obedience and discipline are the Roman way. I stand obedient and ready at your command."

The prefect pondered this response for a few seconds taking it in. He thought to himself, "He does not have an air of cockiness, but rather of calm assurance. There is something about him that is different, yes something…"

Then, he noticed his shield indicating Constantine's cross insignia, shining bright red in the rising sun. This was familiar to him, but he wished to inquire further.

"Legionnaire what is your name?"

"I am called George."

"You ride under Constantine's personal insignia. Did you ride with him then or do you really believe in that sign that he was said to see in a vision?"

"Legate, I did ride with Constantine's cavalry, but I use this insignia not just the honor of it, but because I truly believe that the god it represents is the one true God, Jesus Christ my Lord."

"A Christian, ah! Well George, I see you are stouthearted and not afraid of these tales as my officers are. Thus, I name you centurion and give you charge over the eastern cohort of cavalry. Now lead my army through this forest to the glory of Rome."

Without any more hesitation, George turned about and called out to the cohort now under his command. "Fear nothing. The true God leads us." He then charged in alone without looking to see if anyone was following.

His amazed cohort of cavalry, seeing the fearlessness of their new centurion, all at once seemed to gain courage as they sensed that some supernatural power was mysteriously watching over him. A few seconds later a few brave cavalry rushed into the forest. After a minute or so, the rest of the cavalry took up the charge inspired by the spirit of this fearless centurion. Then the ground rumbled and the forest almost seemed to bend back a little as the mass of cavalry and soldiers surged into its dark folds.

A few hours later, George and the cavalry emerged on the other side of the forest descending on the unsuspecting barbarians, who were completely shocked to see an attack emerging through the haunted forest. However, their chieftain regained enough composure to act. He seized hold of their most prized possession, a sword that was said to have a killed fearsome female demon and rallied his tribe to him as he called out, "Geats, remember your gods. Behold their gift, the giant's sword, Nagelring. It will lead us."

He then led the counter attack driving at the charging cavalry. George seeing this, raced at him leading with his lance and pinned the left shoulder of this would be hero. The blow threw the chieftain to the ground, who still managed somehow to hold onto his precious sword. George then circled back as he saw the chieftain trying to struggle back to his feet and quickly dismounted laying a firm blow to the chieftain's wounded shoulder driving him back to the ground. Then George quickly moved to pin the chieftain down stepping on his wounded right arm before he could get to his feet. Still the chieftain held firmly his precious sword as his arm lay pinned to a rock face. George then struck at the sword laying flush against the rock and broke it near the hilt.

The chieftain seeing his sword shattered called out, "Nagelring has failed me. How is this possible? What magic is this that can overcome the forest demons of Mirkaesir and destroy such a sword?"

Seeing the anguish in the face of the chieftain, George knew then that the Roman legion had triumphed. The rest of the tribe then dropped their weapons in despair seeing their precious sword shattered and their chief pinned to the ground. They fell to the ground in anguish burying their heads in their arms as if it trying to hide their shame, for it seemed to them that their gods were no more. Utterly triumphant, the Roman legion simply needed to herd them into a holding pin, as the fighting ended abruptly right then.

The villagers raced up to George, wanting to herald their savior. Seeing the insignia on his shield, they recognized him as a Christian. One villager called out, "Good Christian you freed us. We thank your god for sending you. The Geats were starving us and raping our women."

"And driving our cattle into that fearful forest where no one would follow. You however, charged through that black forest. You had not fear. Surely, you are a great warrior. You easily destroyed their magic sword, Nagelring. Truly, your god was watching over you."

"A giant among men."

"Mightiest of warriors."

With bright eyes a village elder approached George, "Please Christian, come now and rule over us as our King that we may have the courage to live without fear as you do, men living in freedom body and soul."

George's heart went out to these people that he could see were besieged for a very long time. However, he knew he could not be anyone's savior and thus could never fulfill the role they were asking of him. He paused then reflecting for a moment on how to reply and said, "My good men, you do not need me to be your King in order to live without fear. Accept Christ as your true Lord. He will show you the one true God, the creator of heaven and earth. Through him you will learn true freedom that no marauding tribe can take away from you."

The elder replied, "Hmm, so the power is in your faith. We have to learn more about this. I hear that you have a baptism that makes you a Christian. I will recommend all my villagers to accept this baptism. If it can make you so courageous, it can make us strong like you. Please, though you do not accept our offer, pray for us that we may understand this Christian god that you speak about."

"Of course, I will pray for you and ask the Lord that the peace of Christ remain with this land."

George was reflecting on this encounter as he trotted away saying silently saying to the Lord, "I see Lord their proposal was only a temptation from the world to become a false idol for people. I know this is not your way, but Lord what do you want me to do?" He continued to ponder this thought the rest of the day and into the night.

The next day, as the legate who was surveying the remains of the battlefield, he came across George. "Well you certainly showed your worth in this battle. Son, I could use a good tribune like you. Men like you are hard to find. I could really use you as a leader of my cavalry, for I am sure to run into more of these barbarian hordes. Would you campaign with me as I head north?"

"I appreciate the offer legate, but I have papers releasing me for a sabbatical to pursue some personal business."

"A sabbatical? You showed your steel as a soldier today. You could really advance quickly in the emperor's army with more displays like that. Oh how Roman the legion could use more leaders like you. What are you shying away now?"

"No, sir, that is not it. I feel, well that I have another battle to fight."

"Another battle, for some vagabond noblemen looking to hire private troops?"

"No, no,. nothing like that. Well, I guess it is more of a calling. This battle today has convinced me that I am called to battle for God somehow…"

"So, it is a religious battle of some kind, like Hercules or something. I saw through your actions today that you are a man of determination. In my experience, even mighty generals can't easily shake men like you. I knew a man like you when I was a youth. He was the best swordsmen I had ever seen, but he was not satisfied with just training his body to master some art. One day he noticed clouds peaking down from Mount Olympia as we campaigned near Greece. He insisted on climbing the heights to know what mystical thing was peering down that day. I did not understand it then. I campaigned with him for a few years and seemed like he was always running off whenever he happened upon some story of a mystical mountain or cove. I was always warning him against this. One day he just got up and left, saying, he was called to go off to the desert to find the god that was calling him. I tried to persuade him that we needed good swordsmen like him, but he just dropped his sword right then and there and left. I never saw him again."

"I don't understand this spirit that drives you, but I know by experience I can't defeat it. Go off and pursue your religious mission. You have my leave to go where you will."

"May your god lead you to what are you looking for. Who knows maybe someday I too will come to believe in this Christ whom you believe to be your true Lord. A god that gives such courage in the face of unknown demons can truly bring much virtue to this rickety old Roman Empire. Maybe someday they will tell stories about you also in legendary tales as they do about Hercules and those other figures you hear about."

# Chapter 2

# *A Kingdom without gods*

*M* *eanwhile, in a distance land, another battle was taking place for the soul of a kingdom now long since forgotten.* The wandering of our hero would in time lead him to this kingdom but he knew this not. The kingdom was located in the south of the continent surrounded by three empires all of whom at one time had controlled the area through conquest. Emperors had fought over the territory and much blood had been shed in centuries past. The Greeks, the Romans and Visigoths had all called the land theirs. For generations great armies had ravaged the land, scouring the fields, leaving the people to grope like animals just to survive.

In many respects, the people of the land were much like that of other peoples. Their religion was like that of most kingdoms in antiquity. They supposed that either fire or wind or swift air, or the circle of the stars, or turbulent water, or the luminaries of heaven were the gods. In delight of the beauty of these things, they assumed them such.[2] What distinguished this land, however, was the abundance of wild animals that plagued the territory. None of the priests or wizard's spells seemed able to subdue them making it a wild land to live in. Foreign tribes, who arrived from the sea, decimated the land in centuries past, putting the lie to their gods who they thought were their protectors.

In time, the people of the land recognized all these "gods" to be just wooden statues as the Greeks tore through their lands. For a while, they then followed the Greek pantheon of gods as the people came to admire the wisdom of Hellenistic sages and took on the Greek way of living. Following the example of the Greek gods, they indulged in all sorts of intrigue and indulgence. Likewise, when the

Romans conquered them later they also imitated the stories they heard of fratricide and infidelity among these divine beings. No god, Persian, Greek, or Roman seemed able to help them though as droughts and disease continually struck their land. The people, remembering the failure of their gods through the centuries, looked mockingly at their wooden gods and despised their priests who could not overcome their woes. In rage and despair, the people came to call their kingdom Terrasindei, which means "a land without gods."

Finally, after ages of darkness a light shined through to this people giving them hope. A new religion had come to drive out the despair of the false gods. The people eagerly embraced the hope of Christ in the face of the slavery to gods who they could never seem to please. Peace too finally seemed to come to the land as they accepted this new faith. They then started to mark their days from the birth of their new found Lord.

When our story begins, the land was enjoying this peace, a free land subject to no one, civilized and long since loosed from the subjection of pagan beliefs. For more than a century, people had enjoyed peace, expecting it now as a birthright, while the land grew rich and life became comfortable. People now heard talk of war only in old stories mixed in with tales about monsters, told by men who had travelled to distant lands. For the nobles were now all Christian, having given up their empty gods to follow the one true God and they had long since driven off any wild beasts. The people marked the year now from the birth of their Savior Jesus Christ, more than three hundred years before this time. The days of Roman conquest seemed to be far out of people's minds. Now Terrasindei was left in peace an independent state not subject to anyone. The land too seemed to prosper; green foliage ran through most of the wide-open plains where once great forests were. Farmers tilled the open fields left after the Roman Empire had scoured the forests for fuel and they found the soil was fertile. Thus, farmers prospered, the families grew big and fat, and the merchants started to multiply. Men had become virtuous welcoming the poor, taking care of the abandoned, and defending the weak; they taught their boys to be stouthearted and their young men and girls to be bastions of purity. Therefore, over time the land grew rich through the virtue of man's labor.

The great city at the heart of the kingdom, Valde Venalicium, dominated over the whole kingdom in its influence and grandeur. From the city, one could see the whole of the kingdom, as it was set on a wide bluff above vast plains that opened up all around it. The King's great palace was at the highest point on a small hill jetting up in the center of the bluff. From this palace, the King could just make out the tops of the mountains in the far west and see some of the rock outcroppings that spotted the plains to the east. The archbishop's cathedral, dedicated to St. Michael the Archangel, was set below the palace, making it a prominent reminder of God's providence upon the land. Dusty roads spiraled out from the great cities connected it to a few stone cobble throughways the "highways" of their time. The kingdom as a whole was small by our standards today. Outside of Valde Venalicium there were many small villages that served as centers of trade for the numerous small farms that dotted the countryside. There was one great see or diocese as we may call it, where the archbishop resided and many smaller sees in outlying villages where bishops of lesser significance resided. The land and the kingdom seemed a pleasant place, peaceful and prosperous.

Yet not all was perfect in this seemingly idyllic land, for the passions continued to rage on in man's hearts and the enemy of man's soul was ever ready to take advantage of these weaknesses. In the streets, one could hear the murmuring sound of the beginning of sin. The marketplace was full of these murmurings, a place where people came to trade, hear the latest news, listen to political speeches, barter stories and sometimes sells their souls for passing treasures. Looking around, one could see the various merchants with their tables set up along the street calling out with their favorite slogans trying to entice people to look at their products. At the first booth, one could see a man peddling fresh red apples. He smiled contently as he arranged them. Next to him, a man was selling garlic dangling from a line, calling out, "Good for cooking and curing many diseases."

To the left, an entertainer tried to woo a crowd as he played the clown juggling various items. The choices in the marketplace seem endless and the calls of the merchants to sell their products made a constant buzz in the background. Passing through this scene one could hear a boy screeching in the streets, "Give me candy! I want some. I want some. Give it to me or I will scream all the way to the market."

The embarrassed parents quickly bought something for the boy saying, "Here take this and shut up. Stop embarrassing us."

A merchant observing this was disturbed but remained silent until the child left. Then he whispered to his assistant, "What a scene. Don't these parents have any sense? They just give the little urchins whatever they want, not disciplining them or nothing. Oh yeh, I see many of them. They see something they want and cry until they get it and the parents just give in."

He then drew closer to his assistant and whispered, "That is why I always keep the candy in a prominent place. Cause I know, if the kids see it they will throw a fit until they get it. So, I will sell more, you see."

A young girl passing through the marketplace playfully picked up a ripe fruit while she stole glances at passing young men. She smiled as she was caught drinking in the sight of a handsome young man strolling by. Their eyes met and she noticed the young man also was looking her over. Without shame, she slipped the fruit into the fold of her dress while the merchant was looking away and meandered over to meet the young man presenting her stolen fruit to him as she batted her eyes. "I see you were admiring the fruit from afar."

They both knew what she meant. The young man was not at all taken back by this introduction for many a young woman spoke this way in his day. He replied with a coy smile as he took the fruit from the girl "Perhaps, your fruit is too expensive. Maybe I can shop elsewhere."

The girl, however, like a good marketer pursued him more aggressively, "Oh, the fruit is no charge. What is given secretly is mine to give and I have much more like this. Come with me I can show you how ripe this fruit is. Come with me and we can dance all night together smashing the ripe fruits under our feet. Oh how much fun we will have. Come let us flee this dull place."

The girl then took the boy by the hand and urged him to follow her into dark alley. The boy feigned a little fight before playfully giving in. He threw the fruit on the ground for it to waste away as she pulled him into the darkness of the alley. Few in the market took any notice of this considering such happenings as "part of how life is today."

Passing right through the busy scene one could see an old frail woman strolling in a slightly hunched manner, but in some mysterious way striking a noble stature. She took note of everything around her as she made her way through the street with a measured pace, quietly plodding along. She seemed to command respect even if few gave her much regard. Few dared to make eye contact with her even as all noticed her. She was said by some to be 300 years old, others say older. All knew of her, but nobody ever remembered her being young. She seemed in some way to have always been making her way through the streets, a quite presence always there though rarely recognized, like one's conscience shaping one's values that everyone takes for granted. Maria was her name, Star of the Sea, through which the wind brings new tidings and holds onto old familiar scents.

Maria was talking to a young man as she walked along. "Deary, see those children prancing around their parents like flies around rotten food? It is terrible how little respect they show to their parents; it will be the downfall of this kingdom. I tell you, there used to be great men in our kingdom. Oh, yes great men. They fought off tyrants and respected God and King, but I tell you those days have passed. Now they mock heroes. And look at these young women today, "girls" I should call them, for they don't mature. They are so bold with the young men, not respecting themselves. I tell you they have lost any sense of shame. Don't they have any respect?"

The young man looked a little cross as he was only half listening to her and responded shyly, "Hmmff. Really."

Maria continued, "And where do people go on Sundays around here? You won't find them in Church, that's for sure. They are too busy making money and keeping their stores open. It is 'almighty money' that rules everything now."

The young man looked now more attentively at Maria trying to show a little sense of respect as he said, "But, Maria. Don't you think people are just kind of busy today? I mean there are so many things you can do now on weekends with entertainment and family activities. I don't think they are *intentionally* trying to push God to the side. I mean these store owners they are just trying to make a living. It's tough today and if people will buy things on Sunday, why not?"

"Young man don't you understand, people have become slaves to it all. Oh yeh, they feel they have to make a little more money on Sundays to survive. What they say is that they don't trust the Lord will take of their needs? They don't trust that if they keep holy the Lord 's Day, He will take care of their material needs. Instead, they push aside Sunday worship and force their employees to work these days or else. Thus, everyone becomes slaves to the *market*.

I tell you men do not give the best to the Lord anymore. No, they only *fit him into their schedule*; when *it's convenient for them*. Oh my, if the Lord were to treat them like they treat Him, there would be a lot of things falling apart in the world. Yep, I tell you the order of the universe would fall apart; the stars would fall from the skies and the sun would never rise. For, I guess our Lord might only keep with these things *when it was convenient*. And many of these people can't even give him one hour on Sundays, let alone the whole day. How merciful the Lord is, how merciful."

"But, Maria that's just how things are today."

"Young man, you may think I am behind the times, but I tell you I see everything. Mark my words this kingdom is in for a shaking up.

I say my prayers every day that the Lord will have mercy on Terrasindei, but I know His mercy is not endless. He is a good Father, but a good father will not let his children run around playing with snakes else they will soon get bitten. No, he will discipline them and teach them to stay away from such dangerous things and He will do it in His own way.

"What do you mean, *His own way*?"

"Well, you see there used to be lions around here that did it."

"Lions, what in the world do lions have to do with anything?"

"Well they used to roam around here you see, not many of them, and they were hard to spot, but they were here. I tell you they were always prowling around looking for an easy prey to devour.[3] They seemed to like children most of all, but they got young men and women like you also who were not careful."

"That's a rather gory story Maria. So, how come we don't see them anymore?"

"Well, when this kingdom turned toward Christ, them lions they fled. Oh, the spirit of Christ scared them away. They could not feed on flesh around here anymore, so they went prowling somewhere else. I think though that those lions are not so far away from us yet. You stay awake and vigilant."

The young man squinted his eyes in a puzzled look trying to understand what seemed "weird logic" to him. After a few seconds, he muffled back, "Oh, whatever."

"Oh, I see you don't believe me, but I tell you it was true. I remember clearly. My memory has not failed me. Oh how horrible it was to see those children devoured by the lions. It was not so long ago either. And it was Christ's spirit that drove them off. I am sure of it. So, you better be wary these beasts or something worse could come roaming back into our kingdom. Stay close to Christ then he will protect you from any beast."

"Okay, Maria, whatever you say."

This young man, like other young people of his day, did not give such frightful stories much credence. The young people continued to pursue any entertaining thought that came their way. In the name of "rebelling against their parents," they even went out of their way to find the beasts that their grandparents had said "were driven out of the kingdom."

Finding these beasts for them was a wild adventure, something exotic, the likes of which they had never seen. After many reports about their whereabouts, they even developed a twisted game of thrill. First, a maiden would playfully run into the dark forest in the sight of a young man. After a while, the young man would gleefully follow. Then the maiden would run until she spotted a wild beast and playfully dance near it fawning as if it were attacking her. As part of the ritual, the young man was then to proudly race to her rescue. It was a dangerous game and one that sometimes left the young maidens injured or worst. Eventually their parents came to learn about these games. However, when parents warned young people about the dangers of this game they would reply, "Oh, it is so thrilling, so awesome, the danger is part of what makes it exciting."

The parents not wanting to appear as prudes, just shrugged their shoulders and replied, "Well, what can you do? This is what all the young people are doing today. It is just youth playing games."

Still, they gave their young free reign to roam the streets indulging in whatever pleasure crossed their mind, coming home only when their purse ran empty. Manners started to decay, which was justified because everyone was having fun. The parents only seem concerned when their children sometimes came home with not just bloody knees, but mortal injuries. Even then they would console themselves by making up stories "about how their Michael, did not really know what he was doing" or "how their Felicity was just too young to understand what she was doing."

Often when inevitably, the worst happened and a beast mortally injured a young person, the parents, instead of repenting, would wail at the wind and make poems about the darkness. In time parents and other concerned adults, wanting to protect the children, gave the youth sharp knives instructing them to use them if necessary to fight off wild beasts. They would explain it to them saying, "I know many young people like to play with beasts in dark forests, these days. Take this just in case you need it. You may want to fool around with these beasts sometimes. This at least will give you a little protection."

Parents convinced themselves this was the best way to protect the youth rationalizing, "There have always been wild animals in the forests. Kids will always find such beasts. What can we do, but give them a little protection."

Soon nearly every youth carried such a dagger, which became a fashionable accessory that boys especially liked to show off to each in secret. The youth then came to believe in the power of these daggers and even sought more opportunities to put them to use. Thus, contrary to the intentions of their parents, more youth entered into the dangerous games of baiting the beast and the beast mortally wounded more youth as a result. Meanwhile, the parents bewailed their loss, but still not repenting called for training for the youth on how to use these daggers to fend off a beast.

The beasts though would not follow the youth into the heart of Terrasindei for the land was dry. A drought was upon the land, as all life-giving water had seemed to depart from Terrasindei. To the residents, it seemed that even the water had been pulled out of the air. People could feel the dryness on their tongue when they stuck it out. The drought then became the preoccupation of the minds of men so that they called it the great drought. They complained to each other, "This drought is killing us. We cannot grow anything. Now look even the tourists are staying away from our festivals for dry air stifles the festive mood."

They could not see it was the disordered hearts of men causing the dryness on the edges of men's tongues. Nor could they discern the darkness that was settling in above them just out of the sight of men. What they did not foresee was that some beasts do not need water to survive and thrive when there is dryness in men's hearts. In time, the merchants with their ingenuity found ways to channel water from hidden springs and divert rivers at the borders to supplement the demands of the market. No force of nature would stop them from getting their products to market.

However, the drought of soul continued. People started to grow tired of family devotions while their children played merrily in the streets. People came to forget Christmastide; they reduced Easter to just one day and saw Advent and Lent as just days leading to the next party. However, feasts continued unabated, for birthdays, for friends from out of town, for starting a new job or even when their children seemed bored in the long summer days. Yet, the parties all seemed so dull now; they were a labor to organize and a relief for the host when they were over. They soon then forgot the feasts of old, looking upon baptism as just another party and weddings as celebrations of their beautiful lives. They indulged every desire of their children by giving them fine clothes, toys of all kinds and allowance to play as long as they wanted. For they said, "All is plentiful. What prude would deny their children anything? Besides, the children get upset when I deny them what they want. It is such a pain to hear their moans."

Parents also, with faces painted like adults, vied with their children to be the best at the games of youth. Old age was something they despised. In the market, one could hear the calls of merchant selling their wares to these adults with painted faces. One called out to a middle-aged mother, "I have oils that will give you that sparkle of youth again like a sixteen year old fresh and ready to be kissed. Never let them call you an old maid. Be worthy of yourself. These lotions and oils will turn away the wrath of Morta and bring you the favor of Venus."

Another called out to a slightly balding man, "I have an elixir that will make you strong as Hercules. Look now I can sell you this and throw in the ancient secrets of the diets of gods that will make you live for centuries."

When the fun ended and parenthood bore down upon them, they drank potions that kept them from having to worry more about the troublesome little ones. They even made books of recipes to pass on medicines of sterility,[4] so they could carry on with their merry ways without having to worry about little urchins that might hamper their fun. The young intoxicated by these potions, came to delay their marriages so they could continue their fun into the twilight. Men and women in their twenties often joked declaring they would never take on the chains of wedded life and that they wanted to remain free "to do what I want."

Later when the fun-loving women reached middle age, they often could be seen desperately running after witchdoctors looking for some elixir that would restore the lost fertility of their youth. Such was the sad state to which people had reduced themselves.

There was still hope in the kingdom for not all joined in the dance of merry indulgence forgetting the way of virtue. Old graying grandmothers, slow in movement but keen with intuition, sharpened by the trials of child bearing and homemaking, had quick eyesight that saw what was upon the kingdom. Here and there, an old grandmother would pipe up to her grandchildren. "Now listen up little one. The way you behave is not of the Lord!"

While others were heard to say, "Only the fool follows the way of sloth."

Another scolded her grandchild, "Tsk, tsk. Do you have to take honey with everything? Don't you know if you eat only sweet things you will grow fat and indulgent? Then you will never be able to say 'no' to anything."

These noble women scolded the little ones staring down at their own children, who were the parents of the little troublemakers. They would say, "How can you let your children run around like little dogs yelping wherever they want? Train them in discipline or else they will forget you in old age."

The parents, however, just rolled their eyes and secretly complained to each other out of the hearing of the elders, "How tiresome my mother has become. I love her, but really, I think she is losing her mind always complaining about everything. She just doesn't understand how people live today."

A few devout men also railed against what they saw. One bemoaned, "Have our youth become like wolves that they devour whatever they please?"

Another urged his pastor, "Father you should rebuke these parents today. Their children are no better than little demons. Whatever happened to discipline?"

A small cadre of courageous men even tried to speak out making bold and strident orations against the decaying society they saw before them. Their leader Cholorus one day clamored to the top of a merchant's roof and exclaimed, "Our kingdom is decaying. It is rotten to the core. The people in Terrasindei are becoming slaves to drunken parties. Our children run around like little demons. And what do they really learn in school anymore? They know well how to entertain themselves and the names of all the feasts, even how to make a foreigner welcome during these pagan festivals.

I ask though, can we build a kingdom on such material? Will such as these defend our lands in times of battle?"

However, the typical pattern of reaction took hold of the crowd. One man whispered to another, "I hate these religious zealots who were trying to tell everybody what to do. They are making like new Caesars."

Another whispered back, "Oh, yeh, they are just trying to prop up the rich Church that is trying to push its teachings on us. I tell you Jesus never would say things like this. They have distorted the true teachings of Jesus to prop up their power."

Another chimed in, "I heard all the priests in the churches are really fooling around doing all kinds of terrible things with women and children. I would not trust any of my children to them."

Eventually, the campaign of slander spread amongst many of those assembled so that a few old scurrilously false slurs were repeated and a few new legends were created. Soon the murmuring of the crowd spilled over into violence as they took to shouting down every word Chlorus tried to say. Then the crowd not satisfied simply to censor his words from public oration, took to picking up broken jars, rocks and whatever they could find to pelt him. The worried merchant seeing the angry crowd assembled in front of his store, sought to take hold of Chlorus by his feet and drag him from their rooftops without even giving him a warning. As Chlorus' face slammed against the hard shale of the roof, the crowd cheered and jeered at him twisting *what was really happening*, "Look, he can't even stand by his own power."

"Ah yes, the ground despises him too. It is decaying before his feet."

"He is just one of those drunken people that goes to church all the time. They are drunk with their own delusions and now he falls because he has drunk too much."

As the merchant finally pulled Chlorus off the rooftop with the help of the excited mob they continued to jeer. As the bruised man finally made it back to his feet, he felt the crowd pushing him backward yelling and screaming at him, "Get out of here and take your delusions of power with you."

"We don't want your kind around here."

Chlorus usually a feisty soul, seeing that he was defeated cowered away never again venturing to make such public orations.

In Valde Venalicium the good Archbishop Sanitus also spoke up. Disturbed by the reports he heard about the behavior of the youth and the persecution of good souls, he sought to teach patiently the way of the Lord. He perceived that trouble was crouching at the door desiring to enslave the land.[5] Preaching from the seat of the cathedral he tried to address the whole kingdom saying, "Sons and daughters of God do not forget your heavenly Father and the true home to which you are called. As our ancient scriptures say, 'Stand by the roads, and look, and ask for the ancient paths, where the good way is; and walk in it, and find rest for your souls.'[6] Take this as a calling to come back to *His ways*. Give up your empty parties; seek the joy of the Lord. Do not return to the worship of Pan or Aphrodite like the unknowing pagans of old. Come instead to the feast of the Lord who brings you true peace. Christ has invited you to a greater banquet than the pagan festivals. Do not partake of the food of demons when you can partake of the food of angels. I tell you, 'he who has been willing to joke with the Devil will not be able to rejoice with Christ.'[7]"

On another occasion, he tried to explain to them with a pastor's heart where their actions were leading. "Your drunkenness leads to indulgence, indulgence to debauchery, debauchery to degradation and degradation to slavery to your passions. Those who follow this path start with the trifle of vile dancing, then seek fornication, then turn from the natural to the unnatural, and finally end even in relations with beasts. Return to reason; do not become slaves to your passions."

To the people these words seemed to be lost in the blowing winds. Nevertheless, as a good servant of God the archbishop continued calling out for reform and renewal. He preached to families saying, "Raise your children in the household of God. Teach them discipline, order, virtue and train them in prayer. Do not turn your back to the calling of parenthood by taking the sorcerer's potions that treat motherhood like a disease. Do not give into your lusts and turn marriage into prostitution. Rather, trust in God's providence and seek instead the grace of the Lord that you may give yourself in a godly way to your spouse as Christ did for his bride the Church."

He tried to instill in them a love for the blessing of children, not as burdens, but joys to encounter. He explained, "Seek the blessings of God through children. Remember a child not born is a jewel not found. Take hold of these precious jewels and display them brightly. How we wish to adorn our Churches with these precious gems. Let us fill our temples with fine ornaments of faithful souls who we have trained in virtue. We can trust then that we are helping to populate heaven."

However, few in the streets seemed to pay heed to his call. In a square outside the Church, one could hear men discussing the archbishop's appeal, "Ah did you hear what that stuffy old bishop said now? He said we are no good parents and make our wives prostitutes. I think he wants to make this kingdom into a tyranny, which he runs."

Another man waiting outside the Church while his wife attended Church responded, "Really, I am through with this religion. I hear in other countries that they have gods who enjoy parties, drinking and fine food. I think these parties sound a lot more fun than this old fool. Come with me to the tavern."

Another young man who had just been to the Cathedral with his family saw a young woman as he was exiting the Church. "Heh, how is it going?" She called out to him with a coy smile.

The boy smiled back and slowed his pace trying to avoid the eyes of his parents responding, "Well, you know okay. I was just in Church, listening to that old rag, the archbishop. He was saying like he always does that we should not fool around."

The girl drew closer to him and brushed her hand on his face. "Oh, how I like your face. It is so fine. Don't listen to that archbishop. He is so old fashion. He would not know a good time or *fine* music if he heard it. I could show you a good time."

"Oh really, show me. I want to get away from this stuffy atmosphere."

Thus, it was that they dismissed him as if he were an old fool; a man who did  not understand the modern times they lived in. Nor did they listen to the old women who shook their heads in disapproval as the young walked by. They said to themselves, "All is fun and games. These old people take things so seriously." Thus, by their actions, they proclaimed that they will not walk the way of the Lord.[8]

Despite the efforts of the good archbishop, the passions came to be crowned with glory in Terrasindei. In celebration of these passions the people multiplied festivals: one for Bacchus to celebrate the wares of the winemakers, one for Flora that the florists may benefit from the pull of young love, one for Proserpine to indulge in the selling of fear and death, and a grand one for Plutus that the land may be fertile produce much bounty.

The merchant guilds also turned from saintly patrons to profane deities. They did not consider them real religious patrons, but symbols of their sophistication. Thus, the ironsmiths adopted Hades as their symbol that they may be inspired to work hard, and the shoemakers chose Zeus, who they said must have had big shoes and the flower girls chose Aphrodite hoping all would be under the spell of sweet smelling flowers.

The young people too started to invent new amusements treating the champions of these games as gods, which they cast in immortal bronze. Soon this pantheon of new gods became quite large, while worship of the true God declined. They took from among themselves the most beautiful and gave them the best places at their parties for their fine telling of stories. They made the search for fun and indulgence a business. They sought out young women and even boys who would become slaves to the passions of men for a few dollars. The kingdom became known wide and far as a place for merriment, so that many came from far-away lands to join in the celebrations. Yet, in all this, they never satisfied their lust for pleasure but longed for more.

Archbishop Sanitus upon seeing this preached more loudly and condemned these revived pagan celebrations. He strove against the excessive displays of the storytellers and tried to turn men back from their prowling for pleasure. He even went into the streets railing against the festivals and causing commotion among the dealers. He called men to turn back to true devotion to God and base their celebrations on worship of Him. He urged families to come together in prayer and stay close to their children. He called upon couples to seek the blessing of the priest for their marriages.

He further started societies of dedicated Christians who went out into the public square and rescued those who had become slaves to society's passions. He made houses for the poor in the sight of the rich. He lifted up those who were unloved turning them from the love of trinkets to love of God. He sought to revive the pure festivals of Christ, Mary and the saints calling on all men to give charitably in celebration of these holy days. These actions, however, enraged the merchants, who said he drove off the foreign visitors and dirtied the look of their fine markets by the presence of the poor nearby.

The merchants upon seeing this conspired against the archbishop whispering threatening words into the King's ear. "This man of God is undermining your authority. He is claiming to be the voice of the people. When, really, you are their voice. If you let this continue, the people will think the archbishop runs the kingdom and not you. Listen now do we not support your coffers with our fine wares? This archbishop must learn that antiquated morality cannot come in the way of the progress of our kingdom. We should be a free people and he holds us in slavery. Archbishop Sanitus is completely unreasonable, insane in his preaching. He is destroying everything. He must go."

King Felix listened fearfully knowing the merchant's wealth supported his throne. He turned to his advisors for counsel. Secretly they too enjoyed the fine pleasures plentiful in the kingdom and did not want to dry up the flow of their wine. Thus, the advisors and merchants conspired together to persuade the King that he must act. His advisors recommended to the King, "Follow the words of the merchants. They have the reins of power and wealth in this kingdom. If we lose them we lost everything."

The King doubtful, however, turned toward his scholars. One eager young scholar piped up, "Oh good King, yes, yes, you must act. I tell you this is part of remaking the kingdom into the great kingdom it should be."

"What do you mean *remaking the kingdom?*"

Another jumped in, "Well you see sire, we want to make this kingdom into a beacon for mankind."

"*A beacon for mankind!* What does this have to do with how I treat the archbishop?"

One old scholar then jumped in, "Let me tell you what they mean. You see there was once a great city, a city on the coast that the whole world admired. The people built it up as technological marvel;

there was no religion, but the religion of man. Everything was in harmony as they all saw each other as one with the earth and the heavens.

This city was a true vision of beauty for all mankind. Alas, the city was destroyed and many have forgotten its greatness. However, its memory has been recorded in the reminiscence of man, a dim image of what was, lost in the clouds of time. We can resurrect this memory, make it new and better."

The King listened politely but had a puzzled look on his face. He squinted one eyebrow up and replied, "Hmm, okay. So, I guess you are favor of getting rid of this archbishop also."

The King looked at his scholars and then back at his advisors who were also close by. He felt his mind being squeezed as if under pressure as he peered at both groups around him. His thoughts became clouded and he felt he could no longer take the pressure. Finally, he said, "Well, I don't understand all of this. I mean I am a Christian and everything, fighting an archbishop doesn't make any sense to me, but I guess you all are in agreement. Maybe it will help to make some great kingdom as you say. I don't know if it will or not, but you may do what you want with the archbishop. Only leave my name out of it. I don't want to seem to be against religion, but this bishop seems to be giving us a lot of trouble. If only we could get him to calm down or get another bishop in here, I guess things would be better."

The King's advisors took his comment as permission to drive the archbishop out of the kingdom. The young scholars were the first to jump into action possessed as they were with a fire to change the society. They went to and fro running up and down the streets of the kingdom[9] shouting, "Freedom! Freedom! Freedom! It is time to break free from the tyranny of the iron hand that oppresses us. It is time to throw out the voice that persecutes us. Let us drive from our midst the one that shames our wives and makes fun of our children. Down with the bishop and his tired condemnations! Let us make man free to fulfill himself, follow his dreams and live in peace."

The King's advisors then sent out spokesmen through the entire kingdom to paint fine pictures in the minds of men of a future free from woe. With great swaths of rhetoric, they marked off the focal points of their great masterpiece. They drew the eye of the soul to focus on images of great festivals, where there was an overflowing table of plenty; where all were happy and enjoying themselves as they gorged on the delights before them. They sketched images around the table of master and slave delighting together and even the dogs lapping up happily the left over remains. The wild dreamers became popular and men flocked attentively to hear them relate descriptions of their visions. People flocked to them and soon their disciples started to openly mock the archbishop. Comedians, too, took to the dream making fun of the bishop with gross imitations of him and "respected" men told jokes about the bishop's instability.

Meanwhile, the King remained aloof while his "enlightened" scholars stirred up the people to oppose the archbishop. One of the King's few faithful advisors, Fidelus, tried to get his attention, "Your Highness, have you seen how they are mocking the archbishop. Some young scholars are getting people all excited. They are openly making fun of him in the street. It is getting really bad. I think they might even attack the archbishop's quarters soon. "

The King however, could not be bothered with this for he was busy. "Come on Fidelus, don't bother me with this now. It is almost August. I must get away from this stifling heat. I don't want to hear anything about rabble or scholars, or yelling in the street. People are always doing that about something. No, no, I must get out of here for while and just relax in the shade of our villa. I won't hear anything of this."

"But, Your Highness, they will drive the archbishop out and religion will…"

"No, no. I will not hear anything of this now. I am off in few hours. Just leave me alone. It will take care of it itself. I will hear no more." And with that he ran off to make preparations for his annual trip to his summer villa.

While the King was taking his leisure, the merchants and King's advisors continued to rile up anger against the archbishop. Finally, on a dry arid day in August, they felt a crest of discontent in the kingdom, which had finally reached its peak. Riding this wave of unsettled angst, they rallied a mob of rabble to storm the cathedral. The mob dragged Archbishop Sanitus right out of the cathedral through the public square, all the while mocking and deriding him. They screamed at him as they were dragging him away, "No more with more with intolerance!"

"Jesus is a God of love, but you preached hatred!"

A man laughed at him along the way while he jovially played a trumpet as if in a mock procession as he called out, "Hah, now you can't impose your twisted beliefs upon us."

As the mob dragged him along people yelled out mocking him,

"Now we show the kingdom the true Jesus, one who does not have to impose commandments."

"Yes, take your penances and crosses with you. We will show people the true messiah, who brings light to mankind, then they will know what is really the truth, tolerance and love."

Maria was waddling along with her cane when she heard the raucous and peeked out from under her headscarf. She could see they were dragging Archbishop Sanitus by the arms driving him along like an uncooperative ox. She peered at them with an intense look at yelped at the mob, "You think you bring 'freedom,' freedom hah, rather you call upon yourselves judgment. Yes, yes, the Lord sees your sinful ways. Because of her sinful ways evil will come upon this land and you will not be able to protect your children from the beast that will come upon us. Give heed to the sound of the trumpet of your destruction![10] You bring not freedom, but slavery."

The mob, however, did not balk at her prediction. Many simply laughed saying, "Ah you old fool." Then the trumpeter continued and the "procession" went on.

Finally, they dumped the archbishop in an old shack on the edge of the kingdom. "Here is your new *cathedral*. Don't worry we will give you a pittance. You won't starve. Just keep away from our markets and public squares. Go busy yourself with preaching to poor bent over women. They can be your congregation, those and anyone else who keep their religion to themselves. Just don't show your face in public again or next time it will be your churches that we will tear down and haul their remains out of the city."

Throughout the kingdom, a moan went out among the Christian believers who still held to virtue. A spirit swept across the young and many had visions of a terrible beast to come. They had visions that a fearful shadow was falling upon the land. Some children too had terrible dreams of a dark presence devouring them in their sleep. Yet, the merchants and enlightened thinkers who had driven out the archbishop laughed and called them all fantasies.

Archbishop Sanitus sighed as he beheld his new dwelling, but he did not linger in depression. From the window of his shack he could still make out the castle ramparts of the King's palace and see the cross of the cathedral. He peered at the cross atop the cathedral many a day meditating on the faith for which he was now forbidden to witness to in public. As he fixed his eyes on the cross he took heart and whispered a pray to the Lord, "Oh good Jesus I accept too my cross. Though I cannot physically witness to your gospel, I accept this lot now, this suffering in exile, this imprisonment of silence in union with your suffering. I offer my suffering in union with yours to make up in my flesh for what is lacking in your suffering in your body, which is the Church.[11]

When the King returned, an advisor Seculus came to him, "Your Highness you don't have to worry about the archbishop anymore."

"Really, what do you mean?"

"Well we moved him out so that he will no longer be a bother."

"Moved him out. What do you mean moved him out!"

"Well, we took care of him, planting him in another quarter with help of crowd of people."

"I see. I hope you did not harm him, I mean we don't want to appear against religion."

"Oh don't worry, Your Highness. We will make sure that a new bishop gets in here soon. It will not look badly on you."

The King soon forgot about the incident for the archbishop remained out of sight, confined to his cottage on the outskirts of town. In time, the bishop, dismissed and forgotten, faded away in his little forgotten edge of the kingdom. He soon died, wearing a heap of rags, surrounded by the poor faithful who bemoaned that the King's men had treated their fine bishop as a pauper. To most people his death seemed like a rock dropped quietly into the water with just a little splash, only a slight disturbance in an otherwise tranquil lagoon. The faithful, however, thought to themselves, "Who now will lead us?"

The scholars, merchants and court officials proclaimed that freedom was now upon the kingdom. They rejoiced that they were now at liberty to sell their wares in tranquility. The businesses who sold pleasure were exuberant, for, now there was no one to make their clients feel guilty. The young men made merry with the young women and all seemed happy. They even delighted in the new bishop, a timid fellow, jovial, who liked to get along with people. They shouted in the streets "Now let the gay celebrations go on with no more hindrance."

The kingdom continued to grow wealthy, the variety of entertainment multiplied and the people *felt* secure. They congratulated each other for their fine wares and threw fine dinners with delicate dainties. Meanwhile, wisdom went about the street looking for followers, but none was there to hear her. For the fear of God was lost in the kingdom and with it, wisdom left.[12] License was then crowned as a ruler of the land and the passions reigned supreme leading a procession of slaves in its coronation ceremony. Thus, the people of Terrasindei defiled themselves by their actions, became adulterers by their conduct. Seeing this, the Lord grew angry with his people, abhorring his own heritage.[13] Looking down from on high, He saw the depravity of men in Terrasindei and sighed, for now He must let men suffer the consequence of their choices.

He said to Himself, "Were they ashamed when they committed abomination? No, they were not at all ashamed; they did not know how to blush. Therefore, they shall fall among those who fall; at the time that I punish them, they shall be overthrown. Oh, my people, gird on sackcloth, and roll in ashes; make mourning as for an only son, with most bitter lamentation; for suddenly the destroyer will come upon you."[14]

Unbeknownst to the people of Terrasindei while men laughed, merchants sold goods, and young people made merry a dark shadow loomed overhead. The Lord could no longer confine the shadowy figure and people would soon experience it.

# Chapter 3

# *A Dragon tears into the realm of man*

*L*ooking down upon the kingdom the Lord sighed and turned away his eyes for a moment from the cloth that held the clouds together. In that instant, two terrible claws tore through the weaving of the skies and a dark figure slipped through the ferial net. Thus, the dragon passed into the kingdom of Terrasindei almost completely unnoticed. To the eyes, it looked as if a cloud were passing in front of the bright moon, causing the light to flicker but for a moment. Yet the air did not change, nor the moon shiver as this dark presence broke into the plane of earth, for it was night and this beast thrived in the shadows.

At first, only poor shepherds in isolated fields far from the heart of society *felt* the dragon's presence. Men in the town heard tales of sheep swallowed whole, which were said to be scooped up by a monstrous green winged beast in the dark of the night. Yet, townspeople quickly dismissed these stories as tales of simple shepherds who ran away afraid at the sight of vultures. Even when the farmers complained that their cows where taken whole by a green winged beast, these tales too were dismissed because it was said the farmers were always making up stories to account for their bad luck. It had been about a year since the great drought started and many farmers were really starting to feel it now. Thus, for a while the dragon hunted with few taking notice, feeding on the flesh of poor animals in forgotten corners of the kingdom. The dragon was, yet, only a whispered presence passed on in stories.

A dragon, however, is not like other beasts. Its purpose is not just to satisfy its hunger for animal flesh; for, it is a proud beast. In its pride, it always seeks to dominate its environment, and its hunger is never satisfied. It will not allow any other beast or living creature to rule in its hunting area. Soon the dragon became bolder, daring to attack now even the homes of townspeople under the cover of night. The dragon would descend down out of the shadowy night like a dark cloud suddenly dropping from the skies. It dove upon its unsuspecting prey who felt secure in their warm homes. Cunningly, though, it would stop straight before the roof and touch down on top with only a slight tap. Then with its huge jagged greenish-grey wings, and protruding neck it would peer over the edge drilling with its eyes into the realm of man, terrifying the inhabitants. Often when spotting a child left unattended, it would snap the child up with a quick movement of its jaw eating the child whole in one bite or two at the most. For play also, it would sometimes take adults sumped over drunk.

Like other beasts, it marked its territory; to do this it would spew out its flaming breath of fire in wide circles setting ablaze fields, rooftops and whatever was else was close by. Often, too, it would throw its flames at the foundations of the homes, leaving families to flee into the darkness of the night. Soon, more people whispered about an ominous winged beast, not as the stuff of colorful tales, but as a living presence terrifying people. The dragon then moved from being a legendary beast spoken about in taverns to a real social menace, as people saw the indisputable marks of its attacks seared into walls of homes. As of yet, though, no one had a clear description of the beast, for the only witnesses were terrified parents, stricken with fear, who caught glimpses of the beast as they ran away from an attack or screaming children who saw their nightmares made real.

Simple men with common sense were the first to recognize the nature of the beast menacing the kingdom. In one small village, not far from several farms men gathered on the dusty dirt and gravel road that they called "main street." Surrounding it were a few small cottages marking off the road and the town cookery that marked a sort of center for the village. Here they gathered around an open cooking pit to enjoy a bit of black sausage and jaw about woes of peasant farming. The cook passed out bowls of beans and ripped off slabs of beef, which they gnawed on as they jabbered about the news sweeping the area.

A crusty old peasant farmer commented between bites, "You hear about that green flying monster that they say attacked old John's place. They say it clean took all his goats. I think John been tellin tales again."

Another portly middle age farmer piped back, "No, I heard it was a winged snake. Like a serpent or something, a 'winged demon,' I think they called it."

The cook then cut them both off as he slapped down some wheat porridge into their bowls, "I heard all the stories from everybody that comes here. I think it is just a ball of fire with wings, a demon maybe."

An old man with a walking stick meandering by chimed in, "No, you all wrong. I saw. Yes, I did. I saw it in the moonlight not one week ago. It is a giant bird that breaths the fire of hell. It scared me to death. Yeh, a demon maybe, and if we don't give it some sacrifices it's gonna devour everything around here."

The cook chiming in again said, "Well we all agree it is a thing of terror, ferocious in nature. For me and my children, I am not going be letting them go far out of my sight at night as long as this beast is roaming around. Maybe I will even build a cement cellar for us to sleep in. You just can't be too secure."

Just a little ways away at a cultivated estate, it was apparent not everyone yet believed in the beast. The steward found this out when he spoke to his lord. "Have you heard these tales of a winged serpent? What do you think?"

The lord responded sarcastically, "Oh yes, it throws the flames of the netherworld at people,. I hear. It is said to devour children and set homes afire. I must say, I think these poor souls have let their imagination take hold of them. It is probably just some big fowl which they saw in poor light during some thunderstorm or something like that. Put it all together and it makes for a fine tale. Oh, these peasants are always making up such tales to explain why things go bad for them. Prairie fires happen, lightning strikes houses and even beasts, nature is causing havoc. Why do they have to make up tales about it?"

In the great city of Valde Venalicium the tales of the great-winged monster were yet only murmurs. Few in the city paid any heed to tales of simple farmers. Therefore, they did not pay heed when the moonlight was darkened occasionally at night as a strange shadow passed in front of it. The dragon, however, would soon change their opinion of these farmers' fables.

The dragon soared overhead now peering out over the expanse of the great capital city. If one were to look closely, one could see the eyes of the beast darting back and forth as if taking the measure of the city. The beast seemed to be growing impatient, as if it wanted now to make its presence known to the whole kingdom. It spied a prominent looking red brick building with a thatched roof just on the outskirts of town. It drove at the complex crashing down upon the stone shingles on the rooftop. The violent thud against the roof woke the inhabitants who went rushing out of the house.

As the owner, a rich cobbler named Thomas rushed out, the dragon then leapt down upon the ground right in front of him. The cobbler froze with fear and the beast stared at him intently. Then it spewed a torrent of fire just to the right of the cobbler torching his front door. The merchant still frozen dared not move. Again the beast threw a fiery flame at the building, with a long breathe making sure the whole complex was on fire. The cobbler now cowered back trying to cover his head fearing that he would be the target for the beast's next fiery breathe. To the cobbler's relief, instead of engulfing him with its fiery breathe, the beast simply let out a mighty growl and then flapped its mighty wings as it took off. However, the beast left its mark as it clawed the cobbler's back as it ascended into the night sky. Meanwhile, the cobbler, now bleeding, cowered in fear with his head buried in his hands for several minutes terrified that the beast would return. Finally, some of the cobbler's servants, taking courage, rushed to his side to tell him the beast had left.

That night the dragon attacked other businesses on the outskirts of the great city. Apparently, it did not want to kill any of the inhabitants but simply to terrorize them. Many a servant and landholder gave accounts the next day that they had come face to face with the winged beast that had terrified them by spewing fire all around their property. It seemed the dragon wanted to make its presence known like a lion marking its territory.

The next day, a noted fabric merchant assembled his colleagues to an urgent meeting to address the beast that was terrifying them. After everyone was assembled, he stood up to speak. "I brought you here because we have a situation we must deal with. We…

Another interrupted him. "Situation? How can you call it just a 'situation? A fire breathing serpent nearly killed Thomas last night and you call it a 'situation?"

"Well, well, I was just trying to keep reason. I mean we must be level headed about this."

Another jumped in. "Level-headed! We have to take action. Protect ourselves and find some way to hunt this beast. Yes, hunt it and kill it. This is what I would do with any other beast harassing my chickens or cattle."

The leader called them to quiet down. "Yes, yes, I hear you. I too agree we must hunt it down. Yet, I must say, I have never hunted such a beast. How does one go about it?"

From the back one called out, "We should get a champion, some mercenary or somebody like this who knows how to hunt big beasts!"

At this many chimed in. "Yes, yes, yes, a champion that is what we need!"

The leader seeing this acclamation replied, "Okay, okay! I guess we have decided on our course of action. Let us then pool our money and then we can send out word to find a *champion*, a mighty hunter who will rid us of this beast."

Hearing this, the assembling broke out cheering, "Hurrah, down with the beast! Down with it!"

The affair soon came to the attention of King. One his servants whispered in his ear, "A flying fire breathing serpent has attacked one cobbler, destroying his home and business. I hear the merchants are all excited. They want to hire a champion to take on this beast. Moreover, many peasants also have been harassed by this beast and they say even children have been taken. It is harvest time and the farmers are worried about their crops being destroyed."

The King cocked his head in disbelief. "A fire-breathing flying serpent, you mean like a dragon? Those are only in fairy tales."

The advisor responded, "This is no fairy tale, Your Highness. Even one of our stewards saw it. Reputable people all over the kingdom have seen it. They saw a flying greenish grey beast that breathes fire. It is real."

"A real dragon, hah? Well, I don't know about that, but I guess there is something that is riling people up. Anyway, it is just a beast. I mean, how big a problem is it, really? Can't this wait, with all the other pressing things I have to do?  I mean it is just wild beast that happened to pick on some prominent merchant, unfortunate, but it won't bankrupt our kingdom."

The advisor responded, "Well, yes, you are right. It has only yet really affected one business and I hear the merchants are taking a collection to hire a champion themselves."

"Well then give these merchants a few gold coins as a sign of my solidarity with their cause and be done with it."

Thus, with the wave of a hand and a few words, the King dismissed the beast as if it were like a plague of annoying gnats. The merchants, however, men who knew how to take charge of things, went to work. They flooded into the meeting halls gathering their colleagues to see what they could do about this social menace. Their leader, Faciendo, spoke outlining the concerns of them all,

"Men of action, we gather here tonight to throw off slavery from a force of nature. We who bend the currents of commerce to our will, can surely tame this wild beast. We have in this room, builders, planners, artisans and experts in all things made by men. How different is it to tame such a beast than it is to overcome the problems of the market? Is this more difficult than reigning in the wandering mind of laborers working on a house, or reining in horses carrying a precious load, or redirecting a river so one can put it to use for milling grain? No, I tell you. We need only put our will to this task and we can surely solve it."

Celsus, who prided himself for knowing about all things interrupted. "Ah, yes, talk, talk, talk, what we need is a champion tested in battle that will rid us of this beast."

Seculus, who thought he knew all the ways of the world, responded to this comment with a jab. "What are you proposing yourself as a champion, you old man Celsus? Oh, I know you can't do it. No, what we need to do is put out word among those who can find us a real champion. I have some friends who are veterans of many battles. They keep up with all the young bucks who are looking for battles. I bet they could find us someone to hunt down this beast."

With this statement one merchant stepped forward. "Here is my gold coin. I will back you to find the best champion."

He then threw it in on the table right in front of Seculus. Another then stepped forward. "Here is my gold piece also." Then another and another, soon the table was full of gold coins. Right then the King's servant came in. He announced, "The King wishes to show his solidarity with those oppressed by the beast. He shows this through a generous donation to find someone to hunt the beast."

He then took out a small bag and emptied several more gold coins onto the table in front of everyone.

Seeing this, all shouted, "Here, here! To our champion! To our champion! To the one who will conquer in our name!"

Thus, they sent word out through colleagues. They called on their business partners from foreign lands to send out a message that they were looking for a champion and would pay good money. They threw dinner parties for each other and contemplated the glory they would receive for their practicality in dealing with this social problem.

They would soon find a soul eager to take the part of a champion in a proud figure named Fastidus. He had just come back from a great hunt where he bagged two great black bears and several tall horned behemoths. He was always impatient for the next adventure and reveled in the glory of his triumphs, which made him charming to the women. He was a drifter of sorts, working for a few months here then a few months there earning his way by his triumphant sword. He was a man of good looks and much charm who loved to indulge in fine food and entertain the women while he enjoyed a good drink. He burned through all the money he earned as fast as it came into his hands. As the son of minor nobility, he could always rely on, "good old daddy," to bail him out anyway if things got too thin.

Fastidus was attending a party as usual and got to thinking, "How boring is the company tonight. They keep repeating the same stories. These boors keep complaining about their wives and the stupid habits of their children, nothing about battles, or intrigues, or beasts or anything. At least they could make up something!"

Just then, his merchant friend from the East came in, peaking Fastidus' interest. He thought, "Oh good, things are picking up now. Micas always has some interesting tale to tell, and he knows everybody who is important. I am sure he will have word of an exciting offer from some important noble or something."

Micas made a beeline to Fastidus, giving no regard for others around him. Micas had heard that Fastidus had fought in many battles, hunted great beasts in the wilds of the northern territories and hailed from a proud family with a noble lineage. He had asked around further and heard that he had fought with the Roman legions as an officer in years past in their campaigns against the barbarians. Some also said he had been a mighty hunter who had fought giant beasts in the great forests of the north. When Micas described Fastidus to his colleagues he seemed like a perfect candidate, so Micas approached him on behalf of them.

Fastidus looking for an opportunity for adventure, fixed his ears more attentively as Micas spoke even as he tried to appear aloof by reclining in a lounging posture. Micas did not disappoint as he started into his tale. "I have heard that the land of feasts, Terrasindei, where they love to celebrate Pan, and Aphroditus with great festivities, is plagued by a terrible beast, but not just an ordinary beast. They say it is a winged serpent, which flies and breathes fire, a dragon, a real dragon! Additionally, I hear they are looking for a champion who will slay this beast and win much fame."

Fastidus now stood as if he were at attention in a military lineup and responded proudly, "Why, it sounds like a job made just for me. I have hunted big game, bagged myself two great bears just last month and a few behemoths up north."

He thought, "What glory, what glory, my triumph over the dragon will bring me much fame."

He raised his goblet, without further thought, and pledged to the enthralled listeners, "Surely, I can best this dragon. Who is as fine with a sword as me? Surely, I could make quick work of that beast. With the strength of my arm and the cunning of my wits, I will out duel this beast and bring back one of his teeth as memento for our grand host here. Simply point me to where I can enlist."

Upon hearing this, they all cheered, and Micas raised his goblet in approval calling out, "Let it be so. I will give my pledge of your worth to the emissaries who seek a champion."

When he arrived in the town, the merchants prepared a public gathering and formed an escort to meet him with all ceremonial glory. The merchants lined up to greet their 'champion.' A whole crowd of eager peasants joined them hoping that there was someone who could finally free them from the beast. All put on their best face to please their 'chosen warrior.' The men of great names gave fine speeches proclaiming to the assembled crowds how this social problem will soon be no more. One after the other filled the air with sugary sounding speeches and congratulated each other on their fine plan. The onlookers cheered when their ears were tingled by a fine rhetorical line. Fastidus sat by proudly soaking in the glory of the occasion. After the speeches, the men with round bellies hosted a fine dinner with sumptuous delights often toasting their champion. Fastidus for his part reveled in it and delighted the merchants with tales of his mighty hunting adventures. They all mingled happily in this delightful aura, thinking of how their rich business would soon get back to normal, as they beguiled the nobles and men who were called important.

*Meanwhile, the Lord in heaven was preparing his own champion in a desolate place not regarded by men.*

George was wandering along in the countryside, as he continued his journey in search of the Lord's mission. It was now almost a year since the legate discharged him peacefully from the ranks of the Roman legion. As he was heading out of a local church after the Sunday liturgy, which he never missed, he heard a couple of old women talking.

"Oh yes, it is terrible that the old widow has no one to help her. Whenever I pass by her house, I pity her. It is obvious that the house is in need of repair. It is too bad all her relatives are dead and no one reaches out to her. There must be a good Christian soul who could help her."

George, hearing this interrupted them, "Pardon me good women. I overheard your conversation. I am just now on a journey to do the Lord's will, and I am available to help this widow that you speak about. Will you tell me where she lives?"

They eagerly gave him directions to the house, and he went straight to the old widow's house. He greeted her kindly. "Hello, good grandmother, I am here to help you to fix up the house."

The old woman, called a 'grandmother' in the polite custom of the day, responded with surprise. "Oh, son, I did not expect anyone to come. I have been slowing down for a while now, and I have not been able to keep up this old house. I thought everyone had completely forgotten about me. I expected this house would just fall apart around me just like my old rickety body is doing."

George responded, "No, good grandmother, the Lord did not forget you. I am responding to his call. I heard from someone in the church that you needed help."

She then looked closer at George, squinting with her eyes and responded, "You are a Christian then? But you look like an army officer with that uniform of yours and that insignia. What are you doing here?"

"Why yes, good grandmother, I am a Christian and a military officer. It is precisely because of this that I think I should help you. It is our Christian duty to look after those forgotten and in need. This is also the responsibility of a good officer, to protect the innocent and defend those in need. This, I think is the mark of a true knight."

"But you are so young. Why are you not off chasing adventures?"

George blurted out without pondering his response, "Oh, I have experienced a few of what the world calls 'adventures.' I fought the barbarians in the North. I forged into the wilderness in East to help establish a Roman base. I have been on sea ships crossing a raging sea. Men of arms came to respect me for my courage and leadership. I see all of these 'adventures' now were empty pursuits, seeking the accolades of man. I see now the only adventures worth pursuing are those given to me by the Lord. You are the adventure I am called to today."

"I see. You are most unusual young man, most unusual. The Lord has really touched you."

After helping the widow all afternoon, George left there pleased with himself. Yet, still there was a little unrest in his heart. He turned to the Lord in prayer speaking to Him in his interior thoughts, "What adventure am I really looking for Lord?"

He then wandered about looking for a place of solitude and silence to ponder this question. He finally made his way to an isolated countryside cottage spending a few hours meditating on the way of the Lord. He happened to glance at his sword. He studied it noticing a few defects on its edges, two dull spots and three nicks, "Hmm," he thought, "Can I never keep this sharp? What do I need to do to have a perfect sword?"

He swooshed it back and forth as if battling an imaginary foe. He reflected, "It has good balance, and I know by experience it cuts well, too well. Ah, to shed the blood of your creature Lord, even for a just cause, how sad. Yet, I know the sword is only as good as the man who wields it. Am I fit for your service Lord? And what sword am I to wield in service of your army? Will this worn out blade be sufficient? "

*Terrasindei and Fastidus saw this not though and continued in their pleasant bliss.* In the eyes of men, they had their champion who would soon rid them of this troubling situation. The day finally came designated for Fastidus to go out in a triumphant procession. With great ceremony he dressed himself in gilded armor. He slowly attached each piece of armor in view of all, as if, he was a prime minister accepting his new appointment and putting on the symbols of the office. He slowly buckled his leg armor and fastened his waist garment making sure he was facing the on-looking crowd. He waved to the gathered crowd, who were filled with great expectation at the pageantry of the event. His family's falcon crest showed brightly emblazed on the rear of his fine armor as he rode out slowly with his visor up, so the adoring crowd could get a good view of his handsome face. He thought, "This is my time to shine and I am going to make the most of it."

As he trotted slowly away from the assembled crowd, he pondered how he would be hailed after his triumph. Making his way westward, he slipped into daydreaming. He pictured others speaking about him when they told tales of great heroes. He pictured women running after him because of his reputation. He could see himself walking into a tavern, the owner rushing up to greet him, the customers all crowding around to see the hero and the women turning away from the man they were with to get a peek at him. "Ah," he thought, "How it will be grand."

Then he realized he still had a task-at-hand to slay a dragon. This too got him daydreaming. He started to go through in his mind the spectacular moves he would make to overcome the beast. He contemplated the first encounter, the agility of the beast and his clear superiority. He saw himself maneuvering easily away from the attempted attacks of the beast. He saw himself almost bored with the ease of the battle. He saw himself even playing with the beast a little, to savor the moment of the encounter, wanting to extend so it will make a better tale. Reflecting on this he said to himself, "Ah, and what stories will I have to tell. I will drive my sword through its throat and tear out a tooth from its cold body, which thereafter, I will wear around my neck as a sign of my triumph."

He tried to imagine the dragon in his mind according to the description he had heard about it. Then it occurred to him he had never seen a dragon, but he thought, "It must not be that much different from other great beasts I have hunted."

He had heard the tales that people told of its destructive power reducing men to ashes, and leaving their homes as a pile of burnt rubble, but this thought soon faded as he pictured himself in glory again. He turned his mind to the tales of the great hunts by Germanic warriors as they pursued great bears. He thought of the stories of the wild men of the frozen tundra in the far northern regions who were said to hunt mammoths. He had never seen such beasts, but had heard enough tales describing such beasts, so that he felt he knew them. He had even inserted a few of these beasts into the tales he told about his triumphs; just to add color to the stories. Now though, his story would top them all.

He thought, "Well, I fibbed a little in these tales when wine flowed to impress the maids, and the rich merchants, but I did campaign in many tough battles. I did hunt the great bears in the northern wilderness."

He mused, "I have been in battles with great men. It is true I never lead a charge, but I was in the midst of it and I have never suffered a defeat in battle. I know how to handle a sword and a crossbow. This beast will be nothing for me."

Just then, he noticed a few horses sprinting along to catch up with him. It was a group of rich young townspeople, sons of merchants; they dipped their hats and waved to him as he past. He cheerfully waved back. They came within sight, but kept their distance quickly galloping off after he acknowledged them. He thought, "They fear the dragon so they draw back, but at least they had the heart to accompany me so far, for they want to share a bit in my glory. I will not disappoint them."

Just then he noticed the old woman Maria plotting along. She seemed out of place, somehow without fear when everyone else fled. Fastidus noticed this bent over woman that meandered along slowly when all others seemed to flee. He thought, "Is this woman crazy? What on earth brings her out here now?"

Just then, Maria paused looked up at Fastidus and shook her head dismissively while curling up her eyes and nose in a note of disapproval. Then she continued on her way. This seemed to pull Fastidus out of his daydream for a moment, but then he returned to his fantasies by saying to himself, "No, she is just a bad note in a fine tune. Her presence is just crazy." He then started to hum one of the merry songs he heard in the taverns.

Finally, entering the shadow of the mountain, Fastidus knew he was coming to the abode of the dragon. He started to make his way among the various crevices of the mountain calling out as he went along to taunt the dragon, "Come out beast that I may slay you! Come out! Do not hide! The audience is all here. Come meet your death!"

He did this a little while with no response. Then being hasty for the battle he started to hurl rocks into every cave that he came upon hoping to wake it from his slumber. He continued this until near dusk getting more frustrated at the delay of his glory. Finally, as darkness peaked over the mountain, the dragon arose, darting out from a hidden cave.

The dragon sped straight out of the cave at a great speed then turned quickly and drove into the air so it could survey its environment. Unbeknownst to Fastidus the merchants looked on from overhanging cliffs witnessing the battle. The dragon quickly spotted the mounted soldier. Fastidus lowered his visor and prepared his crossbow with his lance by his side. The dragon turned in a circle then swooped down with great speed like a hard falling rain. Fastidus let loose his crossbow and the arrow whizzed forth striking the dragon squarely in the chest, but the beast did not even slow down, and it seemed even to smile a bit as it continued to dive quickly toward him. The would-be-hero's eyes were now wide open as he desperately reached for his lance to hurl it at the dragon, but it was too late. The dragon spewed forth a spray of fire that consumed him and his horse on the very spot. Thus was the end of Fastidus.

The merchants looking on in their hidden crevices were horrified and taken aback. They hurried away as fast as they could; staying in the shadows for fear the dragon might have caught sight of them. The whole encounter and attack took less than two minutes. The dragon knowing he had displayed his power swooped away into the night triumphantly. The so-called 'important' men with the grand schemes now sulked back into town murmuring in low voices, "This beast is more than we expected. We must strategize differently if we hope to defeat it."

When the townspeople gathered enough courage to venture back, the next day during daylight, all they saw left was the burnt carcass of the horse and the charred body of the knight. One could clearly make out Faustidus' gilded armor, his lance and the sword lying harmlessly by his side. Only the bones and the chain mail survived of the would-be-champion. The next few weeks the dragon burst forth in rage upon the small kingdom pouring out a reign of fire upon random farms blackening acres of crops. He plucked children from the streets, eating them whole and attacked homes seemingly without warning leaving them in piles of ashes. The people of the kingdom were terrified and buried themselves in their homes keeping watch with a fearful eye on the skies above.

# Chapter 4

## *The Failure of man's ways*

*A*s the dragon expanded its terror upon the kingdom, the people started to murmur and throw epitaphs at the King. The dragon had in fact grown in size and its presence now was not easy to miss. It had been about six months since Fastidus' failure. The merchants saw that no one was coming to their shops and discontent started to flow across the kingdom because of the inaction of the King. The King noticed the jeering as he passed by. He couldn't miss this fact when some even hiding in alleys pelted him with rotten vegetables. They mockingly called out to him, "A King, hah, no King to us, but a king of the Worms."

The merchants held secret meetings under cover of night with the leading men of society. After this meeting, the merchants clamored to the King saying, "See now, the beast has even dared to attack some of our brethren, scared people away from the markets, and kept tourists away from our country. We cannot sell our wares, nor even protect our markets. We are scared for our future."

Even some nobles now joined the chorus of merchants with a veiled threat to the , "There is a pressing social problem caused by poor government; perhaps we should find a new way of governing this nation."

As the old stalwart archbishop of the diocese had gone to his reward while in exile, the local authorities petitioned a new archbishop to be named. The new archbishop, Jocundus, wanting to be more appeasing, tried to position himself as a friend to the King. Seeing how the merchants and influential men maligned the King, Archbishop Jocundus tried to establish himself as an intermediary. He proclaimed, "This beast that afflicts us is a disturbing problem that should be addressed by a broad coalition of people from our kingdom." The King smiled slightly upon hearing this, but these words had little influence on him.

The King understood then he must act now or his power and influence would become worthless. He called on his best advisors to bring together the head of the important merchant guilds and the nobles to a great meeting to tackle this pressing social problem. The King's advisors proposed, "We should assemble groups to study the problem with expert advice and come up with a best solution. We can gather the best military leaders, the best hunters, and engineers. They will put their heads together and give us expert advice."

Commidius, a rich merchant, jumped into the conversation, "The dragon has shut down our business to a point where food is rotting in our bins and imports our piling up in storage. And if something is not done soon, we will have to leave for another country."

At this, the King's advisors faces turned sullen and white, but they took up hope again when the King brought forth his expert advisor, Mundatis. The King's grey-haired technical advisor then came forth and the assembly hushed to a silence waiting to hear his address. He was renowned as the genius who had devised the imaginative armaments that helped the kingdom fend off the Asiatic barbarians, many years ago during King Titus' reign when Felix was still a boy. He had long since retired and now spent his time keeping rare company while tinkering with new inventions. The King of old had credited him with inventing strategies and performing battlefield engineering feats that had brought victory to the kingdom when it seemed to everyone like all was lost.

The renowned engineer addressed the crowd. "The King has asked me to come out of retirement to create a strategic plan that will defeat this dragon. In deference to Titus, his noble father, I agreed. Now as you know I helped this kingdom win many battles in the past when the enemy seemed too overwhelming. For me, it never seemed as insurmountable as others saw it. I considered it just a matter of proper study and assessment. This recent problem seems like a similar situation. Here it is not barbarian hordes that we are fighting, but a wild beast, which in my book does not look nearly as intimidating."

"I have done a little thinking about this beast that menaces our kingdom. What I determined is that we need a two-pronged approach: one in terms of security to prevent this beast, or another future beast, from doing more immediate harm, a second to address actively the problem at hand."

"I can say after studying the action of the so-called 'champion' that was hired, one can learn a few thing about the dragon and the reasons for the failure of this "character." *Whom I must say was really a poor choice to engage such a beast.* With help of the King's agents, we investigated Fastidus' background and found he had overstated his experience. In fact, he was known to be a drunkard, a blow-heart, and was prone to exaggeration. It is true that he had in fact been in some minor skirmishes before this, but nothing in his background qualified him to take on a dragon."

"Although the knight was obviously a buffoon, we can take note of some important facts. First, the remains of Fastidus' armor seemed to hold up well to the fiery breath of the beast. This shows us that iron can be an effective protection against the onslaught of the dragon. Second, the dragon has a distinct advantage against a mounted knight because of the swiftness of its flight. Noting both of these facts can help us overcome the beast. The first tells us how to give proper protection to our populace and any future warrior who takes on the beast. In regards to the dragon's swift flight, one can neutralize this with a metal net. I will explain this in more detail later."

"First things first though, we must secure as many buildings in the kingdom as we can. The best way I see this is to invest in iron shielding for the vulnerable parts of our edifices. Of course, the poor will not have the resources to do this, but our gracious King has offered to fund houses of security where they can go in an emergency from the dragon. Secondly, I called a few other old friends from past military campaigns to form a search committee for a warrior that is truly qualified to take on such beast. I will instruct *our qualified warrior* how to use the metal net."

The merchants and nobles conversed among themselves. Some mumbled to each other signs of approval; others only slightly bobbed their heads up and down still a little in doubt. One among them asked, "Explain to me the nature of these iron shields that go around our buildings?"

Another asked, "Who are these military advisors?"

And another, "How will all this be funded?"

After listening a little while, Mundatis, a man of little patience, piped up. "Do not worry. The King will take care of everything with his treasury of gold. Don't get so worried about details, I will explain to all the blacksmiths how to make the shields for your houses and shops. In fact, this will even open up a new market for you, the selling of shields. Now just trust in this boy here, your King."

At this the no longer boyish looking King meekly nodded. Then Mundatis continued. "I will head up the team designing the best fortifications for your houses. I will put the kingdom's best advisors to work on it. We will also make sure your businesses have double fortified walls to protect them. I assembled a good core of military advisors to help me. They will look for the best-qualified warrior to tackle this beast. Let's get on with it and rid ourselves of this bothersome pest!"

Then the King rose up. "Let me assure you, I have selected Mundatis for his engineering expertise and have also assembled the best military leaders in our country to do a thorough search to find for us a *truly qualified* warrior to tackle this problem that our kingdom faces. As a sign of my serious regard for this situation, I had Mundatis prepare an example of a fortified carriage that can protect one from the attack of any beast. He assures me that it can safely protect up to six people in a carriage."

The King then opened a side door and showed the assembly the iron-plated carriage. The important looking merchants looked on with pleasure. The men with old money smiled with smug approval and the zealous young nobles excitedly congratulated Mundatis. They all looked over its details, asked how it rode; saw how it shined as they murmured to each other about the wonder of it. After this look-over, they came to a general agreement that this was a grand plan. Only a few dissenting voices doubted it, but the King's agents managed to drown them out, and make it seem like it was a consensus. The details followed readily as enthusiasm built for this new plan made with expert advice. Mundatis showed his engineering plans to the blacksmiths who devised the home security systems. The merchants got in the act by selling the newly designed shields to their brethren for protection and soon the simple folk followed suit saving up to buy the shields. The King kept his word and made a few token emergency shelters for the poor, though this was far from enough. The military experts got busy putting together the qualities they were looking in a warrior and put out a summons.

The King then sent out emissaries sponsored by the merchants to seek a new champion. They were given instructions to inquire discretely, less word get out, that the kingdom was beseeched by a problem they could not handle, which would adversely affect their trade with other nations. The King's advisors told them to be thorough and discerning in their inquiries to get the best champion for their money; no one wanted a repeat of the last incident. They sought for a candidate who was well distinguished, a proven soldier and savvy about fighting beasts.

Meanwhile, Maria was passing through the streets with her slow hunched over walk. A young man stopped her, "Have you heard the news? The King is sending out his emissaries to find a proven champion this time. Surely, this one will defeat the dragon."

Maria, however, dismissed the young man's exuberance with a waving of her hand saying, "Oh the poor fellow who is chosen. I will pray for him. The poor fellow, I will pray for him."

The youth perplexed by her response did not allow Maria's words to break his spirit and ran off still in excitement.

The emissaries filled with zeal scoured lands in the frozen north. They inquired among barbarian peoples in the south. They even spoke with desert nomads about the warriors of the Far East. After many discrete inquiries and a thorough verification of the background of the proposed champions, they settled on a great champion that came from the legendary city of Athens. His name was Nomineus a soldier for hire who came from a renowned military family. He was known to be a great warrior possessing knowledge of all the arts of war. He was well disciplined, agile with a sword, a keen mind and had a well-tested record in battle. He had recently been a personal assistant to a great prince in the east, whom he had lead on many great hunting trips chasing after great beasts in the frozen tundra of the north. He had fought pirates in the Mediterranean and drove out barbarians in the east. He had hunted great bears in the north and mammoths in India. He had worked with the best generals in the old Roman army and worked alongside engineers making fine machines for battle.

*The Lord, however, took little note of these doings, He continued to prepare his own warrior unseen by the vanity of men's eyes.*

At this time, George was learning to reign in his passions and control the might of his sword. He strove deep into the night practicing his jabs and sparing techniques. He prayed earnestly that the Lord would show him his weaknesses. He had a practice of doing this and found that the Lord helped him to grow strong in areas where he had been vulnerable. He was becoming a master swordsman, but he continued to train. He laughed to himself as he fought an imaginary enemy. "I strike you down demon. You feign of my mind who strikes harder at me than many an enemy, for I can never run from you. Yet, as I fight you I train for the time when this blade will crash against real flesh and blood."

Then he turned his thought to the Lord. "Lord, give me strength and discipline, only make these virtues worthy of you and never let me shed innocent blood."

*Terrasindei saw this not though and continued with their worldly plans.*
*Their* chosen warrior, Nomineus, arrived in the land without gods
with much less fanfare than Fastidus, though they paid him four times
as much, which he gladly accepted. He was a pagan, who did not even
believe in his own gods, but that mattered not to the small assembly
that greeted him. The merchants had a private gathering to greet him,
making sure it was away from the public eye. They greeted him with
more circumspection, but after meeting him, they came to see the
King had made a fine choice in their eyes. They did everything in
private for fear of the last public folly. This also was how Nomineus
would have it for he cared little for ceremony; for him duty is what
mattered. He just wanted to get to the job and be past these
pleasantries.

Soon after meeting with the men of influence, Nomineus was at
work. He first spoke to those who had personally encountered the
dragon. He asked one of the King's young advisors who had
witnessed it. "Tell me precisely how the attack occurred against
Fastidus."

"Well sir, the winged beast drove down as if darkness itself were
descending upon the earth and…"

Nomineus, however, interrupted him, "No flourishing please,
just the plain details. I don't want to know what you felt, but what,
where and when you saw it. Just be precise."

At that the King's advisor continued, "Well the dragon came
down very quickly upon Fastidus right after dark set in. It seemed to
want to pounce upon him."

Nomineus queried, "In what fashion exactly did it attack. Can
you describe it more precisely?"

"Hmm, how do I describe it, 'like a falcon going after its prey.'
Yes, that is it. Fastidus threw his spear at the dragon with no effect,
and then he tried to shield himself, noticing the dragon was
descending quite quickly, but it was too late. The dragon spewed out
a flame of fire and that was it."

Nomineus continued. "Was there anything that survived from the attack?"

"Well, yes, his iron armor. You can see this in the workroom of Mundatis."

Nomineus then proceeded to methodically investigate the remains of Fastidus' armor, asking Mundatis several questions. He noted how it had partially protected him from the dragon's fiery breath, but that it had clear weaknesses that he needed to address. First, among these weaknesses was that much of the flesh of soldier was left exposed. After this inquiry, he devised a plan.

He gathered the best blacksmiths in the kingdom and called on the assistance of the best engineers. He put the blacksmiths to work making a steel house with a small slot for vision and a metal mesh net. He put the engineers to work designing a giant strong steel crossbar that could project powerful arrows. Then he asked them to devise a mechanism to release the steel mesh designed by Mundatis with a simple release of a clasp. To protect himself, he had them design a strong steel shield.

*Meanwhile, George prepared for the next battle in his own manner.* He was preparing for Lent, the great season of prayer and fasting leading up to commemoration of the Lord's passion and death. Seeking to know the Lord's will for him, he stopped in a Church for a day meditating on the heroic acts of the martyrs that went before him. As was his custom, he confessed his sins to a priest, then spent the day in prayer and silent reflection. He spent the day trying to discern where the Lord was calling him next. He called out to the Lord in prayer. "Lord, you led me to take leave from the Roman army. Now what are you calling me to do?"

He waited on the Lord for a while until his mind became fixated on the idea of the kingdom of God. He turned to the Lord with his thoughts as he asked, "What is this kingdom that you speak so much about in the scriptures? You said 'the kingdom of God' is like a man who finds a pearl of great worth in a field and sells all he has to obtain the field. What does this mean, Lord?"

He noticed a mosaic depicting the Blessed Virgin Mary and started to meditate on its significance. Then in a moment of inspiration, he felt inspired to give his sword over to the Virgin and let her lead him. He drew out his sword placed it at the foot of the mosaic as he prayed, "O Mother of the true Lord Jesus, you through whom my Lord sought to come into the world pray for me that I may now dedicate my skills and my entire being to His most majestic service. True Lord of my life I seek service in your kingdom. I will be satisfied with no lesser lord."

"I offer myself to you now, take Lord all my freedom, all that I have and call my own. I place my sword at your service; it is yours to do as you will, may it help to bring a kingdom of peace. I lay this before you as your true possession. Only lead me to where you want me to go, what you want me to do, keeping me always in your love and grace."[15]

After this heartfelt prayer, he waited silently, pondering the mosaic. He studied its details and noticed it was a depiction of the Mother of God in some sort of mystical scene. It showed her as the woman from Revelation with twelve stars above her head, and the moon under her feet. This inspired a thought. "John's apocalypse depicted this woman as fighting a dragon. I remember now that the holy bishop spoke of how this woman represents the Church, pure and virginal, who bore the followers of Christ."

This meditation brought a question to his mind. "What significance is the dragon? I know not. What I do know Lord is that I am a part of this battle as a follower of your Son. Show me Lord how I am to enter into this battle."

The Lord in time would clearly show George where he was leading him. For now it was sufficient that he was inspired to continue pursuing the Lord…

*Back in Terrasindei the thoughts of men continued to contrive their own plans.* On a mild spring day, Nomineus called together his assistants and detailed his plans. "I have studied the patterns of the beast and noticed that it likes to come out at night just after dusk. I believe this is because the beast sees better at night, a fact we can use to our advantage. I also noticed that the beast emerges every night from the same crevice, low to the ground then quickly soars into the skies. This gives us a tactical advantage. We know from where the beast emerges and thus we know where to set up our offensive devices.

I have prepared certain devices with the help of our good blacksmiths. You will see here an enclosed steel room with a small slot, three walls and no floor. This is my safe-room that will protect me from any fiery onslaughts that the dragon can throw. From this safe room I will shoot out some finely sharpened steel arrows with high-powered catapults. In order to keep the dragon at bay, I also had the blacksmiths make a strong steel mesh chain. We will cover the dragon with this mesh using a catapult device right as it emerges from its cave. My strong assistants will then hold the dragon down with chains. I designed this steel net to hold down a whole horde of elephants. It will allow us to entrap the dragon and then finish it off."

After his speech, the assembled leaders gave him congratulations. Many spoke great words about him, congratulating him on his ingenuity. He thought to himself. "This plan is well made. I have tracked every move of this beast, noted its weaknesses and determined a plan of action. The steel mesh I designed could withhold ten mammoths of India. The steel house can stand up to the flames that devoured Fastidus. I have accounted for all things. My backers heartily approve. It will go smoothly. Then these people can get back to their daily lives and I will move on to the next job at hand."

Nomineus then set out to put his plan in action. He headed to the western edge of the kingdom where the dragon made its residence. He made his way through the ravines and rock out cropping until he finally made it to the great mountain in the west where the dragon made its lair. He waited patiently until sunset came, at which time the beast typically emerged. He lay in wait at the edge of the crevice from which his scouts told him the dragon usually exited. Meanwhile, his assistants prepared all the devices. Some town officials stood off at a distance watching anxiously, with much more caution this time. They hid themselves behind a rock where they could still see the happenings, but where sure to be safe.

Just as Nomineus expected, the dragon came screaming out through the crevice soon after sunset. He released the lever for his trap. The net spread out over the dragon as the beast flew out trapping it and completely stopping its momentum. The winged-beast dropped to the ground all balled up in the steel mesh. The assistants held tight holding their lines with cables at a safe distance. As the dragon struggled in the trap, Nomineus shot a harpoon directly at the beast's head striking it with great force, while he remained safely in his steel house.

*However, something was wrong.* The harpoon simply bounced off the dragon's head stunning it for a moment. It did not pierce its scales and the dragon soon shook off the effects of the strike. The dragon pulled itself up on its feet taking the whole metal net along with it as it set itself aright. It then spewed out a mighty flood of flames. Nomineus, though perplexed by this unexpected failure, was at present protected within his steel house. He withstood the flames calmly. He reset his harpoon for another shot while he instructed his assistants to pull more tightly the cables to constrict the dragon's movements.

Just then, something else happened that Nomineus had not foreseen. The dragon tore its way through the steel mesh with a mighty flap of its wings, shearing apart the net in several places. The assistants seeing their mortal danger dropped their cables and fled further away from the scene. Nomineus was shocked. He exclaimed, "Ten mammoth elephants could not do that!"

The dragon then rushed at Nomineus who now had only his steel house to protect him. Nomineus in desperation fired another harpoon, which the beast seemingly without effort caught in its mouth and flung to the side. Then the dragon drove at the steel house overturning it and leaving Nomineus exposed to the onslaught of the beast. Nomineus seeing his deadly state grabbed his steel shield and held his ground, knowing now this was his only hope. The dragon shot forth a stream of flames at the would-be-champion. Nomineus tried to shield himself behind his steel shield, but the flames were too much. The head of the flame seared his hands and leaped up over his shield scorching his hair through his mask. He dropped the shield as the hot metal started to burn the skin off his fingers. He fell to the ground at the pain of the scorching.

Then the dragon grabbed the shield clasping it with its mouth and threw it derisively to the side. It then seemed to stare at Nomineus with piercing eyes drilling right through the very skin and bones of its prey, into to his very soul. Nomineus stood face to face with the beast. He knew this was the end of his life. He lay dejected on the ground in pain and mysteriously transfigured by the dragon's eyes. Just before the dragon's final fiery assault, Nomineus was heard to utter in despair. "The beast is not from this world. Nothing made of man could defeat it. Only a god can strike down this beast."

Then the flood of flame came upon him and the would-be-champion breathed his last.

*In the heavens above God looked down upon the scene and mused over the folly of men as he continued to prepare his hero.*

# Chapter 5

# *God Prepares His champion*

A s Nomineus was engaging in his mortal battle with the dragon, George was on pilgrimage to a Church of the Roman martyrs. This Church preserved the relics of those early Christian heroes martyred under Nero. As it was the season of prayer and fasting, he was meditating on the Lord's passion. He spoke to the priests who tended the small shrine, hearing the stories of the martyrs and their courage in the face of trials. He listened as they detailed how the Christians with no weapons stood up to lions and gladiators. He heard of their courage in the face of torture and their steadfast hope that upheld them to their last breath. He listened attentively to the priest who said Mass over the tombs of the martyrs.

After the Mass, he stayed and prayed pouring his heart out to those brave souls who he considered his friends in heaven. "O good souls, who died in Christ, pray for me that I may have the courage to face evil and remain steadfast until the last. Pray that I may have the grace of the Lord to overcome my weakness. Bend the ear of the Lord that he may see the trustworthiness of my pleading that I may have all the weapons of Faith to confront the work of the evil one."

*As George was praying thus, the kingdom of Terrasindei was deteriorating.* The dragon had become enraged after the battle with the second champion. It took out its rage on the townspeople, going out now more frequently than before. It had reigned over the kingdom a year and half now. It attacked now seemingly random houses at will, even at times devouring whole families in one night. The dragon followed a horrible ritual; it would land on top of a home attracted by the smoke from the father's secret sin. The father would try to fend off the dragon, but was no match for the beast who would soon devour him. The mother would try to hide the children, but to no avail for the beast would eventually find them, then engulf the whole family with a mighty blast of its breath.

All the merchants and the King could do, in response to this horror, was to clean up the burnt remains of the homes removing the sight from the eyes of tourists. For themselves they prepared more and more elaborate security systems to protect them from the fiery breath of the dragon. The merchants, however, continued their festivities, for the dragon though fearsome was only one and could not be in all places at once. The party must continue as the saying goes. "Let the drunk be pushed to the side and my problems too, but let the party continue."

Thus, they carried on their feasts as if no dragon existed and hid any signs of its presence from the sight of tourists, who came from far off lands. They made great preparations for the spring holidays, making their products look nice, decorating the streets for the thousands that would be coming. Whether it was in celebration of the Lord Jesus' birth, or the coming of the spring fairy, it mattered not as long as they could have a great party and sell many goods.

However, the dragon did not pay heed to times or seasons and was growing more ferocious in its desire to reign over the kingdom. As the season of high feasts came upon the land, the town was making merry with many celebrations, full of colorful parades and funny costumes, which attracted many people. The dragon recognized this time as opportune to strike. It broke its normal pattern and ventured out during daylight on an overcast day. The dragon circled above the festive gathering, remaining at first unnoticed as it popped in and out of the cloud cover. It surveyed the scene looking for the best place to attack.

Then it dove down from high up on a group of unsuspecting young men, just out for a good time. It overturned their wagon throwing them to the ground violently, one suffered a gash in the head, another had his ribs broken from the weight of the cart and others suffered serious injuries, a few scurried away. The dragon was not finished though, and it circled back blasting fiery flames upon the tents of merchants, who were selling their goods, causing many to flee. It then circled back again and started to bear down upon the people now running in chaos. It grabbed hold of one small innocent boy with its hind legs and soared high into the air with its prey. Then, to the horror of everyone, the dragon dropped its prey from a great height, and the crowd watched as the innocent little boy fell to his death. It then swooped back lashing at women and children randomly. The crowd was terrified seeking anywhere they could to hide.

Yet, in the midst of the chaos, a group of men dressed in grey cloaks and long beards remained undisturbed. They calmly walked right out into the middle of the market place as the dragon bore down for its next attack. The people watched these mysterious figures attentively. To the wonder of all, as the dragon bore down upon them they remained calm, raising their staffs over their heads, pointing them directly at the beast, as if they were going to engage the beast. Suddenly, to the shock of everyone the dragon stopped in midair seeming as if to confront an invisible wall. It halted some few hundred feet away from the mysterious figures. The dragon then started to back pedal with its wings, as if an unknown force controlled it.

Then one cloaked figure waved his staff in a circle, as the others stood firm with their staffs fixed pointing at the dragon in the air, and the beast followed along with the pattern traced by the circular movement of the staff. He swirled his staff toward the skies in some sort of mystical rhythm, and the dragon followed the dance traced out for it. The people were amazed and started to come out of their hiding places to see the sight. All continued to watch in wonder forgetting the horror they had just seen of the innocent boy plunging to his death and the chaos in the market, save the grieving mother of the dead child. They stood transfixed watching the magic of the men cloaked in grey. As the eyes of all were fixed on the director of this magical performance, the grey-cloaked maestro gave one last swirl of his wand, as if directing the dragon to fly off, and the dragon followed the path traced out for it perfectly fleeing from the scene.

The people were immediately beholden to them. They quickly encircled the grey-cloaked men peppering them with questions. They spoke smartly with very fine words saying, "We are wizards, keepers of the secrets of men and enchanters of nature. We have studied the laws and mechanics of the cosmos above and the earth below. We know the secrets of the spirits that dwell in the heavenly bodies and the forces that move things on the earth."

The people were instantly delighted and the merchants all acclaimed them. The shoemakers, market owners, and sellers of festive goods, all came out of the stores curious to see who had saved them. The presence of these grey-cloaked men mesmerized everyone, so that a sense of lightness and laughter filled the air.

There was general rejoicing, save Maria the faithful soul, who was wandering through the market. The crowd had not taken note of her presence. With a contrary tone, she turned with a gruff face as she looked at the wizards, and yelled out rather loudly, "No, no, do not fall under the spells of these enchanters. They are vile men and deceivers. Was it not just a few generations ago that your forefathers worshiped pagan idols and fell for their evil advice? No, no, no, do not follow them!"

At this, the light-heartedness of the crowd dissipated a bit, and the crowd seem to part for the frail old woman, who had been passing through their midst. Yet, the parting of the crowd was just their way of dismissing her, like a group of teenagers turning away from an unpopular character. She seemed like a voice shouting in the wind, which did not hear it.

One merchant dismissed her with a smile responding, "These men are not fiends; they saved our town, and clearly they know how to control the dragon. How bad can they be?"

Another clever young man chimed in, "They are no more evil than the engineers who transverse rivers or the doctor who knows the secrets of the bodies. They are scientists of the ways of nature who know how to control its forces. They are not bad."

With this, they drove off the annoying voice. The crowd then ran off quickly to exalt the wizards. From the crowd one could hear a voice proclaim, "Let us usher them to the King and demand that he give them a place of honor."

A large crowd then started to rush off in enthusiasm toward the palace. A huge spontaneous assembly then formed outside the palace demanding that the King come out, so they could acclaim the heroes of the day. The great mass of people disturbed the King, but he recognized he must say something to them. In a fluster, he came out on the balcony and proclaimed to them, "I hear these men have done the kingdom a great service today. Be assured, I will greatly reward them. Please let them come into my palace and enjoy my hospitality. I will hear the words of wisdom that these men have for our kingdom. Let them be my guests."

Despite his public proclamation supporting the wizards, the King was unsure and fearful. He did not trust the wizards; his Christian upbringing seemed to speak against it, but he thought, "What else am I to do in this situation, only the wizards show any power over this beast?"

He passed by the chapel where his daughter, Procuvera, was praying. She was kneeling with head bowed, looking very intent, as she poured out her soul. The King thought, "Ah, my beautiful daughter, how innocent and faithful she is. The sight of her is surely like seeing a newly blossomed daisy, in contrast to the garbage heap that is the politics I face every day."

"How are you my dear sweet daughter?"

"Oh, just fine my good father."

He did not feel so 'good' just now, but he did not let her see any of his interior distress as he smiled slightly.

"My father, I am so excited. I have to tell you a great story. I have just now heard about a wonderful story of a true martyr of the good God. Her name was Philomena; she was the daughter of prince."

The King wanting a distraction listened quietly.

"It was said that her parents became Christian and baptized Philomena because she was miraculously cured from the danger of death. As she grew, her parents were pleased that she took a vow of virginity when still a tender girl. But when the Emperor was threatening to start his horrible persecution of the Christians, her devout parents sought an audience with emperor."

"Well, it seems that the evil emperor took an unnatural liking to Philomena. To win her he promised to call off his war and leave her parents in peace, if only, they would promise to give her in marriage to him. Philomena, a true maiden of the most high, would not turn away from her true Lord and did not accept to break her vow of virginity."

"Her parents tried every method to induce her to break her vow of virginity. Telling her, You were too young when you made that pledge. It was said, her father also became very angry and threatened her with all sorts of ugly words. Her mother too broke down and both of them got on their knees begging her to cede to the emperors demand for the sake of their family, their people and their kingdom."

"But she boldly replied, No! No! My vow of virginity, is more important that any earthly considerations, whether it be you or my country. My kingdom is heaven."

"She was then handed over to the emperor who tried to induce her to marry him, but she refused as a good noble should have done."

The King continued listening while thinking, "How innocent she is, how innocent and pure, my daughter, a beautiful young lady now."

"Are you listening, papa?"

He replied, "Oh yes, continue," as he smiled slightly.

"Well then the emperor had her scourged, so that her whole back was full of blood. It was said she would have died had not the Virgin Mary appeared to her and gave her healing balms. He then tried to drown her, but the angels saved her from that fate, then he tried to kill her with arrows and lances, but these darts turned back on the archers. He finally had her beheaded. Oh, how glorious it is father to hear such stories of faith. Surely, father you are nothing like that evil emperor. Thank the Lord those times are over." [16]

At this last statement, the King drew back a little at the comparison of himself to the emperor, but managed to respond sheepishly, "No, I would never do anything like him. Christianity is protected in my land."

"Oh father, I know this. We should honor the martyrs such as these. I want to give an offering to beautify her tomb. I will write to the curator of her tomb offering money and commanding them to place an anchor, arrows, and a palm. Oh, oh, and under the palm I will put a javelin and a lily." [17]

"My dear daughter, do as you wish. Whatever you want to send for this tomb I approve. Just ask the treasurer."

The King walked away pondering the contrast between the sight of his lovely daughter and the wizards. "Ah, I used to believe in such tales. My maid told them to me when I was a child. I remember how wizards were such evil figures in such tales, but now I am adult, and I must put away such children's tales for the reality of the politics I face."

He then whispered while walking away, as if, trying to convince himself, "No, I must support these wizards. They are the only hope to overcome the menacing beast that attacks my kingdom. What good are lovely fables for fighting dragons?"

A court servant then stopped him, "My Lord, Fidelus, your regent has assembled a number of concerned Christians who wish to have an audience with you. There is also a mother who claims her child was killed in the market today by that dragon."

"Oh, yes, bring them in. I will hear them in the official court chamber."

Fidelus speaking for all of them said, "As even Nomineus recognized, this beast is beyond natural powers. I warn you, turning to these warlocks is to turn to the very evil, from which the dragon came. Your Highness, who comes from a noble line of Christian kings that threw off paganism, should not turn back to the bestial ways of your forefathers."

The words of the faithful Christians stirred the King's heart for a spell, but soon other voices, knowing the King's vacillating nature, seduced him with a contrary message. The leader of the merchants came marching up with a great procession of important men who ushered the wizards into the presence of the King. Their leader spoke flattering words to the King. "My lord, majestic King, and wise leader of the realm, I beg your attention. I know that your forefathers served our kingdom well by establishing trade routes with our neighbors. They watched over the development of our markets. They made sure the annual festivities were well furnished and kept our land secure from marauding bands. In times of war, they brought together the Kingdom's best engineers to make weapons of war. They fought to protect our ancestral inheritance, ushering in this time of peace we now live in. We have always been pleased with your reign and your concern for social problems. We ask you now to take the advice of these masters of nature's arts; only the wizard's show hope to overcome this beast.

At this, Fidelus shot back, "Nature's arts, rather the devil's black arts. Do not heed him! He will…" The merchants, however, clamored louder drowning out his remaining words, and the whole assembly broke into a confusion of small groups arguing. Finally, the King broke in saying, "Calm down everyone. I will take counsel with my advisors and consider all the viewpoints. For now, these grey-cloaked men may stay here as our friends."

Fidelus tried to intervene to dissuade the King from this act of tolerance, but the ruffians hired by the merchants pushed him to the back of crowd and muffled his voice. All during this commotion, the wizards watched quietly without making any comment. Behind closed doors, the King sighed a breath of relief commenting to his aides, "At last, I am free from that pressing crowd. Don't those Christians know I must run a kingdom? I can't please the merchants if I drive away these wizards. I know they are not Christian, but they do seem to be able to get rid of this problem vexing us. I want no more tales of monsters and heroes, yes, no more tales. I must face the naked reality of politics."

The wizards and court officials were perplexed at the last statement of the King, but they knew they had won him to their cause. Thereafter, Fidelus had little influence in the court, and the King's officials only invited him to official gatherings as a courtesy for he was an old friend of the King's father. The King allowed him to speak as he will, but people treated his words like the speeches of children that one does not take seriously.

*While souls were contriving to turn the King's heart to the wizards, God was preparing his humble servant, George, in the crucible of obscurity and trials.* George was following the path of a pilgrim trusting that God would show him where he should go next. It had now been two years since he left the commission of the Roman army. As he was journeying one late afternoon, he noticed a strange darkness creeping over the land, too early for the dusk and too dense for storm clouds. He sought shelter in a nearby forest thinking it may be an unknown storm. However, the darkness dipped down now right to the earth and soon even filled the forest so that he found himself soon lost in it. He drudged along in the thick darkness that *felt* like it was closing in upon him from all quarters. It became stifling.

He peered around him in fear and continued to trot along with trepidation, making his way only by recognizing the open dirt that kicked up under the horse's hoofs. Soon he ran into a brush. He attempted to dismount, but before he could secure his horse, it suddenly broke free and fled into the darkness. Thus, George was alone in the dark mist that seemed now almost to suffocate him. He started to say some vocal prayers, but his words seemed to choke and would not form. He tried then to form prayers in his mind, but images of darkness ran through his imagination, so he could not keep hold of any holy thought.

In desperation, he pulled out his sword to try to combat the impending fear that pressed on him now from all sides. Just then, out of the darkness a swine charged right at him. To save himself, he speared the beast with a quick stab. He sighed, and thought, "Just an animal, but why do I still feel this foreboding? I can feel the darkness pressing against me. What is this that I am battling?"

He continued to drudge along with his sword drawn in front of him, almost as if cutting through the darkness with the edge of the blade. He attempted to turn over prayers in his mind, but could not keep a whole prayer connected. He walked gingerly along through the seemingly endless darkness, for though his senses were at a peak, he could see nothing more than a few feet in front him. He thought, "Is it night now or still late afternoon? I know not in this darkness."

Just then, a dark phantom like figure jumped out at him. He slashed at it with his sword, but the sword just passed through the dark void, and he no longer saw the phantom. He wondered, "What is that?" Then to his astonishment, he *felt* another presence creep up over his back. He twirled around and slashed at the presence, but nothing was there. He was not sure if it was just his imagination or real. He continued to struggle forward in the darkness trying to get away from the area where he felt the presence.

Suddenly, another obscure image seemed to appear to his right. It was like a beautiful woman beckoning him to come forward. The image intrigued him, and he felt himself drawn to it for at least this was something he could recognize. Her beauty gave him a momentary sense of peace, but this peace was broken when the woman smiled coyly and started to slip off her robe as if she wanted to flirt with George. The knight's senses then came back to him, and he realized the evil deception. To drive away the image from his sense, he turned violently to his left. However, to his horror he saw the same seductive woman beckoning to him from that direction. He turned completely around, and tried to backtrack quickly away from the location. To his horror, he now  saw before him a multitude of seductive images swirling around him wherever he looked.

In desperation, he started to slash at them with his sword. The images seemed to dissipate a bit when he slashed at them, but then they would reform and his battle with these images would continue. With his heart pounding, he stumbled along for a few fierce minutes of battle with these unwanted images now crowding around him on every side. He slashed this way and that, but he could not get rid of them. Finally, he put down his sword and closed his eyes while he continued to stumble forward saying a prayer in desperation, "Oh good Virgin, Mother most pure help me."

Suddenly, he found himself tumbling down a hill. He caught himself with his hands, but continued to roll on his side bouncing off rocks and brush until finally he came to a rest at the bottom of a small ravine. He sat exhausted and in fear, fatigued by the fight, he thought, "I should rest here, at least it provides some protection from whatever lies out in the darkness."

He thus curled up in a ball and attempted to sleep hidden from the elements in the small ravine. He could not find any solace in his dreams though. He felt a presence creep over him nudging him to wake up. He looked around and saw an imposing black figure, causing him to draw back in fear. He looked around and was no longer in the ravine but on top of a cliff overlooking a devastated land. Fear seized him, as he now realized he was looking over the edge of a steep cliff that careened down farther than his eye could see. He stepped back and beheld a black land, spotted with small fires peeking up through crevices in the land. He thought, "Where am I, who am I, what am I to do?"

He felt the presence again creeping behind him. He reached for his sword, but it was not there. He stepped back and realized it was one step too many...

He then jolted up realizing it was all a dream and he was still lying in the dark ravine. Just then, something seemed to pierce through the darkness, an obscure figure with light encircling it. As it drew closer, he could see that the figure seemed to emanate light illuminating everything around it. He could see the translucent figure approaching the top of the ravine. He instinctively struggled toward the light feeling he could trust it. His senses now became keen, and he had an intuitive feeling that he should pray as the figure approached. His mind cleared and prayer came to his mind. He prayed, "Oh my good Guardian Angel guide me that I may know the Lord's true presence and be protected from the shadows that pursue me."

He climbed out of the ravine, struggling toward the light, seeing that the darkness seemed to dissipate around the illuminated figure. He now could make out the features of the figure. It was a majestic sight, a giant, well- built man with huge wings, who was brandishing a massive sword and carrying a linen bag. George knelt before the figure recognizing he was standing before an angel of God.

The Angel spoke, "Rise, chosen one. You are a son of God. Be not afraid! I am Michael, the Defender of God, Chief of the heavenly hosts. I come to give you help in the battle you must engage in. The Lord has seen the plight of the people in Terrasindei and heard their cries. He wishes to send a deliverer to overcome the dragon that ravages their land. You are he, who the Lord of heaven and earth has chosen."

George was transfixed before the heavenly vision, but after a little while, his senses came back to him and his fleshly humanity asserted itself. He asked, "But how will I fight such a beast? A dragon's power is not of the earth."

St. Michael stared back at George with a solemn, stern face and calmly replied, "Be not afraid. He who is the Word has decreed that you will be helped. He has prepared a sword for you to combat the dragon. This sword has been purified by the blood of the lamb and was steeled through God's fiery justice. It can cut the soul away from the spirit and joints from marrow. [18] It will be a judge to unveil the heart of the one wielding it. No created thing can stand against its blade. It will pierce the head of the dragon and cut into its flesh."

After pronouncing these words, the Archangel opened a linen bag he was carrying in his hands. He unveiled a gleaming two-edged sword, emblazoned with words on both sides. One side said in Latin,

"Spirit," the other side, "Truth." The handle glistened with gems of jasper and the edge seemed to emit some glow reflecting light from its blade. The moment George took hold of it the Archangel disappeared leaving George in the vacuum that had parted the mysterious fog.

He stayed there the rest of the night meditating on his encounter with the angel and the mission to which the Lord called him. He pondered the nature of the beast he was to engage, questioning himself, "What is this beast that I am to fight? What are its dimensions? How is one to attack a flying beast with a fiery breath? From where does it come? Surely, not of earth, but some dark region of the sky not known to man, as the stories tell so."

He looked down at his sword emblazoned with the words "Spiritus," and "Veritas." He thought, "With this I will slay the dragon. How, I know not, but I trust that you Lord will provide. My Lord Jesus, I trust in you, but help my unbelief. Show me how to conquer this beast. I know through you I can do all things."

# Chapter 6

# *Mystical powers revealed through darkness*

**M**eanwhile, *the dragon that was thought to be subdued was very active under the cover of night.* Though the wizards had driven it away during the festival, it now made its way back to its former hunting grounds under the cover of clouds. It sought its prey shrewdly; under the cover of darkness, it sought to hunt women who made their living at night. Few noticed these night attacks for society had forgotten these women. Only when the dead carcasses of their bodies started to appear in increasing amounts did anyone take notice, but by then the people had become completely enamored by the wizards. For, they noticed that the dragon dared not to disturb their festivities as long as the wizards walked openly in the town. They considered these unfortunate souls then an acceptable price for society to pay for peace and prosperity.

Despite their growing popularity, the King stayed aloof of the wizards, tolerating them but not inviting them into his inner circle. He had let them stay in quarters at the palace, but he would not consult them. Procuvera, for her part, never took to them feeling a cold chill whenever she passed them in the hallway. The King, however, was not such a sensitive soul and made a point anyway to keep them out of his sight. He would parade them along with him when he was in public to make an appearance that he was supporting them. He in his own way felt that same chill, but stifled his conscience so that he would not acknowledge this in his thinking. The wizards recognized the King's aloofness, but they patiently bided their time as they made secret plans.

Janus, the headmaster of the wizards, looked around at the King's servants for a ready target. He found one in a middle-aged steward named John, a butler as we might call him today. He overheard him speaking in the hallway with the other servants. He could tell he was a talkative fellow, very outgoing, one who always had an opinion about everybody. The steward would often joke and speak about the tales he had heard in the tavern the night before. Janus observed how John attracted a crowd when he told these tales. When his fellow servants crowed around him in delight to hear his stories, he became like a little King with his court around him. Janus concluded John was a perfect target for manipulation.

Janus called over his chosen target in the hallway, "Pardon steward, ah, John right, please come here?"

John jumped to attention. "Yes, it is John. What can I do for you?"

"Well, John, I wonder could you fetch me a good quart of strong grappa. I hear you know your drinks."

John smiled. "Oh yes, indeed I know all sorts. You couldn't name one I do not know. I know of that drink that you speak about. You can get that liqueur, I think, from some of the merchants who travel in from Crete from time to time. I will fetch some for you."

Janus reached over to drop a gold piece in John's hand. John looked at it amazed. "Sir, this is a bit much, don't you think?."

Janus smiled and glanced back at John with wide-open eyes, ignoring the question and replying instead, "My good boy, what do you think about this beast, the dragon, running around everywhere, attacking people at night?"

"Well, I think it is just horrible, really horrible. I mean it just ripped apart my cousin's neighborhood and Mickey's tavern was knocked over the other night and…"

Janus broke in. "Well you know, we wizards could take care of the beast if we only had the King's ear."

"Well, I reckon you could sir. I've seen you all in action. You don't fear no beast. I mean, you just stand there when the beast comes flyin down upon you and wave that wand without any fear or anything. Yep, I bet the whole bunch of you could readily take down that beast."

Janus looked at John now with an intense look, "My good John, I tell you we could tame that beast in no time, if we only had the support of our King, but you see he invites us into his palace, but he does not trust us."

"I see, sir, well, I think you are fine fellows. Maybe the King will change his mind soon."

Janus then closed the hand of John over the gold piece, "Good man, you don't worry about how much I gave you. Now go get that grappa and you have a fine time yourself."

Meanwhile, the dragon started to cause more trouble burning some storage bins at the edge of town, burning some piles of crops, and causing a great deal of grumbling among the merchants.

Janus, for his part took to asking, John many more favors like this and soon won his confidence while he sent a bit of wormwood loose in the palace. Soon he could overhear John telling his tales, with a typically too loud a voice, about how the wizards could take down that dragon thing if only the King would let them loose. Within little time, all the servants were on the wizards' side. At night, they rushed home after long days, where their wives would be waiting for them with meals and they would listen to all the gossip and stories the women had collected during the day. The servants would interrupt their eating whenever they heard about a new attack of the dragon and complain to their wives, "Oh, if only the King would turn to those wizards. They would best it for sure."

In many a home the servants made similar exclamations to their wives. John and his fellow servants likewise would grumble and complain as they downed their mugs at local taverns. Soon, a discontent grew over the populace of Valde Venalicium.

A few weeks later, a large angry crowd assembled outside the King's palace. They had enough of the beast's attacks. The populace knew the wizards resided with the King. They now came in an angry mass to the King's palace demanding to see the wizards. The timid King peeked out a curtain from the safety of the palace interior. They were in the great room and all his ministers were present.

Seeing the urgency of the situation the King turned toward the closest page saying, "Summon for me, Janus and the wizards. Only they can appease the crowd."

As the page was hurrying off to get the wizards, the King paced back and forth sort of speaking to himself sort of addressing his aides. "Do you see that crowd? How am to deal with this? And all over that dragon? I thought it was subdued. I thought I could avoid having to deal with those pagan wizards, but I must deal with the situation as it is. I must be practical. Yes, I must be practical about this."

His court just sat idly by, watching him work it out in his mind as they remained silent. Hearing all the commotion, Procuvera made her way to the wall outside the great hall so she could hear the discussions. After a few minutes, the wizards made their way to the presence of the King. The King greeted them, ignoring protocol. "Finally, you are here. Look, look at this angry crowd. They are here because of that blasted dragon. You must help me with that beast. I know you can do something. I heard you did wonders with that beast at the last festival. I know I have not really welcomed you here. I admit it is because you were foreigners and pagan wizards you know. I did not trust you, but I see now you are our only hope."

The wizards delighted to have finally an audience with the King and proceeded to explain to him, "Lord King, we are at your humble service. We are skilled in the ways of nature. We have studied the ways of men and beasts. We know how to influence both of them through our sciences. We have often dealt with beasts such as this one, which have appeared in different places. In times past, even one from our company in Persia was known to domesticate one of these beasts and keep it for the service of King Astyages.[19] We wish to be at the service of humanity. If you take us into your service, we can help you to overcome this affliction that besieges you. We only ask for a fair compensation for our work."

The King listened with attention, but a divided heart. Within him stirred a feeling of distrust coming from his Christian background that urged him to listen with caution to these pagan warlocks. Yet, a sense of urgency took hold of him as he saw the despair of the people, clamoring for some action. Looking out at the people and then back at the wizards, he paused in silence for a moment. Then he shyly commented, "Continue, I will hear you out."

The wizards taking this as their cue felt now the King was starting to hearken to the words. Janus then spoke up, "This beast cannot be driven out all at once, but we can control it through ritual sacrifices."

The King's suspicious heart grew weary at mention of this, but just then a rock crashed through the window and all heard the shouts of the clamoring crowd outside. This caused the King to draw back and he turned urgently to the wizards saying, "Okay, you are now my only hope! Give me a plan before this crowd tears us apart."

At this, Janus urged his assistant Lumenoire to come forward. He looked intently at the King, smiling calmly to pacify the King's worried face then started in. "We have seen these beasts in action. They tend to devour everything within their sight. I have seen burnt out ash heaps of villages left after the attack of such a beast. If we were not here, you would have to worry, but you need not be anxious since we are here at your service. We can take care of this with only a few little sacrifices, for the good of the whole kingdom. You have children here who die of disease don't you?"

This question caused the King to draw back a little. Despite this, he responded with a timid voice, "Yes, of course, why do you ask?"

"Well" Lumenoire said, "These little ones can serve to ward off the attacks of the dragon."

Procuvera who continued to listen from just outside the great hall overheard this remark. Her heart jumped and her mind fell into confusion trying to comprehend what she had just heard. She clasped her hands together and dropped her head trying to take it in. "What is this they are asking for?" she questioned herself.

Just then, a guard came rushing in to warn the King that the people were threatening to break down the castle doors. The king turned back to the wizards hurriedly exclaiming, "Do what you must, but keep it quiet for now." He then ran out to calm down the angry crowd.

Fidelus called out from the far end of the hall exclaiming, "No, don't take heed of them your Highness. However, the King's general shouted him down, "Shut up you fool. No one cares what you say anymore."

The King for his part glanced at Fidelus when he made this remark, but just turned back to wizards without comment as if Fidelus did not exist. Fidelus knew then that he had lost all influence at the court. As he slumped away depressed, he saw the good princess Procuvera, full of beauty and virtue in contrast to the scene he had had just witnessed. He turned to her and quoted a verse he remembered from the book of Wisdom, "When they had resolved to kill the babes of thy holy ones, and one child had been exposed and rescued, thou didst in punishment take away a multitude of their children; and thou didst destroy them all together by a mighty flood."[20]

Right after he said this, Procuvera heard a baby's cry in some far off corner of the palace. This cry drew her attention away from the King's dialogue with wizards. The child shrieked and then suddenly stopped. She was not sure if it was the child of some maid in a distant corner of the household or her imagination. With that sound though, Fidelus' words pierced her heart. She walked away from King's court and turned her mind inward imagining in her inner eyes a little one who would no longer scream. "Is this sacrifice of convenience the end of the little ones our kingdom? Could a mother really do such to her children? Could a King do such to his people?"

She tried to push such thoughts away and studied intently instead the wall that lay before her. "May I become part of this wall, a statue even, but let me not think that such a thing could happen in my kingdom."

The King popped his head out from a watchtower. The people upon seeing him turned from their plots to burn the ramparts and waited for the King's words. The King called out, "My people do not be so anxious. I am taking control of the situation. See now the wizards are right here with me."

With a gesture then he urged the wizards to hurry to his side. They happily complied and waved at the crowd while standing next to the King. The crowd was appeased and soon dissipated, as did the ruffians the merchants had hired, who had been exciting the crowd to their frenzy.

After the crowds dispersed, the King pondered the words of the wizards in silence, "What is this talk of sacrificing little children? I am not sure what they are getting at. My good grandmother who was always telling stories of Christians standing up to the immorality of pagan Rome would never approve. Yet, what choice do I have? Either I bring these grey wizards close to me and give heed to their advice or the crowds will overrun my palace."

At first, the King had the details of the wizard's plans kept secret. He also hesitated to implement them fully, vacillating because of his innate suspicion. However, the wizards kept urging him, "It is only a few small infants that we need. Just give us the ones the mothers don't want."

When talk of this came up, the King would change the subject and speak about how the wizards must be seen publicly at all the festivals. The King kept dragging the wizards out with him to public appearances, where they would say magic words and perform mystical rituals that they said would ward off the dragon. Secretly, however, they kept urging him to allow them to start the sacrifices. The King put them off them for a few weeks while the dragon continued picking off forgotten souls for its prey.

However, the dragon would not wait for the King to do it; it sought to remind the kingdom of its prowess. One night the wife of a rich merchant was walking alone enjoying the nightlife in the kingdom, when the dragon swooped down upon her taking her in an instant into the dark night sky. The husband not too far off had just turned his sight away from her for a moment. When he turned back in her direction, he caught a glimpse of her held tightly in the claws of the dragon, as it was taking her into the night sky. The distraught husband upon seeing this event called in vain for someone to help. When no one came, he collapsed in a fit of exhaustion.

Later that same night, after downing several drinks, he made his way to the King's palace banging on the door in a rage. The guard who answered the door recognized who it was and rushed to inform his superior who passed word to the King. The King, knowing this merchant was one of the most influential men in the kingdom, rushed to greet him as a show of concern. "Come in my good friend. I just heard the horrid news."

The merchant though was in no mood to be consoled. "I've lost her. She was killed by the beast! That beast in me, or in the air, or wherever it is, that beast took my love! No children now. We were planning to start our family now, but there will be no children now. My love, there will be no children now! My plans, our plans destroyed. Broken, all broken, my dreams, your dreams, destroyed. How could such a beast destroy me, I mean her, take me, ah, her? It has taken everything from me."

The onlookers clearly saw he was drunk and was babbling, but through his blundering speech, they could recognize that the dragon had taken his wife. It was known that she was getting to the end of her childbearing years and was desperate to have children. The rumor was that they had been taking measures to avoid having children early in their marriage, for the wife was very busy with social affairs and they did not want to spread their wealth among too many children. It thus, seemed even sadder that such a grand social light had come to such a state.

Upon seeing the spectacle the rich merchant made, the King now felt he *had to turn to the wizards*. In the cold of that dark night, he turned to them, "Tell me what you need to fend off the dragon?"

They discreetly suggested, "We only need a few little sacrifices of unwanted little ones from desperate mothers."

The King sighed, knowing want they really meant, but latched onto the words, "unwanted little ones," forcing himself to believe it was true. Then after murmuring a little groan, he bent his head down and whispered to the wizards, "Okay, go look for suitable sources quietly. Just don't make a big deal of it."

They soon found a desperate poor woman without a husband. An intelligent good-looking young wizard approached her. He knocked on her door, a poor little cottage, which nevertheless the woman took pride in, keeping everything tidy and in its place. A scared bedazzled face peeked through, "Hello? Are you here to help me with my child? I hear someone was here to help me with my pregnancy?"

The handsome young wizard smiled gently, "Oh yes, I am here to help you with your problem."

He slipped in quietly making sure to keep a mild manner and gently disposition. He asked, "May I sit down? I want to hear your story."

The desperate woman replied sheepishly, "Oh yes, sit, please. I want to tell you what I have been through. No one has taken anytime to listen to me. I did not mean for it to happen. He said, 'he loved me.' I thought he would stay and be with me, but it was a lie. I want to do what is best for the child, but I am afraid. Here it is. I don't know what to do with it."

The flush faced woman presented the child to the wizard. She held onto the child nervously rocking it while they continued to talk. The young wizard sat quietly listening to the mother's story interjecting only, "I understand. I understand, yes you tried the best you could. Do not be afraid. I know some people who can take care of the situation."

The woman was delighted, "Great tell me what I can do. I have no income, no one to support me with this child."

The wizard replied, "Well, let us do the best for you. You can't have a future unless we see you through this situation. Don't worry all will be well. My colleagues and I have seen many situations like this and seen mothers through this with little or no pain."

The woman interjected, "You have, great tell me what I must do."

The young wizard related, "Just follow me, bring the little one with you and it will soon it will be all over. We can take care of the problem and make sure the little one feels no more pain."

The woman was puzzled, but without seeing any other solutions, she followed hoping out of desperation that this young man, with a trusting face, could help her through this. Thus, like a sheep led along a perilous path toward green fields, she followed by instinct. She thought to herself, "I am not sure of this, I want to do the best for my child, but I can't. I love the child, but I can't help it. How can I love a child like this in my situation? How can I take responsibility for it? It is only a little sacrifice."

Therefore, she followed along in a moping manner. Thus, the wizards had their first sacrificial victim, an innocent little child cajoled from his mother by the promise of safety and freedom. The young wizard led her to his colleagues. As they took the child from his mother's embrace, they assured her. "It is for the best. Do not worry your child will no longer feel any pain."

She left weeping and murmuring to herself, "I had no other choice. You must understand my little one. I had no other choice. I am doing the best for you. Please forgive me."

They took the child to an open field later that day. There they had prepared a cold flat stone altar about seven feet in the length and three feet in width, long enough even for a man to lie on. It was located close to the cove from which the wizards knew the dragon emerged. One wizard made sure the altar was completely clean, pure and sparkling, sterilized of any impurities, while another chanted a spell, "*Non tse snafni. Aut oitpo tse. Etcer sicaf utef odneicifretni. Mulos srap sirtam suispi tse. Irtam ispi tecil mutroba erarap. Sutef non tse sunamuh.*" [21]

They left the child screaming, without love, or comfort on that cold flat stone. Just after dusk, the dragon came swooping down attracted by the cries of the child. To the bystanders it seemed, as if, there was a little sly smile that appeared on the face of the dragon as it recognized the baby. The dragon circled down until it came to a perfect rest on top of the rectangular stone altar. It planted its two feet on either side of the child as it landed softly upon the altar. The toes with its sharp protruding hawk-like claws bent down over the edges of the altar. It peered down at its prey staring at it for a moment. The child in terror, screamed with a shriek that could pierce the soul. The dragon picked at the babe and it screamed in pain. Then the dragon like eating a worm tore the child apart with its mighty jaws. Even the wizards could not look upon the horrid scene. They distracted themselves in the ecstasy of mysterious chants losing themselves in the smell of their incense.

Fidelus told the faithful Christians about the horrid decision of the King. The faithful bemoaned this decision, recognizing that now there was upon the kingdom an evil worse than any dragon. The dragon had only attacked their bodies but these sacrifices attacked the soul. These faithful Christians took to the churches praying, fasting and beseeching the Lord that he would send them deliverance. A few courageous leaders among them organized prayer campaigns and spoke up against the presence of the wizards, which they recognized were ushering in a return of paganism.

However, the sound of joyous festivals overshadowed the words of courageous Christians. The wizards at these festivals, playing their parts, stood proudly as saviors of the kingdom. The King made sure the people knew he sponsored them. He walked openly with them at the events, proudly introducing them as artists and technicians of nature's ways who would protect them from the attack of the beast. Soon they demonstrated again their apparent worth with a public show of their power. During one great festival, the people saw the dragon hover over the crowd like an eagle surveying its prey.

The wizards, however, stood proudly without fear posing in some sort of predetermined formation. The dragon circled down as if descending rapidly upon its prey, but just then the head wizard thrust his staff suddenly into the air. At that, the dragon seemed to stop in midair. Then a second wizard drew a circle and the dragon followed in a circular motion along the path traced out for it. Then a third marked a zigzag up and down to which the dragon followed also. Then all the assembled wizards waved their staffs in some sort of mystical ritual and the dragon seemed as if it were dancing along to the rhythm of an unknown song. It was like an orchestra at work; all the onlookers were amazed. The tourists who had come from afar for the festivities thought it was a show commenting, "What a wonderful spectacle they are putting on this year!" not knowing that this was a wild beast. All lauded the wizards and the King was much pleased.

Thereafter the public celebrations in the kingdom were peaceful and well attended. The dragon mostly stayed far away from the festivities and the few times it ventured by, the wizards would chant mystical spells that seemed to drive it away. Each time the dragon would seem to dance at the chant of the wizards and would then fly away as if it were following the wand of an orchestra director. One could hear their chants in the street and others took to saying them also in imitation of the wizards, "Ovlos eanimef. Ovres muus xov mutcele. Ovres xov tu muluvrap mutroba."[22]

The wizards, however, kept returning to the King to ask for more sacrifices, saying they were necessary to keep up their power and to make sure their spells remained strong. It seemed the dragon was growing and they needed to feed it more so to keep it content. The King recognizing how popular the wizards had become, hired men full-time to search the alleyways and forgotten corners of the town for lowly women that the world cared little for.

They most often told the same well-prepared story to each desperate mother. The wizards and their assistants cajoled desperate women into offering their babies for sacrifice with tales of false relief from their sufferings. The wizards, through the mouthpiece of local witches, commended these women for helping to fend off the attacks of the dragon. They even told them they were really doing something noble.

The sacrifices went on for months and the months grew into years, slowly the practice became accepted. Despite the forecast of the wizards, their mystical incantations and sacrifices did not completely control the dragon's movements. It seemed that the beast did not keep its hunger within the bound of the official sacrifices. Repeatedly people whispered stories about how an unsuspecting home had been attacked in the middle of the night and all the inhabitants were devoured. The King's men would hush such reports spreading counter stories about how such things rarely happened.

Procuvera became increasingly alarmed at the actions of the wizards and she sought to learn everything she could about their doings in secret. Still though she was afraid to act publicly, she only listened in on their conferences with the King. She was afraid even to abide in her maidservants; however, they soon surmised her disposition. One night a maid saw her milling about the court while the King was consulting the wizards. She noticed her pressing her ear to the door and making painful expressions while listening. The maid quietly approached and surprised the princess with a question, "Can I ask the King's courtiers to help you with something?"

"No, no, I am okay, um, I was just, just trying to see if the King was busy. I mean, if he had time for me. I won't need your help. You can go."

The servant then shuffled quickly away, but she noticed the pained look on the princess's face. She could recognize the princess did not approve of the wizards.

Soon people began to whisper that the King was not in complete control. Procuvera heard these whisperings also as did the King. The wizards, however, would soon soothe any worries the King had by performing with their magical wands and saying new spells. In the streets, they called out, "Arebil sanimef. Avres sui muroe idnatpo. Mutef sinimef rep ut erecifretni taecil."[23]

Soon after these seemingly mystical words, the dragon would disappear for a while.

Slowly, the King gave in and the sacrifices of the little ones became a common ritual, which by its' increasingly frequency became more well-known through the kingdom. After a while, some mothers without any anguish, simply wanting to be rid of children were depositing their children at the doors of the wizards and witches. Yet few objected, for the festivities continued unabated. Still the wizards said there were not enough offerings to keep the dragon at bay simply through unwanted children. Soon thereafter unplanned attacks started again. The King could not hide the attacks forever and more people came to complain to him about the dragon. The King turning to the wizards asked what could be done. The wizards suggested the King call in his jesters for entertainment and call upon his best rhetoricians to relay the following spell in the form of a benign message. It read:

"People of Terrasindei, we your guardians need your help to protect the health of our nation. We call upon the citizens of this great kingdom to aid us. Help us keep your kingdom safe and healthy by doing your part with little sacrifices. All men live with the reality of beasts. They are part of nature. Through our scientific arts, we know how to keep you safe and free from the attacks of the beast. We came to protect your freedom and to keep you from the oppression of the past. Preserve the freedom that you hold dear. Do not give into the fear mongers who tell you false stories. The best advisors are working studiously to keep you safe and free."

The King was a bit puzzled at this. He asked Janus, "How is this a spell? It sounds to me like simple political rhetoric. What power can such words have over people?"

Janus replied, "Words have power in themselves. They mean what we make they mean. And if they do not say what we want them to mean we twist them, mystically alter them and transform them until they have the effect we want. The power of the words is in the intention of the speaker. I have many years' experience in wrestling with the mystical power of words and know how to tame them to my will. The tone of voice one uses when pronouncing them, the frequency they are used, and whether one speaks them with a smile or not, can change their influence. It is all part of their mystical power.

Speeches and spells are alike in the hands of a skilled orator. Many times one needs to say a spell repeatedly to reach its full power. Likewise, one often needs to repeat well-crafted slogans, bound together with twisted words, to reach their full effect. Spread this spell far and wide proclaiming them with a smile and emotion, repeat them often and then you will see the power they have."

The King glanced down at himself after this little explanation about, 'spells' and 'words' as he had a hint that the wizard seemed somehow to be berating him in a secret way. Then he looked smartly at himself, making as if he were checking out the cleanliness of his clothes, while he was really pondering whether this strange power of words was affecting him now. He decided his sheepish look showed a sign of weakness and thus replied boldly to Janus, "Do as you will. Caste your spell, speak your mystical words. Let the wind carry it to the ends of kingdom. You have my leave to do as you will."

The speech had its intended effect, the number of willing sacrifices started to increase. However, Janus felt that many more such spells were necessary to reach the intended goal. He thus had the King call a public assembly of the people. He had one of the King's officials mount a podium to give a speech, the words of which he had devised through his secret arts. The official spoke thus, "People of Terrasindei our King feels your pain. We all must sacrifice for the sake of the common good. The King has decided to choose only from those little ones who are not wanted. We will not ask more than you are willing to give. These sacrifices are necessary for all of us to maintain our way of life, the freedom and pleasures we enjoy now."

The crowd was pleased at this proposal and applauded loudly the speech. Unknown to them, Janus and the other wizards, even as the official was speaking, were saying to each other, "There will not be enough infants to sacrifice born from prostitutes and loose women, but this will alleviate their concerns for now. We will speak pleasant words to them and advertise this campaign in a compassionate tone. Then there will be little opposition."

As Janus was exiting the platform after the speech, he encountered Princess Procuvera. Their eyes met. Procuvera inwardly studied the features of Janus. She could not hear the secret whisperings of Janus to other wizards on the stage, but she just had a sense that there was evil in his eyes. She peered closely to look behind his eyes and keenly reached out to a get a sense of his demeanor. Behind his sparkling brown eyes, she noticed what seemed like an evil spirit at work and felt a wisp of cold discomfort. She wanted to turn away like a little girl frightened running to her mother, but she knew she must not do this. Instead, she forced herself to stare intently at Janus defying the cold evil she felt pushing her down.

As Janus crept out of the sight of the princess, he whispered to another wizard accompanying him, "She will be a problem. Women are often problematic. They are always going around caring for someone or something. And when it comes to children, too many of them will do anything to protect them. These types of women have no pragmatic sense, too feminine they are, I tell you. Oh yes, women, like this princess, reason by *love, as if love had its own logic.* Our spells have little power over such fools. It is best to just isolate them, persecute them and get them dismissed as, 'fools who live by their emotions."

"Whatever you do NEVER, I say NEVER acknowledge that their arguments have any merit; simply dismiss them out of hand. Yes, this is the best way to deal with them. We will have to bring in a woman of real intelligence, pragmatic to the core, not weakened by any feminine delicacy for little lost children. She is a true equal to us. I will send for her now."

Janus then sent out a messenger to seek his friend, the mistress of witches. He had known her many years and had helped to train her how to use the spells of persuasion. She had become quite adept with these spells, adopting them by inserting a feminine appeal to justice and fairness. When they met in the evening, Janus greeted her cordially, "My dear Mortepulchra, it has been a long time. I am eager to see how you have faired over the years. I hear you have become quite influential in changing public opinion, a master of shaping the thoughts of society."

Mortepulchra stared back at him coldly, "Yes, yes, indeed I have studied this art and I have learned many spells that draw people's affection. I hear that you have managed to plant yourself in the King's court. You have established yourselves as tamer of beasts, I hear. Now, my old friend, tell me how I can help you?"

"Well, my dear, if you could help me with some spells to influence the affectivities of the general populace for our plan."

"Yes, yes, I hear it has something to do with sacrifices for the sake of the beast. Oh yes, these are always necessary. Human beings are beast too. Too many people forget this. We are just the smartest of beasts. Nature has a way of reminding us of this.

Yes, I can help you. It is the genius of liberated women to nurture the beasts of nature within them. We cultivate it; we bear it; we hold it within ourselves. Then it is ready for you wizards to manipulate and control it, but you need us first to bring it forth from our bodies. Always remember women are the masters and mothers of nature. You too must serve this Master, She who is great."

Janus was a little put off by this as he stared at Mortepulchra intensely, but then he regained his senses and responded in a kind sly tone, "Oh yes, I worship also the Mother of beasts. It is She who gives us everything useful. It is from her that we get our raw materials."

By giving this reply, he was playing with her idea while still maintaining control in his own mind.

Mortepulchra recognized this mind game and smiled. "I see you are still in practice with your clever spells. You were using a spell of influence there with twisted words. Very good, but you need something more powerful to overcome my interplay, but you knew that didn't you? You were just playing with my thoughts to see how I would react."

Janus smiled back at Mortepulchra. "You remember me too well." And with that they departed.

Meanwhile the wizards continued to hound the King. They enumerated the fine words they said to the people, how their spells were really taking hold. They hinted to him that they must press on now to continue their work. Erotes, one of the wizards, urged the King, "We have strengthened your hand now Your Highness, through our words, but more is needed. There is need for more offerings to the beast and those that will offer them voluntarily are not enough. You must establish a lottery so that we can have a greater pool of sacrifice to appease the beast.

Let me introduce Your Highness to the mistress, Mortepulchra. She is a master of nature's arts; she knows the minds and hearts of women, and the enchanting words that will bring them to our doorstep. She can help with the campaign to promote the lottery."

Mortepulchra approached the King with a smile. "Do not worry about the beast, it is but a little pet in the hands of one who knows how to take care of its needs."

At first sight, the haunting beauty of Mortepulchra entranced King Felix. The sight of her instantly drew him in so that he forgot everything else about him. Just as he was about to lose himself in his fantasies, the image of a terrible black monster seemed to be tearing into his mind. This jolted him back to reality and made him realize that there was something strange about her. He paused to catch his breath and then thought, "The sight of her, her tone and very continence is magnificent, but terrifying, she is attractive but repulsive, she draws me in but it makes me want to run as far away from her as I can. What is it this power that is before me?"

He contrasted in his mind the sight of his beautiful daughter. He thought, "Oh, how different is the sight of her. She is purity and charity, sweetness and hope. Nothing in her continence scares. What then, am I afraid of in this creature before me?"

Mortepulchra smiled breaking his train of thought and said to him, "Do not be afraid. We only come to help. I know the secrets of nature. The dragon is one of nature's many children. Nature is my sister. I can tame the dragon, one of nature's beasts. I know what food it eats and how to subdue its appetite."

The King hesitated, "Okay, yes, you may proceed, but wait. I am not sure. What do you mean? You are a witch, yes? Did not our good God condemn your kind in the Old Testament? Is not your work an evil craft?"

Mortepulchra smiled again as her long black hair shimmered, "Oh, no I do not practice the dark arts. I only help people with my magic. Wiccan is an art that works with nature to tame its secrets and bring it to the service of humanity. We believe in the God that is within. She is all around us and She can be called on through the powers of our positive intentions. We have learned wisdom through following Her who is within. To turn our powers against others would be to break the harmony of nature. What I can do here is to keep nature in accord with Herself. We simply take little ones not wanted by one branch of nature, but that can serve as fertilizer for another. Nature is our Mother and we learn from Her the ways to keep balance. These little sacrifices help to keep balance. As long as one does them with a good intention then nature will remain in harmony, and peace will reign."

The King looked down at his feet. He knew she was talking about more sacrifices of babies even if her words befuddled the actual acts. His head felt dizzy and clouded as if some force were pressing against it. He tried to shake off this suggestion for more sacrifices, which seemed to be pounding on his head causing a small headache, but he could not. He looked at her and tried to look in upon himself. Then he looked back at her. Something in the haunting beauty of her eyes drew him in, and at once he found himself blurting out, "Yes, yes, do as you will. I guess I would not want to hurt nature or anything."

At that, the pressure against his head subsided and his headache went away entirely. Soon thereafter the public all received notices delivered to them with a strange message about a lottery to gather offerings to keep the kingdom safe.

*The Lord in heaven looked down upon the kingdom and sighed. He looked around and asked among the luminaries.*

Who will deceive the King, so that he will go and fall?  And one appeared before him, "I will Lord."

"How?" the Lord asked, "I will go forth and become a lying spirit to the King's advisors.

"You shall succeed in deceiving him. Go forth and do this."[24]

# Chapter 7

## *Cloaked secrets revealed*

*I*t had been two years since the dragon started its reign, and the wizards had now firmly established their influence in the kingdom. Despite the widespread zeal for the plan of wizards, not all in the kingdom had lost their sanity. Some in the kingdom abhorred the sacrifices the kingdom offered. Here and there, if one looked closely, they could see women with tired looking faces complaining, "The kingdom is going to the devil."

In other places, hearty men, with well-worn hands complained, "It just ain't right. We keep feeding that devil beast running around everywhere and giving no heed to our Christian faith. It just ain't right."

Even occasionally, astute and meditative intellectuals would pine to confidents how the culture in Terrasindei has reduced man to a slave to the dragon. He is now lower than the cows in the fields, which at least run when their predator comes to take them.

A few bold priests stood against the crashing waves of the culture preaching strongly against the child-sacrifices. These true shepherds were not afraid to warn the flock of these predators, even in the face of revilements and scorn. Fr. Pneumatus, a strong figure, preached boldly, "Do not give into this abomination. Turn away from these sacrifices that only feed the gods of pleasure. Do not remain enslaved to your passions. Take hold again of your sonship in God, and do not lower yourselves to the state of swine. Your Father wishes to welcome you into his home and feed you at the finest banquet if you will only turn from these vile ways."

However, most people, intoxicated by the lure of comfort, looked at this shepherd with blank stares as if he were speaking a foreign language. Only a few brave souls took to heart his calling. They formed a group made up of those who sought to overcome the scourge upon the land, but the voices of true shepherds were few, and thus the faithful who stood against the tide where likewise few in number.

Archbishop Jocundus, appearing tall and proud as he publicly sought friendship with the King's officials, was thunderously silent about the sacrifices. To the faithful, he seemed like one of the mosaics on the wall, a tiled facade of a true hero without any real life. He was a friend of the King and dared not speak too boldly, for fear of losing his favored status with his lordship. When a few brave young men stood up courageously speaking against the abominable sacrifices in the public square, people mocked them for their witness. The archbishop rebuked their action and distanced himself from their discourse saying, "We Christians stand as a unifying people in this kingdom. I cannot support the divisive rhetoric that a few radicals displayed today. We should witness rather to a spirit of dialogue recognizing that what unites us is more than what divides us."

After hearing the statement of Archbishop Jocundus, the zealous young men abandoned their campaign and moped off after facing ridicule from the so-called 'civilized' members of their *own* Church.

In this depressing situation, the devout bemoaned to the Lord beseeching him, "Lord what shall we do?"

They gathered in the church halls of the few faithful shepherds and consoled each other in the dark, while they prayed for the Lord to end this scourge upon their land. In secret, though, they continued their opposition to the wizards. To many of the faithful the actions just did not seem right and they felt, somehow, they that must continue to take action. Such souls, antsy for action, came to cluster around a prayer group meeting at Fr. Pneumatus's church.

After one of these prayer meetings, Bacchus, a devout and brave soul, was meditating on their intention that night, which was to overcome the work of the infernal dragon. He felt a sudden urging to find the meeting place of the wizards and spy on their doings and noting their spells. At first, he thought to himself, "This is imprudent. I am not one to go sneaking around. I came here to pray and let God work on it."

But as he continued walking down the lowly street that night, he could not shake off the thought. He thus argued with himself. "Surely, you know where they meet? You see these grey-cloaked figures frequently meeting at the lodge not far from your house. It would be so easy just to listen in on their conversations. What do you have to lose?"

Finally, feeling overwhelmed by this inspiration, he decided to hide himself near their lodge where they normally met. He made himself out like a beggar in a dark alley around the corner. For the first time really scrutinizing their meeting place, he noticed its features. It was an inconspicuous darkish brown, stone cobble house. He thought to himself, "Hmm, it looks so normal."

After seeing the last of the grey-cloaked figures make their way into the meeting hall, he hid himself just outside a window, so he could listen to their conversation. The wizards were discussing their plan for dealing with the dragon, "We should continue to feed the beast's honor. The quantity of food is not as important as the beast's honor. As long as the dragon feels it reigns over the region, it will be appeased."

Another said, "Oh yes, in Persia I hear they honored one as a god that kept it at bay for years. It became like a court pet, so docile was it."

Bacchus was horrified at this last statement; it seemed to confirm his opinion of the wizards. Yet, there was worse to come that night. Late into the night, they discussed stratagems, back and forth. It was like listening to the writers for some macabre theatre production.

Bacchus continued to listen to their conversation. He heard them say how their public demonstration of control over the beast would help them to create a stronghold in the kingdom, which in turn would allow them to address other social problems. He heard one say, "Of course, we must pay our due when the time comes."

To which another replied, "Oh yes, we will all pay it when it comes due."

Bacchus was puzzled at this statement but continued to listen. He then started to realize that some of the voices were familiar, like he had heard them somewhere in public before, but he could not quite place where. They continued speaking about how they would educate all the children in the arts of nature; how their children would benefit from being loosed from the chains of the rigid Christian dogmatism that held Terrasindei tightly. Their leader proclaimed, "We will destroy this society and remake it in a better way."

After a while, Bacchus reflected how disturbing it all seemed that despite the morbid topic the whole meeting seemed to be very orderly. There were no passionate outbursts; they seemed to be generally in accord, and there was no disruptive little groups interrupting the discourse. It seemed as if the combination of little orations seemed as a whole to make a spell that had power over the listener. As he was thinking about this, he noticed the door open, and a very sullen-faced looking cloaked man slipped out of the meeting hall with a few others following. He just caught a glimpse of his face but not enough to allow him to recognize him; however, he could tell it looked very grave and withdrawn. The man also seemed to mope along betraying a depressed spirit. Following his intuition, Bacchus followed the small group, shadowing them to see where they were escorting the sullen-face one.

This small group of grey-cloaked wizards weaved through darkened corridors remaining hidden from the lamps that shown in the night. The sullen face one, which the others seemed to be leading on, looked pale and somber, but he continued on dragging his feet like an animal, pushed against its will. As they passed in and out of the shadows, Bacchus observed how the light seemed somehow to collapse close to the face of the sullen one; it was if there was a darkness forming in the air around him. He said to himself, "What is this that drains the light from the air? What power is at work?"

The procession finally stopped and mounted a slightly raised platform where political leaders often gave public addresses. At night, however, the square was dark, and the platform stood silent only holding onto echoes of proud speeches in the imagination of those who looked upon it. Bacchus looked on with curiosity. Upon reaching the platform, one of the three companions of the sullen faced wizard took out a string that he had hidden in his cloak. He attached it to the wrist of the sullen-faced one and tied the other end to a post on a podium. As the moonlight peeked through the rooftops highlighting the center of the platform, Bacchus could just see glimpses of the wizard they prodded along the way. He noticed that his face now appeared stone cold, as if he were in a trance and living through some terrible dream.

Then to the utter astonishment of Bacchus, the three wizards receded back a few steps, and *the dragon appeared from out of the folds of darkness.* Yet, the wizards did not seem to fear the beast. At the sight of the dragon, they did not rush away or even seem to take much notice of its presence. It was clear that they knew the dragon was present and had no concern. Without any apprehension, they then calmly took off the cloak from their pale faced comrade and then spoke to him in a solemn tone, "Now is the time for you to pay your dues. You have been given a prominent place in the order of nature. You served her well, now you must return to your true master."

After these bizarre words, they turned their backs to their colleague, receding into the shadows while the dragon drew closer. The drama of it caused Bacchus to affix his eyes to the sight of the now stone cold figure of the man. As the other wizards slipped away, he recognized the face of the man; he was a royal official who was once prominent in the kingdom. Now this former luminary in the King's court stood face to face with the dragon. It just then struck Bacchus that they had tied him to the same podium where in years past he had given prominent speeches.

As Bacchus continued to watch attentively, he noticed that the royal official's face now turned from a stone faced hew of blue to pale white and contorted with a look of utter fear. No longer in a trance, the former luminary now bent back like an animal fleeing from its prey. In an even more bizarre turn that surprised Bacchus, the Dragon itself broke the silence. Saying, "I have given you power to rule and hunt in my name. Now it is time for me to take back the flesh that is mine!"

The official screeched back, "Yes, I have served you, but please, no, I am not ready!"

Now in terror, he tried desperately to untie himself from the small little string, but was not quick enough. The dragon opened up its giant jaw and swallowed the former luminary whole with one huge bite. Bacchus drew back at this sight, horrified. He murmured under his voice, "How, why, what just happened? Lord, I commend his soul to you. "

Bacchus slipped away into the night pondering the horrible image that was now seared into his mind of the terrorized wizard desperately trying to untie himself from the weak little a string. He thought, "What a small little thing that held him tied to that post. An attachment he made himself, a weak little strap not even a rope, but strong enough to hold him though when the beast came upon him. I see now these wizards have no real power. The beast holds the power to make men enslave themselves. These men only pretended to be in control, while they were deceiving themselves and us. It is rather this intelligent beast who is their true master."

Bacchus brushed away the sweat he noticed dripping from his forehead. Right at that moment, he made a resolution. I will oppose these wizards with every ounce of my being. I must not rest. I must not waver. I must not stop, until we disperse this evil cohort. I see that this beast destroys human nature; it not only devours the body but also kills the soul, encompassing the whole man with its hunger.

The next morning, Bacchus gathered some of the other faithful who opposed the dragon and told them the horrible truth of what he saw. Some believed right off, as it confirmed their fears, others doubted, saying they could not believe such horror existed. Soon, a cohort of brave Christians joined in a pact to oppose the wizards and the dragon who they served. They agreed to spy more on the workings of the wizards, and the dragon, to see how they worked in collusion to allow this evil to come upon their land. Putting their trust in God, they left their meeting and went to the Church to commend their plans to God for the safety and welfare of their land.

Thereafter, a few stalwart Christian souls took on the task of spying on the wizards. They too witnessed the terrible conspiracy of the wizards who were in collusion with the dragon. Likewise, they started to shadow the women who some said were offering their newborn children as sacrifices to the dragon. They observed the despairing faces of the mothers, their cries of terror when the wizards took their baby from them and the horrible scene of the innocent little ones left on cold stone altars to die. They saw Calvary repeated before their eyes, but not for redemption, rather as a sacrifice to the passions of men. Many then vowed that they would do everything in their power to prevent these sacrifices.

Some of the faithful Christians marched to the gates of the King's palace demanding an audience to address the terrible outrage that was going on in their land, but royal officials would always dismiss them saying, the King had no time. They then went to the public squares to warn people of the horror in their midst. However, the merchants who were fond of the wizards, made sure a clutter of noise drowned out their speeches. Despite the seeming uselessness of their efforts, the Christians in face of continued despite the contrary spirit that fought them. They persevered in pray and spoke to anyone who would listen. They trusted the Lord had a plan that they could not always see. Bacchus urged them on,

"We must be faithful, however bad the situation looks. God can overcome; He will overcome if we trust in Him."

The Christian cohort organized themselves into a unit trying to fight the dragon, while they prayed that God would deliver them from this plague. They consulted a faithful young priest Fr. Cristalta, who helped them to organize groups to campaign against the wizards.

They went about their work with great dedication, sacrificing their free time to the endeavor. They roamed through the public markets speaking to anyone who would listen about the terrible deeds of the wizards. As a result, they soon recruited faithful souls to the campaign. Among them were even some good pagans who were outraged at what they heard.

Not all was easy for these hearty Christians and their companions. The royal officials hearing about them speaking against the sacrifices in the public square, would often harass them, preventing them from talking at all. Further, they would hide their agents in the crowd to rouse people to call them names and ridicule them. Meanwhile, the dragon itself became furious at the opposition and started to attack a few houses of the merchants to show its power in the marketplace.

The King, seeing the anxious faces of the merchants, called his royal officials together with the wizards. "What is this I hear, that the dragon is attacking the merchants again? Do we have control over it or not?"

Janus pied up. "It is a few bothersome Christians. They are not heeding the call of Archbishop Jacundus for dialogue. They are stirring the anger of the beast. They are not willing to confirm to the reality of the situation. This beast is here to stay; it is no use working against this fact. These troublesome Christians will not accept this. They are arguing that the beast cannot be controlled and thus oppose our truly effective means to control it. They have been harassing the women who offer their unwanted little bundles. The result has been to exasperate the beast and cause it to lash out more. We must act against them."

The King looked on the wizards with a distrusting eye, but also recognized anxiety in the face of the merchants. He looked down and turned his thought inward, but before he could hear the voice of his conscience, he turned back to them. "Do what you want only relieve me of this anxious group that is always pressing upon me."

The wizards thus sought every means to harass the Christians, exclaiming that they were the cause of the increased activity of the beast. They used this as a pretext to offer even more sacrifices to the dragon. For its part, the dragon was never appeased; its appetite seemed to grow every more, so that, more and more sacrifices seemed to be necessary in the eyes of the wizards.

The King had an uncomfortable feeling about all the actions of the wizards, but he continued to appease them by allowing them to seek whatever they needed for the new sacrifices. The wizards, seeking to soothe the minds of the mothers who had heard rumors about the terrible sacrifices, decorated the altars to make them look more comfortable. They created rituals so that the mothers could say, "good bye," to their little ones with 'dignity,' and they hired kind looking women assistants to speak compassionate words to those bringing their children. These women would tell them, "All will be okay. Do not worry. You must do this now; it will make things better for you."

Meanwhile, within the same palace walls, where King Felix placated every whim of the wizards Procuvera was becoming more and more distressed. She saw how the wizards were clamoring around her father and heard whispers of more "sacrifices." Finally, getting courage, she cornered one of her maids and asked her directly, "What is this I hear about, 'children being sacrificed?' Have you heard about any such goings on in our kingdom?"

The sheepish maid replied, "Well, Your Highness, I hear that the wizards, your majesties' servants, have been looking for young pregnant women all across the kingdom. I hear rumors that they are trying to convince to take their children out to the fields. Then after that nobody sees them anymore."

After hearing this, Procuvera walked away from her maid and hid herself in her room for a while lost in an argument with herself. "Oh, I wish I could remain a girl forever, a pretty little girl without any cares. I used to love it when my father caressed my hair and how mama when she was alive complimented me on my good posture.

Would that I could go back to *playing* the good princess of my childhood dreams, yes, yes, in those dreams the kingdom was always so nice, the people so gracious and papa was a grand King."

She tried to picture herself as a girl, posing as the proper princess in procession with her father and mother, the King and queen, but suddenly the image was shattered as she pictured a mother in the adoring crowd holding an infant. All at once, the mother seemed to grow into a rage and strangled the child right in front of her. Procuvera then turned her thoughts violently away from her daydream and buried her head in the bed as she wept profusely.

Despite the propaganda of the wizards, the quiet opposition of the Christians started to have an effect. The number opposing the dragon began to increase; even some merchants, seeing the beast was beyond the control of the wizards, joined the movement. Some mothers who had given up their children for sacrifices had come to repentance. They too now joined the fray to make up for past sins and witness to life. The quiet campaign of these faithful souls then continued in hopes of eventually ridding their land of this beast, even as the wizards and the King's officials tried to oppose them at every turn. Throughout the struggle, the good Christians stayed close to their priests relying on the power of the sacraments, while they offered their own prayers to the Most High.

*The Lord in heaven who is never silent foresaw their prayers and directed the champion he was preparing to come to their aid.*

# Chapter 8

# *A True knight sent from heaven*

I t was spring, nearly two and half years now since George had left the Roman Army corresponding with the time in which the dragon had reigned over Terrasindei. As George was approaching the outskirts of the kingdom, Bacchus was praying in a small outdoor chapel for God to deliver them from the scourge upon their land. The faithful Christian had his head bowed, but something caught his attention out of the corner of his eye. He saw a foreign knight, looking strong and fearless, with a cross emblazoned on his shield. There seemed to be a strange aura that surrounded him, emitting a sense of peace, even as he proudly carried his sword by his side. He knew this was an answer to his prayers. With the first sight of this noble knight, he instinctively knew he could trust him even with his very life. Running to greet George he called out, "My lord, my lord what brings you here?"

George replied, "I have come in search of the Lord's will. I seek to enter into battle for Him. The Lord has sent me to do battle with a dragon. Have you seen any in these parts?"

At that, Bacchus the stalwart Christian, knelt down and started to weep with joy so that he could not immediately answer him. After a few seconds, he regained his composure and replied, "We have been waiting for a champion such as you. You are the answer to our prayers. Yes, there is a dragon in these parts. I am among a small group of faithful Christians who have been trying to oppose it. Please come with me, and I will introduce you to the other faithful who have been in this battle with the dragon. We can answer all your questions. Come now!"

Bacchus led George to the small cadre of Christians who had been battling the dragon. Word spread quickly among them that a foreign knight had arrived who seemed to be an answer to prayers. The small cohort assembled quickly in a house next to the Church, and George entered into the room where the curious crowd was gathered. Bacchus then introduced him to the waiting crowd, "Here is the answer to our prayers. His name is George. He says he is here heeding a call from God to fight a dragon."

Spontaneous exclamations poured out from those assembled. A devout old woman called out, "The Mother of God sent him. She is praying for us."

Another called out, "How did you find us?"

George tried to respond humbly, "I was just trying to follow God's voice and…"

Another excited Christian interrupted him, "Tell us how you will kill the dragon?"

George started to answer, "Well, I have not yet even heard where the dragon lives. I trust the Lord will lead…"

Before he could finish another interrupted, "Notice how strong he looks." Another called out, "He is God's giant."

George now was getting abashed at all the attention. He finally broke in, "Slow down, slow down. I am a trained soldier. Please, all things in their proper time. Let me see the lie of the land first then I will engage the beast. Tomorrow, I will scout the dragon and its lair. First things first though. Tell me where am I? What country is this?"

At this, the crowd laughed and started to disperse. George stood there baffled still awaiting a response, but recognizing that he was accepted. As the crowd dispersed, a young man who had been waiting patiently made his way to the front. His name was Sergius, an aspiring young scout with ambitions to enlist in the Roman army. He smiled shyly and mentioned in a matter of fact tone, "You are in Terrasindei, the land without gods. Welcome, I am so glad we have an experienced knight who can direct us in battle. I am eager to learn anything I can from you. First though, let me show you where you will be staying tonight."

The next day, the Christian cohort brought him to a two-room stone cottage for a meeting. This humble little cottage had become a familiar haunt for the little Christian cohort, a home for their ideas, a place for strategizing and place for solace. Yet, it was nothing much to speak about. In years past it was used as a living quarters for a family of ten in the cramped style of the day. As was the manner, there was a fireplace in the center to warm both rooms and cook small items. The rooms, which were once divided, now lay open to each other creating one big great room. The cottage had passed to the estate of Lady Kathleen, a pious Christian noble who supported the work of the Christian cohort. She had made the cottage into a meeting hall for charitable purposes. Her servants had thus set tables near the east wall with chairs and an open space toward the west wall.

From the outside, the cottage did not look like anything special, just a plain stone house with a few small windows adorned with wooden shades. Its walls had a typical purplish-grey hue owing to the clay mortar used in the area to bind the stones together and roof was a shade of burgundy, as it was covered with stone shale serving as shingles. The cottage was built to last, but was not much to look at, just perfect for the cohort, a good foundation but not much flash. In time, the Christian cohort came to call the little cottage "Domus Spiritus" but this is getting ahead of things. Now it was simply a convenient location to brief George. Sergius and the other members of the Christian cohort met him here, explaining to him the nature of the dragon, its pattern of destruction, and the evil it had brought upon the land. George listened, took mental notes and asked many questions. He was disturbed to hear how far evil had progressed in the kingdom. However, he believed firmly that the Lord had called him here. Thus, he looked forward to matching his sword with the dragon so to vanquish evil from the land.

George turned his thoughts to the Lord. "Well Lord, I trust in you. I am not sure how I am to engage the dragon. I know you have a plan and that I am part of that plan. Show me what to do next."

After the meeting, he put his heart to prayer and waited on the word of the Lord.

Meanwhile in the King's court seeds of dissension against the wizards were germinating. Princess Procuvera became increasingly distressed over the appalling actions done to the innocent little children. She whispered to herself meditating on the horror of it all. "How could they kill these pure little ones? These wizards and evil shamans do not bring relief but grief. My Father and his court should take heed of the wisdom imparted to us in the tales told by our nannies. They warned us of wizards, witches and dragons. Oh, I believed, I have always believed. Now I see I am in the midst of one of these stories now. Will it turn out well? Lord, I pray that it does."

Procuvera heard whispers from court officials about the small cadre of Christians opposing the dragon and the wizards. Generally, the court officials derided them with grumbles as the greatest obstacle to their work. She surmised then that the work was having some effect because of the aggravation it caused the court officials. Finally, one of her maids got the courage to address her directly about the work of the Christians. In private, she whispered to her, "I have seen your distress over the mothers sending their children to their doom. I can see Your Highness that you are disturbed and saddened because of this. I want to tell you, I know some of those who are opposing the dragon and seeking to rescue the precious infants. They are a brave lot."

Procuvera brought the maid closely and whispered to her, "Come with me into my chamber, and we will talk privately."

The maid then explained, "My Lady, I know there is a small group of true Christians in my poor parish that have been covertly opposing the wizards. Pardon me, my Lady, if I speak against the King, your father, but I must tell you the truth."

Procuvera smiled and touching her on the shoulder gently said, "Do not worry. Continue, I share your concern. I have come to see that these wizards have gained too much influence over him. Please continue."

"Well, my Lady you see these brave Christians have been opposing the wizards in word and action. Some even have been following the wizards as they turn their spells on desperate mothers to influence them to give up their children to supply their sacrifices. Sometimes they manage to intercept these mothers along the way to the altars of sacrifice and speak a few words of hope; too often though they fail. Others hide near the places of sacrifice and try to snatch the innocent little ones left on the altars before the dragon comes to devour them. They are so brave. The wizards though have convinced the King to put more guards out, so it is becoming harder and harder now to rescue them from their terrible fate.

Still others are trying to oppose the wizards with speeches that stir up the people. The wizards though, have hired ruffians who disperse them whenever they try to speak. Now we have renewed hope, for we just heard a foreign knight has arrived in answer to a calling from God. We believe he is an answer to our prayers. You could be a great help to us, Your Highness."

Procuvera thought to herself, "I see, I can no longer live in my daydreams. I must face the truth. I must now live like those heroic queens I remember from the tales of childhood. "

Summoning up courage then as she recalled the queens in the fairy tales, she responded boldly, "As my loyalties lie first to the kingdom of God, I pledge you my full support as a princess of God's kingdom in any way I can help. Be wary though, for I see I must keep this discreet as of yet. The wizards are everywhere, and they have great influence in the palace through the power of their spells. My father, the king seems to be increasingly succumbing to their spells. If they are willing to do this to the king, I am not sure they will hold back from harming a princess."

Seeking to witness the horrors for herself, Procuvera arranged to sneak away one night with her maid. She passed through the shadows dressed in the garb of one of her servants. Her faithful maid directed her to a place where the wizards would meet the women, a dirty street, just behind where marketers sold their goods. Merchants clamored in the background arguing over the price of goods. The two waited in hiding near a darkened alley littered with few shards of broken jars and other trash thrown aside by those passing through the market. From the darkened alley, a desperate looking woman peeked out with some object wrapped tightly in her arms. Procuvera noticed a hooded man greeting her. As he greeted her he took off his hood, smiled and spoke in a gentle tone as he directed her to come along with him. Procuvera could see the man was young and handsome, a contrast to the task he was undertaking. Procuvera and her maid shadowed them for several blocks. As they drew closer to the place of sacrifice, several more wizards met up with their cohort, forming now a kind of procession to the place of sacrifice.

Procuvera noticed the demeanor of the woman who seemed like a broken thing, not much different from the shards of the broken jars outside her residence. She seemed like a zombie with sullen sunken eyes just prodding along only the aggressive gestures of the wizards seemed to push her along now. The wizards were now murmuring some chants that became like a morbid hymn for a deadly procession to the place of sacrifice. Meanwhile, the young handsome wizard spoke soothing words to the mother saying, "It will be alright. It can't even really think yet. See, it does not protest. It will just hurt a little bit, this sacrifice. The procedure won't take that long then it will be all better. Don't worry that the beast will not bother you anymore after this."

They weaved through the streets until they came to an open field, a remote location that would not attract the attention of the townspeople. The area was spotted with many rock outcroppings, among which the wizards had chosen a rather flat one for an altar of sacrifice. Procuvera, who was following, now hid herself in the crevice of a rock with her maid. The woman uncovered what looked like a pile of rags revealing a child, which she was directed to place on the cold stone altar. She then turned and ran away instinctively, fearing not the dragon, but a pitiful feeling that seemed to enclose in all around her. The wizards watched from a distance, and the princess peered upon the scene from her hiding place. Suddenly a brave Christian woman, Veronica, rushed up and sought to grab the innocent child from the altar, but an arrow swooshed in her direction, and she ducked to avoid it. Then another arrow whooshed by her head causing her now to seek cover, pinning her down just a few feet from the stone altar.

The King's soldier then appeared commanding her away from the altar with crossbows at the ready. Veronica reluctantly pulled back and they ushered her away from the scene. Then the grim sacrifice continued as the princess looked on. She witnessed the winged beast circle above taking measure of its prey. Then suddenly, it swooped down and pounced on the innocent little one. With its giant jaw, it could have swallowed the child whole, but instead it tore and ripped at his limbs picking the infant apart. The child could be seen convulsing trying through instinct to turn away from the pain, but the dragon kept picking him apart. Only after a few minutes was the whole child devoured. Procuvera wanted to rush out and stop it, but she knew she was no match for the dragon, or for her father's evil guards that stood watch over the murder scene. Therefore, she wept silently burying her head in her hands. When it was over, her maid urged her to flee from the sight, but she could not move for a while overcome with the horror of the sight.

Finally, her maid whispered to her quietly, "Your Highness, it is a horror, I too weep. You could not have done anything for this little one, but come and we will show you how you may aid us in many ways to stop this horror in the future."

After a while, Procuvera regained her composure and slipped away from that sight. Her sadness remained for a while, but soon it turned to rage as she thought about how her father perpetrated this, even providing guards for the gruesome scene. The bile in her stomach started to build up as she wiped the tears from her eyes. She turned to her maid. "I pledge now to do everything in my power to fight the dragon and my father's participation in this evil. May our royal name be restored!"

The rest of the night Procuvera could not sleep, as she had the horror of the gruesome sacrifice imprinted on her mind. She slipped out of bed and knelt on kneeler before the crucifix, she whispered to our Lord, "Lord, how can this be overcome? What horror. What horror! How am I ever to get this scene out of my mind? But Lord, should I really want to be rid of this image? The blood of these children is on our royal house. How are we to be cleansed of it? Oh good Virgin, show me how to be a good queen like you."

She then felt a deep sense of peace flow over her, and it was as if a refreshing song was sung to her soul. She rested in that song for a bit, causing her to become completely relaxed so that her mind became as one, and she knew then what she was supposed to do.

The next day, she ventured out in disguise to seek this band of stalwart Christians who opposed the dragon and the wizards. She secretly started to give them financial support and recommend to them others in the palace that might offer help for their cause. She started to spy out the plans of the wizards and her father's cohorts listening to their conversations about the sacrifices. She then passed any information she gathered onto the small Christian band.

The brave Christian princess even went so far as to oppose her father's soldiers when she heard the wizards talking about more sacrifices. She planned a ruse, wherein she would hurry to meet the procession and interrupt it, demanding that the soldiers address some concerns she had about a supposed administrative matter. This slowed them down enough to allow time for the small Christian band to intercept the mother on the way to the place of sacrifice. When the soldiers were distracted, the Christians worked on convincing the mother not to kill her child. Procuvera practiced this tactic the next few times the wizards went out for their ritual sacrifice, thus, saving the innocent ones from death. Each time she would whisper a little prayer that the Lord would protect her from the wiles of the enemy as she sprinkled holy water around her carriage for protection.

The dragon, noticing that it was now losing more and more sacrifices became furious. Circling above one night, it spotted one of the wizards about. Ignoring its bond with wizards, the dragon pounced upon the unsuspecting wizard pinning him to the ground, demanding an accounting of why its meals were slowing down. The wizard in terror, face to face with the jaw of the dragon exclaimed, "It is that princess, the daughter of the King, the one who rides in the royal carriage with a rounded contour. She has been distracting the guards and interrupting the sacrifices."

This was enough for the dragon; enraged that the princess dared to defy its authority, the beast prowled that evening with a keen eye for the carriage described to it. Finally, it spotted the carriage and drove down fiercely upon it seeking to tear the carriage apart with its mighty claws and rip apart the princess' body. However, as it came crashing down upon the carriage top the beast felt as if there were barrier opposing it. Its claws bent back in pain, and the dragon fell back on its hind side crashing to the ground. The carriage, which should have been crushed by the weight of the beast, was simply flipped on its side but remained intact.

The confused beast made its way to its feet seeking to turn the carriage and the princess into ashes with its fiery breath. However, its breath suddenly became stifled and it waddled away trying to grasp for air. The dragon was now completely bewildered and recognized some force was driving it away from the carriage. Just then, the wizards raced to the scene and said some chants, as if they were driving off the dragon. The dragon fled knowing it could not break through the strange barrier that protected the princess.

The wizards then rushed to the King and reported everything that happened detailing how the dragon attacked his daughter, apparently because she had been helping to oppose their sacrifices.

The wizards demanded that the King rein in the princess or they said, "We cannot guarantee the safety of your daughter."

The report shook the King, and he was inwardly appalled at the gall of the wizards that now make demands on him. He thought, "I see now they do not really have control over the beast."

The next night, the dragon wreaked havoc upon the kingdom, attacking randomly whole families and disturbing the businesses of the merchants. Many angry merchants protested to the King that these attacks had interrupted their business. The wizards now pressed him for more sacrifices, which they said, "He must do it quickly." The King fled those pressing upon him hiding in a forgotten room, the palace chapel. He buried his head on a dusty kneeler and for the first time in a long time, he prayed to God earnestly for the safety of his daughter.

The brave Christians heard about the attack on Procuvera and sneaked into the palace where she was recovering. One of the Christian cohort, let in by the maid, tapped Procuvera on the shoulder. She rolled over with a befuddled look and asked, "Who is it? What do you want?"

"Oh good princess, God bless you for your bravery. I am one of the Christians opposing the dragon. I want to give you good news. A Christian knight, named George just arrived in the kingdom. We are sure he is the one, we were praying for that will deliver us from this beast. I think you heard a little about him before."

Procuvera smiled back, as life seemed to flood back into her face exclaiming, "Oh, I have heard about him, but I did not hear his name."

The Christian replied, "George."

"A good name, I will pray for him and offer the little sufferings inflicted on me by the dragon for him. When can I meet him?"

"Tomorrow, after you are recovered. We will arrange it."

When the appointed time came, Procuvera sneaked out escorted by one of the faithful Christians. So as not to draw attention to themselves, they dressed as a band of plainly dressed Christian peasants. They escorted the princess through the dark corridors of the capital. They weaved between buildings, to make sure no one was following them, until they came to their meeting place.

Finally, they reached their destination, where George was waiting to greet the noble princess he had heard so much about. She was struck that he did not have a fine form or comeliness that would draw one to him. He did not strike one as handsome and beautiful at first sight.[25] However, there was a mysterious sense that drew one to him, as if he were a bearer of truth. To the astonishment of all, the princess came before the knight and knelt before him saying, "O true knight of Christ, I perceive in you the presence of one who bears the light of your Master. Will you rid our kingdom of this woe that is upon us?"

George a little bit astonished replied, "Please, please Your Highness. Who am I that you should kneel before me? No, it is I, who have come to serve. I serve in the army of God. Behold, I have been given a sword for this purpose emblazoned by St. Michael himself with the words 'spiritus' and 'veritas'"

At this, the Princess was very pleased. She then proceeded to tell George of the recent history of her kingdom. She explained to George how the morals of the people had been declining for years and how dragon came upon them after this decline. She explained, "The King, *if you can call him that*, my father, sent out two champions before you whom the dragon killed. One was a proud fool, the other I had hope for, but I see now he fell because he relied on human means. After this, those wicked wizards came and proclaimed that they could tame the beast. I was a bit weary of them, as I saw they had grabbed control of my father's attention. They performed many tricks making it seem they could dictate where the dragon would go and what the dragon would do. They said we only needed to offer a few sacrifices to make their magic work.

In reality, those evil fiends sacrificed of innocent little children so they could gain control over the kingdom and in truth, it is the beast that even controls them. I learned this thanks to these brave

Christian souls who have risked their lives confronting the beast. I have seen the lies of these wizards with my own eyes and beheld their terrible sacrifices.

Now the dragon wants to attack me, but I see how the Lord turned the beast back when it sought to pounce on me. Don't heed the reports that it was the words of the wizards that turned it away. This is a lie! I saw that dragon draw back before the wizards came. I think it was the power of Christ, for I had my carriage blessed, and I pray every day to Him. The dragon drew back because of this. I know it! Beastly, beastly is this dragon and those wizards. They are conspiring with that beast. I see it all now. We must use every ounce of our strength to oppose this beast.

Now we have a true Christian warrior to combat the dragon. I want you to know, I am at your service in whatever way I can help."

As soon as Procuvera returned to the palace, her father, the King met her. He asked, "Where have been? I have been looking everywhere for you, since I heard of the attack. I am sorry this happened to you. I have been weeping and praying all night for your safety."

This statement caused Procuvera to draw back; however, a sudden burst of boldness overwhelmed her. She straightened herself up proclaiming, "I have been out trying to undue your evil policies. Your weakness has given the dragon power in this kingdom for too long. You authorized the sacrifices that feed the dragon. You permitted innocent little ones to be offered as sacrifices to the beast and for whatto make it seem like you were ruling? Really, you are no King, but a slave to this beast just like those wizards with their false incantations."

At this, the King cowered back like a dog that was just kicked. Sheepishly he replied, "Yes, I know what you say is true. My conscience was bothering me today when I tried to pray for your safety. I am not sure the Lord can hear the prayers of a sinner like me. I am sorry, so, sorry. I was only trying to protect myself, but really to protect my reputation. What can I do to make it up to you?"

Procuvera, urged on by an impulse of the Spirit, blurted out, "Just this night I met a true Christian knight, named George, who was trained not by men of a vacillating spirit or by the machinations of proud military thinking, but by the Spirit of God. A brave Christian cohort fighting your policies for some time now is aiding him. They introduced me to him. I tell you he was sent by God."

"Yes, my dear you have been right all along. The presence of these wizards disturbs my spirit, but I need them still. I will meet your knight nonetheless, maybe he can give me some hope that this will come to an end."

Meanwhile, George attended a meeting with the cohort of Christians opposing the dragon. All the Christians were fasting in keeping with it being a Friday during Lent. The assembled Christians went through in detail the rituals of the dragon and the way the wizards offered the gruesome sacrifices. They explained to him the terrain in which the dragon lived, how it hid itself in a cove and the nature of its habitat. While they were discussing these points, there was an unexpected knock on the door. It was an official of the King saying, "I come in the name of the Princess."

With some trepidation, they opened the door to the finely dressed courtier. The official explained, "Do not fear, the King has heard of you. He has recently grown weary of the wizards that surround him. He wants to meet this new champion brought by God."

George pondered for a minute this proposition then turned his mind to God seeking wisdom. He then responded. "Yes, tell the King I will meet him and hear his request." The Christians stood in shock, but praised the Lord for this unexpected turn.

The next day, the court officials escorted George to the King's country residence, a place he retreated to when he wanted to be away from the public eye. George waited there praying and wondering where the Lord was leading him. Finally, at dusk the King arrived in a windowless black carriage like the ones the military uses for escorts, something one would never expect to be carrying a King. The King stepped out in front of the backdoor and quickly made his way to the room where George was waiting.

The King greeted George, "I am happy to meet you. I am sorry to come to you in such a place, but I cannot trust all in my court. I see now some are in conspiracy with that dragon. The attack on my daughter has opened my eyes. That dragon demands my daughter for sacrifice now, and the wizards want me to give in. Knight of God can you help me?"

This plea of a father who seemed simply concerned for his daughter moved George. "Be not afraid. The Lord can conquer the dragon. He has dominion over the heavens and the earth."

The King felt a sense of peace when he spoke to George. However, he remained hesitant as he remembered the failures of the other would-be-champions. Thus, he queried George further. "Why should I trust you, when others have failed at this same task?"

"Your Highness, I can understand how you may be weary. I served in the Roman legion for many years. I know a good general would always test his soldiers before entrusting them with important tasks. Then he would make sure he has the best tools for the job. Likewise, my Lord, the King of heaven has tested me in many ways. It is only through struggles that I have made my way here. I have heard of the failures of the soldiers sent before me from your daughter, Princess Procuvera. She believes that they failed because they trusted in human means."

"Human means you say, knight? So, what do you have that is different?"

"Well, Your Highness, I have been given the proper tool to vanquish the beast."

"Your Highness, if you will allow me, I will unsheathe my sword and show this to you."

"Yes, feel free. Show me the reason I should trust you?"

George then slowly unsheathed his sword and held it with two hands presenting it to the King saying, "Behold the sword that was given to me by St. Michael himself. He told me it was purified and tested by virtue. Note the words engraved on it "spirit" and "truth." In this I trust that Spirit of God leads me in all truth."

The mysterious light that seemed to emanate from the blade mesmerized the King for several seconds. He felt a tremendous sense of awe at the sight of it and a bit of fear, knowing he was a sinner. Recognizing this sense of awe, he knew the Lord was working through this knight. After a long pause he then responded, "Yes, I can sense that the Lord is with you. I commend you do all in your power to combat this dragon. You have my royal commission." Then the King departed slipping away in the same black carriage as before, retreating to the safety of his palace.

# Chapter 9

## *George breaches the dragon's lair*

Georges was eager to engage the dragon after meeting the King. He turned to the Christian cohort assembled in the cottage, "My spirit is really alive here. Oh, how wonderful this is. The Lord seems to be truly leading me; you were praying for a savior, I was fasting and praying for the Lord's will and now the King is asking me to engage the dragon. I have a sword given to me for this purpose. What is there to wait for? Let us get at it and be over it."

At this, one wise old grandfather cautioned him, "Young buck, don't be so hasty. You just got here. All you young people always wantin to run before you consider things. This kingdom is all full of evil. You don't know the ways here. I would suggest you just go look about first."

George looked upon the old man kindly smiling, "Dear grandfather, I appreciate your words. Do not worry. I will scout out the dragon's lair first. Trust me. Surely, the Lord is leading me. What is there to worry about?"

As soon as George broke his fast on Saturday morning with a big meal, he set off toward the remote western boundaries. The Christians prayed for him with some anxiety. He scouted out the dragon's lair noting the possible exit points and the rocks that encircled the enclosure. He took counsel with the small Christian cohort who advised him that the dragon usually exits at twilight. Being thorough, George ventured into the exterior corridors of the dragon's cave to spy further. He carried blessed candles with him that he left at various points to give some light along the way. He wound his way back and forth into the heart of the dragon's den, until finally he came to a spot where the air was fowl and his mind was numbed. He thought, "I smell the stench in the air pressing upon me. So this is what evil smells like? It seems to even choke off the air itself."

As the air grew more stifling and the smell worsened, he came upon a small nest of eggs. It was the dragon's brood of seven hatchlings about to be born. George wondered, "How can such a beast have a brood? Where is its mate? Truly, these offspring are not from God, for all things created by God were made to give themselves to others. I guess, this beast makes offspring from secret arts of its of own design."

He quickly dispatched the evil offspring lest they spread further evil in the kingdom. He slashed with virtue dashing the eggs into pieces. Then he stealthily wove in and out of the shadows as he went more deeply into the lair. Finally, in the depth of the cave where all natural light disappeared, he came upon a wide-open spot probably 100 feet across and 50 feet high. As he lit a candle near the edge of the opening, he spotted the dragon curled up in a ball, sleeping as it does during the day. He sneaked closer to the dragon until he was right upon it. As the dim light flickered in the cave, he could see glimpses of the dragon's greenish-grey backside glimmering in the shadows. He could make out part of its massive wings curled up under its belly as it slept, and he could see the hardened scales on its backside. At this sight, he pondered, "Hmm, the beast looks so tame asleep."

He felt now he could almost touch the dragon and questioned himself, "I came here to spy, but I am so close. Why should I not strike now and be done with it?"

A nagging thought came to him that he must be patient and wait on the Lord's timing. However, he dismissed this idea, as he said to himself, "But has not the Lord delivered the dragon into my hand here and now? Yes, now is the time to strike."

George slipped into a position to attack the beast, stealthy drawing closer to the dragon. He positioned himself close to the backside of the dragon, away from any attack of its fiery breath, and raised his sword high above his head as he sought to drive it deep into the dragon's flesh. He was sure his blessed sword would pierce right through the dragon's scales. With a tight grip on the handle, he drove the edge of the sword mightily down on the dragon with an overhead thrust. To his astonishment, the sword jerked to the side, not at all piercing the dragon's flesh, but only glancing off.

Then in horror, George realized his error, the dragon awakened in a terrible rage. The dragon quickly twirled around to see what thing had disturbed its sleep. Its instinct was primed to pounce on the intruder, but George realizing the peril of his situation jumped to the side and took hold of the dragon's wings knowing the beast could not spew his fiery breath at his own wing. The beast feeling its foe cling to its wing flapped it mightily, while George held on for dear life. After several mighty flaps, the beast paused growing tired from the effort and rested its wings for a moment allowing George to slide down right onto its back. Now on its back George tried to renew his attack and made several stabs at the dragon, while he harnessed his shield on his backside. Still, his blessed sword did not seem to do much harm to the beast, as he only managed to knock off a few scales. George thought, "What went wrong? Do I not have a blessed sword given to me by St. Michael himself? Why then won't it pierce the dragon's flesh?"

This thought only lasted an instant though, for the dragon after a seeking vainly to grab this pest on his back twirled around faster and faster in a circle. George held on with all his might, recognizing he was safe from the beast's fiery breath while on its backside. Exasperated the dragon stood erect and sought then to smash its foe with its backside against the wall of the cave. Seeing this, George slid off the beast's back and leaped to the side onto the ground just as the beast crashed against the wall.

As beast continued to smash its backside against the wall, George moved around to its front and courageously drove at the dragon with his shield in front of him before the beast could recognize where he was. The beast dropped down, but George continued to drive at its jaw right as the dragon was about to snap at him. George's slashing sword seemed to annoy the dragon so that the beast pulled back its head. In the small confined space, the dragon could not maneuver well, and George hacked a few more times, but still without piercing its flesh. The dragon feeling itself backed into the wall, raised itself on its hind legs and attempted to crush George underneath him. George jumped back against the wall of the cave, but he realized he was now face to face with the dragon and pinned against the wall.

The dragon then spewed forth its fiery breath. George hid himself behind his shield holding onto it for dear life, even as the flames spilled over the shield burning his hairs. The dragon shot out his fiery breath repeatedly attempting to burn through this medal shield that protected George. At last, the breath of the dragon was exhausted, and George dropped his red-hot shield, which seared his hands as he held onto the metal handles. As the dragon was catching its breath for another blast, George ducked away into the shadows. He then raced through a corridor leading away from the dragon and quickly fled the scene leaving his shield where it was.

As he leapt out into the daylight, he wiggled his hands blistered and red from the fiery attack and brushed a few of his hairs from his head that the flames, which lapped over his shield, seared. To his great relief the dragon did not pursue him, apparently fleeing from the bright sun. George dejected, tired and suffering with burns to his hands and parts of his body, struggled away in the noonday sun. He crept back to the Church where the Christian cohort awaited him.

The Christian souls seeing him with burnt, torn clothes and a blackened face were shocked. They believed he went out just to scout the dragon. After the initial shock of his appearance, one Christian sheepishly asked, "Did you fell the dragon? Did you triumph?"

George swallowed haltingly trying to regain a gentlemanly continence then replied, "No, I did not triumph. I killed some of its evil offspring though. I did engage the dragon, but came back only with my life and this blessed sword. I did not mean to engage it, but seeing the dragon right there, I thought, 'Now must be the time for me to strike.' Therefore, I drove at him, but my sword could not pierce his flesh. I have been proud and I failed."

Though the Christians were disheartened at George's defeat, they sought to alleviate his sufferings. They placed healing balms on his wounds and pondered together the mystery of how their Christian champion could have failed. As they were bandaging his wounds all were in silence. He broke the quiet saying, "I am sorry. I know I acted too hastily. I did not wait on the Lord; I acted before it was the Lord's time. I just got a lesson in humility. I must pray now and see what truly is the Lord's will."

That night, the dragon showed that George's audacious attack, which had killed its offspring, did nothing to deter it. In response, the dragon burst out furiously in the dark of the night and laid waste crops in the field, destroying whole farms and laying wreck to entire fields. The King seeing this terrifying display of power by the dragon was disheartened that the Christian champion could not quickly dispatch the beast. It caused him to pause and think again whether he should trust the Christian champion and his cohort. The wizards, however, hearing how the King had asked George to intercede when Procuvera was threatened, determined to keep the princess completely away from any doings of the dragon.

**Recovery and Preparation for renewed Battle**

A few days later, George was in Church meditating about his encounter with the dragon. He hesitantly raised his dejected head up and meekly asked God, "Lord, why did I fail?"

He ran through in his mind every detail of the encounter with the dragon every move it made, the look of the dragon, the scales that protected it, its jaw and its mode of attack. He thought, "What was I thinking at that time? Yes, consciously how to attack the dragon, but what did I feel in my soul? Lord reveal this to me."

He delved more deeply into these memories examining the emotions that he felt during the battle, a fiery desire to engage the dragon and a feeling that he was doing something important, noble, for which people would remember him. Thinking over this he thought, "Yes, I acted proudly. I tried to overcome the beast through my own strength alone. Teach me Lord, how now to engage this beast. Teach me your ways."

Then George turned back to the Lord and asked, "Do you really want me to use my skills for your sake? Might it be better if I just pray and you slay the dragon yourself? I was a failure when I acted. You gave me this sword, but I acted too hastily and could not slay the dragon. Perhaps you can choose someone else of better character. Give the sword to someone else." The Lord however, seemed silent to George's plea.

George bowed his head and continued to pray for many more hours. Finally, after pouring his heart out to the Lord, he felt an inspiration to open up the gospel book. He raced his finger over the text then let it light where it will. His finger stopped on a story midway through the Gospel of Mark, the story of Jesus driving out the demon from the possessed man. It said:

Someone from the crowd answered him, 'Teacher, I have brought to you my son possessed by a mute spirit. Wherever it seizes him, it throws him down; he foams at the mouth, grinds his teeth, and becomes rigid. I asked your disciples to drive it out, but they were unable to do so.' He said to them in reply, 'O faithless generation, how long will I be with you? How long will I endure you? Bring him to me.'

They brought the boy to him. And when he saw him, the spirit immediately threw the boy into convulsions. As he fell to the ground, he began to roll around and foam at the mouth. Then he questioned his father, 'How long has this been happening to him?' He replied, 'Since childhood. It has often thrown him into fire and into water to kill him. But if you can do anything, have compassion on us and help us."

Jesus said to him, 'If you can! Everything is possible to one who has faith.' Then the boy's father cried out, 'I do believe, help my unbelief!' Jesus, on seeing a crowd rapidly gathering, rebuked the unclean spirit and said to it, 'Mute and deaf spirit, I command you: come out of him and never enter him again!'

Shouting and throwing the boy into convulsions, it came out. He became like a corpse, which caused many to say, 'He is dead!' But Jesus took him by the hand, raised him, and he stood up.

When he entered the house, his disciples asked him in private, 'Why could we not drive it out?' He said to them, 'This kind can only come out through prayer.'" (Mark 9:17-29).

He realized then why he could not defeat the dragon right off. "Yes, Lord I see one can drive out some demons only though prayer and fasting. Such is the demonic beast that I am battling."

The next day, George gathered the dejected Christian cohort. They met again at the cottage. They were curious to hear what he had to say, but some stayed aloof, as they had lost confidence in the first impression of their hero. George addressed them, "I know you are all dejected and some believe that you were sent a false prophet. I too have wondered why the Lord brought me here. I asked myself was I following the right 'spirit?'

I tell you, I am just one who is trying to follow the Lord's will. I am no prophet, but perhaps like Elisha, a pruner of sycamore trees, just a simple soul. Yet, I see the Lord has chosen me and I have tried to respond, but I took up the cloak of a hero without discernment. I am a simple swordsman who wishes to give his talents to the Lord.

Yesterday, I prayed all night seeking the Lord's will and the reason for my defeat. After listening for a while, I believe I know why we failed. I say, 'we' because I realized it is not a battle I can win alone. The Lord gave to me the passage from scripture indicating that this beast is not like those known by man. It comes from another realm and no human power can defeat it. This beast is of a spiritual nature and thus can only be defeated through prayer and fasting.

The Lord showed me the nature of this beast; it is not like a demon possessing a soul, but rather a spiritual force infecting this kingdom. In order to defeat it, we must work together. We must fast and prayer together so to bring to light the spirit that we are battling. We must fight together; we must counter this beast at every turn. We must stand tall together in the face of its fiery breath and endure all trials. We must commit to this battle until the end and trust in the grace of the Lord.

As a swordsman, I present to you my sword. See it and recognize its worth. I know swords, their worth, their power and their might. They must be tilled by fiery coals that burn off all their dross. This one was presented to me by St. Michael, the Archangel, and I see now, it must be have been born in the midst of fiery suffering, which is much hotter than the breath of the dragon. It was given to me to know that the blood of the martyrs has burned away its dross before St. Michael presented it to me. It has a fine edge that is kept sharp by the Spirit that cuts through flesh and soul.

This sword however, is only as good as the one behind it. I tell you this swordsman cannot win this battle by his skills alone. Having fought in wars, I tell you also that a lone swordsman never wins the battle. A sword can be wielded in only one direction at a time, but in battle usually there are attacks from all around one. The good swordsman knows he needs others to protect his back and overcome the spirit of defeat that overwhelms the lone warrior. Only unified and faithful battalions win battles, not lone warriors who think they can take on an army alone.

I ask you now to enter into this battle with me, to endure the trials with me, to help burn away the dross from the swordsman you see before you that he may be worthy to wield this blessed sword. Be the faith and courage behind me! Come plead for me to that Spirit which keeps the blade sharp. Now I take out my sword and place it before you. I commend any brave souls to take hold of the hilt of this sword and pledge to fight this dragon to the very end."

After this oration, there was a few seconds of meditative silence, while George held the sword straight down, blade first in the middle of the Christian remnant. The sword, which had gleamed before, was now more an ordinary steel grey. In a courageous move Sergius was the first to take up the challenge, exclaiming, "Yes, I will take hold of that hilt. I know nothing about swordsmanship, but I can pray and fast. Teach me how to wield a sword and I will fight too."

Then another called out, "I will stand behind you" and another called out, "I will be your courage." Then another, "I will make sure your blade is always kept sharp" and many others proclaimed similar words. All then took hold of that hilt proclaiming, "We pledge now to continue this fight until this dragon is killed!" As all took hold of the hilt, hand upon hand the sword again gleamed with the mysterious glow.

# Chapter 10

## *Training the steel of a warrior*

The next morning, George was walking by a local blacksmith when he spotted Sergius. He was curious to see what he was doing there. "So, Sergius, what brings you here this fine morning?"

"I am preparing to fight."

"You are and how is that?

"Well, I got some iron ore here and wanna commission this blacksmith to make me a sword, so I can fight that dragon and whatever other evil comes our way."

"I see you are just rearing to fight?"

"Do you have any experience?"

"Well, no, but after seeing you and your courage even after your failure, I just want to take up arms and fight."

George replied with a stern look, "So, you think you are up to the challenge of being a swordsman? Do you really know what you are getting into?"

"What does it matter? I just wanna fight. I get that the blacksmith to make me a sword and then we can get at it. I mean you can train me a bit, right?"

"Novices are always so eager, but they rarely know what they are getting into. Nevertheless, this eager spirit can carry you far."

"What do you mean?"

"Well, you will learn in time, but first things first. Let me see your iron ore."

"Okay here it is. Do you know anything about sword making?"

George investigated the sampling of iron ore that Sergius took out of a pouch. "Oh, I know a good deal. I studied the art of swordsmithing as some call it because I always wanted to make sure, I got the best. You have to delve into it yourself if you want to make sure you have the finest weapon. I found along the way that swordsmithing can be an act of prayer, requiring patience, penance, and long-suffering. It will take a lot of pounding and firing. You have to have a lot of patience. Are you up to it?"

"What do you mean making a sword can be an act of praying and all that?"

"You will learn in time. The first thing, is to steel your ore. We got to mix in some carbon as hardener to make some good steel from your mix. This will give some good virtue to the mix."

"Come with me now, Sergius, into the blacksmith's shop and we will get at it. I will show you the work we must do to forge this sword."

As they popped their head under the roof of the open aired workshop, George greeted the blacksmith, "Good day to you my good man. I wish to show this novice your fine art. Please sir, tell me your name?"

The blacksmith, whose face was covered in soot with a long grayish black mustache and ruffled unkept hair, replied simply with a grunt saying, "Yeh, yeh, do what you want. You pay. You can watch. My name is John, ah, sir."

John looked at George with a peculiar look, for few wanted to see him to do his work and never before had a knight entered into his humble workshop. He, however, recognized something different about this knight; he showed John respect in his greeting. All the other so-called noblemen in Terrasindei treated him like a dog shooing and pushing him around. This knight's politeness surprised him, and he did not know how to respond. He wondered, "Who is this knight that speaks to me as an equal? His face is that of a foreigner. Why is he lowering himself to work with this peasant to make a sword? I am not sure I completely trust him. No man speaks so kindly without irregular motives."

George directed Sergius' attention to the clay-lined kiln. He explained, "See this oven here. This heats up much hotter than does the fireplace in your home. This is where iron ore will be first separated from the slag. Our good blacksmith, John, will try the mixed ore in the fire for a time heating it so that all the dross is burned away, the slag loosens from the ore, separating during the process. He then must hammer off all the crusty slag from the outside to get the pure ore. It can be a lengthy process taking a skilled hand. If one does not pay close attention to his work, he will not get pure iron, but a poor quality mix of iron and other elements that will not make for a very good sword. Is this right, my good John?"

John was trying to hide his curiosity as he checked out the strange knight that seemed to know so much about his trade. When he heard his name, he simply grunted back, "Yeh, yeh that is how you do it." He was becoming more interested in this knight with each word, as it not only seemed he was polite, but that he truly respected his labor as a blacksmith. He had never seen this before.

George continued, "You see, in this act of burning away the dross, we get our pure iron. When I see this part of the process, I think of the Lord burning away the dross of sinfulness from my soul. The Lord burns away my sinful tendencies through the trials that he permits me to undergo, only his skilled hand can do this work in me. I know I must allow my soul to be purified in this fire. If I resist too much, I become like this mixed ore, poor material for a tool of God.

As it says in the Proverbs, 'Take away the dross from the silver, and the smith has material for a vessel; take away the wicked from the presence of the King, and his throne will be established in righteousness.'[26] We should then strive to be righteous nobility who have allowed the Lord to purify us from our dross."

Sergius listening with intent interjected, "I see my lord, but how is that you have such a fine sword as you do, such as I see peeking out from its sheath?"

At this, George slowly and lovingly unsheathed his magnificent sword and held it up in the light to display its glory. They then both stared at it in silence in admiration of its beauty. It seemed so much more glorious now to Sergius than when he had taken hold of its hilt before.

John the blacksmith now felt a bit uncomfortable. He did not know how to react in the presence of George who possessed this strange mystical sword. He drew back hiding a bit in his workshop as he beheld this sword. In all his years of smithing, he had never seen such work. It gleamed with a brightness one could not describe, seeming to glow from its very core. Its edges were perfect with no defects whatsoever. Looking at it one seemed to be drawn into another world. Finally, John broke the silence saying, "Truly sir, it is beautiful."

George smiling slightly replied, "Ah, this sword is a special gift of grace given to me. It was forged not by human hands, but by the fiery justice of our Lord. No human blacksmith could make such a sword. Its virtue is beyond that of all human doings, but alas, after my failure I see I am not yet worthy of it. I see, I must learn humility from lesser swords so I can wield properly this great sword."

Our good blacksmith is right though, you will need further materials. You will want to mix some steel in with the iron to make fine material. I can also help you to acquire some secret graced material to help it keep its character. From this then we can make a fine sword."

Sergius interjected, "So, how long will take to steel it or whatever you said? And when can I get this secret material? I mean, I want at the fight."

George shook his head slowly saying, "In time I will show you how to acquire the steel and the yeast to give your sword a good character that will resist stress, which will make it difficult to break. However, this process takes time. You must be patient. Now let us allow the blacksmith to start the fiery work. Good day, good John, we will check in with you later."

John replied, "Good day to you, sir."

As they left, John thought, "There is something not of this world about that knight. His sword showed this clearly, but his whole way of acting, his kindness and charity. It is not common, no not all. And how could he see my sweaty tiresome work as an act of prayer. How strange this is? Does God really burn away the dross from our souls like he says?" John started up the fire for the kiln in quiet meditation, as he pondered these thoughts.

George then urged Sergius on, "Hurry now or we will be late for an important part of your training."

Sergius queried, "Training, what are talking about? I don't even have a sword yet."

"I mean training your soul in sacred silence and prayer."

Sergius followed along without questioning, but wondering what he meant by this. He tried to pray, but he thought as they made their way through the streets, "What does this have to do with training to be a swordmaster?" They continued in silence. Sergius not wanting to speak after George had spoken of 'sacred' silence.

Finally, they reached the local church. George broke the silence, "Ah, we are just in time for Divine Liturgy. Have you eaten yet today?"

Sergius, replied, "Yes, I had breakfast already."

"Ah, what a pity, then you cannot partake of the food of the Lord, but nevertheless you can receive God's gift of grace by beholding his great sacrificial banquet. Come now with me we must prepare our heart to receive our Lord. Later, I will explain the importance of fasting to receive him in a proper way."

They sat together in silence as George bowed his head and seemed to bury his mind in deep meditation as he threw off all distractions around him. Sergius, not used to this type of prayer, looked curiously at George and at the few assembled that day. He noticed how George was content in his prayer and focused during the liturgy. All were silent in the room contemplating the great Mystery unveiling before them. Though Sergius was uncomfortable in this silence, he felt it would be impolite to break it.

He thought, "Why are these souls so intently worshipping here on this day? It is not a Sunday. This seems so different from other liturgies. On Sunday, so many seem to be rushing to the liturgy, some come after the opening prayers, some right before the readings and some leave right after the unveiling of the great Mystery. Yet, here all sit intently, even before the opening prayers. This is not the type of prayer I am used to. What does it have to with being a swordsman and how can such an active soul as this knight enter into it? Why does this difficult silence not distract him?"

As the liturgy continued, George focused his attention at times squinting his brow, as if, really trying to capture what was going on in the liturgy, at other times just seeming to watch peacefully and silently. Sergius, meanwhile, continued to squirm and could not wait until the liturgy was over. He hurried outside as soon as it was over where he had to wait a few minutes before George joined him.

Immediately Sergius broke in with a question. "What does this quiet prayer have to do with training to be a swordsman?"

George then smiled again nodding his head a little, "You listen, but you do not hear. You look but you do not see. Yes, yes, I could feel your distraction during the liturgy. In time, the Lord can teach you the meaning of silence. In this silence, we can hear the voice of the Lord. In this encounter, we can see the sight of the Lord with the eyes of the soul. In this mystery our Lord trains our hearts in His ways."

Sergius interrupted this discourse, "But still, I do not understand how this inactivity has anything to do with wielding a sword."

George then explained, "Well you see it is not enough just to wield a sword, but one must know the right time to use it. We can both learn from my first encounter with the dragon. I wielded it at the wrong time. Now you can see that I have the marks of burned hands and singed hair to show this. In order to wield the sword at the proper time one must know what battles to enter into and which to avoid. One must not jump in too soon or remain a coward, who never wields the sword. I have found that much of the battle consists in waiting. Waiting for the proper time when the enemy is vulnerable, waiting in hiding, waiting in difficult situations, waiting with little food, waiting where it is hard to sleep, waiting with men with rough personalities, waiting, waiting, waiting. The good knight will wait until the enemy is vulnerable when he also is tired, hungry and angry, but because he has learned to control himself in the silence of the waiting, he will triumph. For the good knight has not allowed himself to become a prey to his own demons in the silence, but to become a master of his own soul."

Sergius pondered this for a while, as they made their way to the little cottage where George was staying. They had to pass by the blacksmith again. George urged Sergius to stop in. "Let us see the progress that our good smith has made. Hello, John how far have you gotten now?"

"Well sir, I managed to take off all the dross from the rough iron. Should we mix in the carbon to make our steel now?"

"Oh, yes, my good John, you can mix in the carbon and start pounding out the pieces, but don't set into it a slab yet, I want to add a little leaven to the mix. Keep up your good work. We are not in a hurry. I have to teach my student here a few lessons about how to use a sword before he is able to wield it. He has to earn his steel."

As they make their way into the streets, John thought, "A yes, this man really knows swords. He will make a good hard and sharp one for that mate of his, but what does he mean by 'leaven' and how does one earn steel? Leaven, maybe he means throwing some junk in there like the bakers, ah, but for them it is not 'junk.' I never thought of that, I guess for bakers it is really the important stuff. So, what important stuff would you put into making a sword? Hmm, anyway none of my business, I will see when it comes to it."

Sergius and George conversed as they headed into the street. "Sergius, as I told John there, I will get you your steel to make your blade hard, but don't lose sight of what has already been done."

"What do you mean? All I have, as yet, is a few slabs of tin."

"No, you forget, we have removed all the dross from the iron. This is the first step. Before you can build strength, you must burn off all the dross. He has separated it from the mixed elements. This is what you must do with your soul. Remember how you fidgeted in the chapel. This is a sign of a soul not yet at peace. Find those mixed elements in your soul that keep your attention from being fixed on the Lord. Allow the suffering you will enter into to burn off the dross in your soul.

The Lord is continuing to do this with me. I still have some mixed elements in my soul too. I recognized this after my failure in the battle with the dragon. May the Lord purge all these elements from my soul that I may be His sharp instrument to do with as He wills."

# Chapter 11

# *A Battalion is formed*

As the weeks went on, Sergius became more active in the Church, so that people noticed him more at the daily liturgies. Others noticed that he seemed to becoming more disciplined, prayerful, and courteous. Maria, plodding along slowly with her crooked cane, passed by the cottage of the Christians, accompanied by a middle age man and a few women. Upon, spotting Sergius she commented in the direct unashamed manner of old people. "Look, there goes a fine young man. That good Christian knight is giving him some discipline and showing him the right way. I see him praying all the time, helping people and no longer bouncing around like a no-good loafer."

She then tapped her cane on the wall of the cottage saying, "See this here cottage. This ain't no church, but I tell you it is a house of spirits. Yes, a house of spirits."

The middle-age man responded, "Do you mean it is has some wandering spirits in it?"

"No, no, no. It is a home of the Spirit, the spirit of God. I have seen good Christian souls coming and going here, and I have seen that good Christian knight come here recently. I tell you the spirit of God is working here."

The middle-aged man reflecting on this, and seeing the newly acquired virtues of Sergius, later sought out George saying, "Excuse me sir, I hear you are looking for some people to fight the evil dragon that afflicts us. Well, I am not sure I am called to wield a sword, like this young strong buck Sergius here, but I am willing to provide my strong hands to support any campaign to oppose the dragon."

Later a woman who had accompanied Maria, seeing the disciplined attitude of Sergius stopped George. "How can I help to oppose the dragon? I too know how to work hard. Let me help."

Another woman after hearing her friend take the courageous step clamored also to George, "I too heard about those terrible stone altars where the children are left to die. I am willing to suffer whatever danger is necessary to snatch those little innocent ones from those cold altars. I may not be able to fight with a sword, but I am quick on my feet with a child in my hands.

An older woman overhearing this conversation was inspired also. She tugged on George's cloak to get his attention saying, "Good sir, I am getting on in years and can't run around like these young people, but I promise to be your prayer warrior. I will offer whatever suffering the Lord wants to give me, ailments, pains, aggravations, even ridicule for you and the cause of defeating this terrible dragon."

George then reflected on these people running to him. "Ah, Lord, I see you are calling me to form a cohort, a battalion of simple souls. You do not choose the mighty, Lord or the proud of heart. Yes, Lord I see this is not my task alone, but it must be a work of the Christian people. It starts with this small remnant. They will be the small cohort that stirs the culture of this kingdom to repentance."

George then with the help of Sergius assembled the Christian battalion in the small cottage and prepared them for battle. He addressed them. "We come together in this small cottage, which I hear has come to be called a "House of Spirits," a fitting name for a place where the spirit of God is really working. My brave Christian cohort the Spirit of the Lord has gathered us together here. The Spirit draws us here to stand up against the dragon that attacks your land. As I look around one could say, 'in the eyes of the world that the lot of you do not look like typical warriors ready to battle with a dragon.' In the eyes of the world, not many of you would be counted great figures. Before me, I see frail old women, slightly rounding middle-age men, tiny little women who could be knocked over with a simple whiff, and only a token number of hearty young men.

However, we do not look with the eyes of the world, rather we see with the eyes of faith. The faith that gave Gideon the courage to attack much greater numbers with only four hundred picked men, the faith that gave David the courage to charge the giant Goliath, the faith that inspired Judas Maccabees to charge a vastly superior Assyrian army. It is this faith that inspires. It is this faith that directs us, and it is this faith that will protect us. Recognize we are fighting an evil beast that arose from the darkness. This darkness has a multitude of hosts to help it. However, there is a light that pierces that darkness and that light is the light of Christ. We trust in this. We hope in this. We live in this. Christ too has his heavenly hosts and multitude of legions at his service. He has not forgotten us. He leads us now into battle. See now he has sent his commander, Michael, to give me this sword to guide us forth into the fray. Fear not for our Lord goes with us.

So, what shall we call this battalion of the Lord? Hmm, of course, St. Michael's battalion after our patron and protector. He will guide us. He will defend us and he will lead us to final victory through the grace of Our Lord. I am sure of this."

The brave cohort responded, "Yes! Yes! Yes! We will follow! We will march forth in company with Gideon, David, Judas and the host of heavenly armies. Onward we go; onward we go; no fear in the Lord."

George then continued, "Listen now, this is what we are called to do. We must oppose the dragon at every move. We must, 'be sober and alert for our opponent the devil is prowling like a roaring lion waiting to devour us' as good St. Peter said.[27] This is a call for vigilance. We must scout out the place of the dragon and oppose it wherever it attacks. We must go out to the places of sacrifice and rescue the innocent ones from the places of their doom. Let us not let a single innocent child perish while we are still breathing. We must oppose the wizards and their spells. We will stand up and proclaim the way to overcome this beast, even if the King himself continues to oppose us, for we fight with a sword of truth and battle for righteousness. Fight, fight, fight, always be ready; always remain vigilant.

"I need you all. In the Lord's plan, you all have a part to play. I will lead in the Lord with my sword. I will wield the sword, some will strike with the arrows, some will agitate the dragon, some will grab the little ones from their place of sacrifice, some will be scouts, and others will be there to heal the wounds that our battalion receives in battle. As a good St. Peter says, 'Each has received a gift, employ it for one another, as good stewards of God's varied graces; whoever renders service, as one who renders it by the strength which God supplies; in order in everything God may be glorified through Jesus Christ. To Him belong glory and dominion forever and ever. Amen.[28]

I commend you also not to fear the spells of the wizards that oppose us. I declare to you that the words of a devout Christian are more powerful than the spells of a hundred wizards, if spoken with conviction and faith. The testimony of our faith is much more powerful than any dragon or spell. Our witness shall bring life back to this kingdom, now so engulfed by death. We will show them another way, the way of light that leads to life overcoming the dark that leads to death. Through our struggles, sacrifices, prayers, and fasting we shall overcome this dragon. The Lord has promised to me, his servant, and to you his faithful servants, that he will answer our prayers. Now let us take strength from the bread of life so that food of angels may nourish our souls for the battle."

Kathleen, upon hearing the oration of George, dubbed the cottage, "Domus Spiritum," meaning "a house of spirits." She thought it fitting as a good code name, which was not without a bit of humor. For through the eyes of faith one could see the 'Spirit' working there, but in the eyes of the world it could also mean a place where people were under the influence of different sorts of "spirits." This gave a convenient cover to explain the great number of people who frequented the establishment. In time, this would prove a truly fitting name for this place, for souls felt much inspiration and dejection here, made many plans and strategies, and felt hope and despair. There was always a constant need to discern the 'spirit' that was at work in the house whether it be of the Lord, of man, or of the evil one.

After praying, George assembled them the next day at Domus Spiritum. He laid out his plan to the battalion. "My courageous colleagues in battle, I prayed to the Lord yesterday and worked out a strategy for our battalion. Here is what we will do. First, I will assign Sergius here to reconnoiter for me. He will scout out the patterns of the dragon, reporting to me every movement of the beast he observes. To do this, he will camp near the dragon's lair. He will mark every time the dragon enters and leaves, sending a signal to the patrols as to which direction it is heading. Then our other troopers will rush off to follow the path of the dragon.

I have instructed him to communicate this information with a lamp. He will use a lamp to send out a strong steady light whenever he sees the dragon leave a cave. He will then circle with the light the direction in which it heads. To make sure it is clear, he will light a lamp in a particular window: facing north, south, east or west, depending on which direction the dragon heads out. Others stationed throughout the kingdom, will keep vigil waiting for the lighted signal to appear. When they notice the signals, they will put a lamp in their windows to acknowledge that they received it.

We will put a cross shape overlaying the light, so one can distinguish them from other common lamps. It is the cross then that will lead us, and it is under the cross that we must find our protection. Finally, when the patrol encounters the dragon, I have developed special metal tipped missiles that we will shoot from a giant crossbow. The metal tips alone will not hinder the dragon, but I will add a special blessing from the priest to make them more effective against such an ungodly beast. This front line patrol will especially need your prayers, as will we all."

When darkness covered the kingdom, the battalion soon was at its work and one could see them in action.

"Look, Sergius, is that a cross of light you see above the building?"

"Ah, yes, I see the light circling around. Quick, send a signal to the others the battle is upon us."

He raced to the cabin they had established as a safe house and flashed a lantern in the western window. Thereafter, followed a whole series of signals sent from house to house throughout the kingdom directing the battalion as to the exact location where the dragon was headed. As the dragon descended, the battalion rushed to the scene guessing where the beast was about to attack in order to engage it. George turned to Bacchus, whom he had come to trust implicitly, "Do you have the missiles blessed by the priest?"

"Yes, we prepared everything. Here they are with the giant crossbow."

"Okay, here I go, pray for me that I may have strength for the battle and be protected by the Lord."

George then crawled out and hid himself around a corner that offered him some shelter from a potential attack of the dragon. A thought struck him as he peered up at the descending dragon. "Hmm, the dragon has grown in size."

However, he had no time to ponder this observation. Just as the dragon touched the roof of the house, George shot forth his first missile. One could hear it, "Fsst! Plunk! Clunk, clunk, clunk." Then there was a slow vibrating metal sound as the missile thudded on the ground.

The missile hit its target directly, but it did not pierce the dragon's skin. George expected this. After his first encounter with the dragon, he knew that not even St. Michael's sword could pierce its flesh. He recognized it was not given to him yet to pierce the flesh of the dragon. However, he hoped that the blessed tip would, nevertheless, aggravate the dragon. This it did.

The dragon turned about when the missile hit it. Although no blood came forth, the beast drew back flying away from the scene.

Then it seemed to claw at its own flesh, as if trying to rid itself of an infection. It then quickly drove into the air away from the scene.

George turned to his cohorts. "Ah, see it is the blessed tip that irritates it. See, I told you that the blessing would inflict pain upon the dragon."

In this manner, they worked to oppose the dragon wherever they could. When they spotted the dragon, they would try to rush to the scene to oppose it. These attacks usually happened in the shadows. It became obvious to the battalion that these attacks were a lot more frequent then the wizards let on. Their task was difficult and often futile, as there were few in the battalion and the beast was very quick. After gaining some experience, they developed assault tactics. Their usual method of engagement was to race to the scene where George would lead a formation. He would take the point while two others would peel off to the right the other to the left. They would then engage the dragon with steel arrows blessed by the priest.

George had heard about the terrible manner in which the wizards offered sacrifice to the dragon; Christians who had witnessed them described the sacrifices to him. He also heard about those who were already valiantly trying to save the infants from the altars of sacrifice. To further their heroic work, he wanted to have a specially trained division to undertake this endeavor. Thus, he organized other members of St. Michael's battalion into a rescue team to oppose the ritual sacrifices. For this division, surprisingly, he chose mostly women. After he assembled them, he explained to them their duties. "I brought you here to this gathering to be part of a most important division. You are called to be the last line of salvation for the innocent little ones. I chose each one of you, not because you were the strongest, quickest or most fearsome, but because you have courage and steadfastness. These will be very important qualities for your assignment.

I need you to go out to the places of sacrifice to rescue these children from the very brink of death. If you cannot save them from death you can be there with them as they go through their Calvary; a sign that we did not run away when Christ was suffering in his mystical body."

The assembled group replied enthusiastically and soon they were at their task. George wanted to witness their first attempts at rescuing the children. The rescue division went out to a place of sacrifice where George had them hide close by behind a cleft of rocks. They had worked out a method, whereby some women would continue their efforts to dissuade the women from their sacrifices, but if this failed, they would send a signal to the rescue division. This night they sent a signal to this division and directed them to which sacrificial altar the wizards were proceeding.

George explained to the division, "Okay, now wait here until we notice the wizards appear with the little ones. Do not try to stop them from placing the child on the altar of sacrifice. From what I understand, there are many of them who help to prepare the altar. No, wait until they have cleared the area and wait for the dragon to pounce upon its sacrifice. This is the time then to run and try to rescue the child from the place of sacrifice."

The division then waited hidden behind the cleft in the rock as instructed by George until after dark. Finally, they noticed the wizards coming. The wizards prepared the area as normal, now with the help of some witches who sterilized the altar with their hands as they said some weird sounding spells. The wizards lit candles to mark the altar for the dragon and placed these on the four corners of the altar. They then placed the sacrifice on the altar and everyone retreated to a cliff overlooking the scene. This is when George called out to his division. "Okay now, rush out and grab the child."

A few women then ran out together. The idea was that two would run out in case one tripped, or was hindered by something; then the other could continue with the rescue. On this occasion, both reached the altar of sacrifice, and one grabbed the child just as the dragon was circling overhead and was about to descend on its prey. Both then ran off quickly from the scene and slipped into the dark shadows. Owing to the contrast between the light of the candles and the dark of the shadows, the dragon's night vision could not track them as they raced off.

George congratulated them. "Well done. The Lord watched over you tonight. How awesome is it that we could save the life of this little one. Hurry now, let us bring this child to a place of safety."

Many a night the rescue division continued their efforts. They would hide in the cleft of the rocks until the wizards left the scene and then would grab the innocent ones before the dragon could swoop down upon them. This enraged the wizards who learned to keep watch over their sacrifice and thus stopped many attempts to rescue these innocent victims. The dragon too started to become more aware of their actions, and sometimes they were almost killed themselves as the beast sought to fend them off. However, a strange force always seemed to keep the dragon just far enough away so they had time at least to escape when the dragon attacked them.

Seeing the difficulties, the faithful cohort, however, became more ingenious and sought to put more effort into counseling the women against abandoning their babies, so to prevent the sacrifices. Often they found later that many mothers would thank them for this intervention. The cohort through these means was able to save a few of these innocent ones and stand as a witness to life against a society that did not regard them.

The wizards recognized that the women of St. Michael's battalion were becoming more successful in dissuading mothers from offering their children as sacrifices. To counter this, they commissioned witches to help them, who came disguised as midwives. The witches developed a "best practice," for convincing women to give up their babies for sacrifices. They would greet each mother with smile and pat her on the shoulder saying, "I know it is difficult and you may be a bit confused, but it is for the best. The little beings at this age don't know what is going on. Do not worry they won't feel much and will not understand anything. It is only like a little animal yet, like a plant that is just budding.

Now, now, I will accompany you along the way so that you can say goodbye to the little bud. Don't worry it will be over soon."

They learned it was best to take the children away from the mothers before they got to place of sacrifice. Meanwhile, the witches would give the mothers a bit of opium telling them, "Take this, it will help you calm down."

Afterward, they would give them a potion telling them, "Take this medicine home with you and take it once a month so that you will never have to face this choice again."

After investigating this "medicine," the good women of the battalion exposed the truth about them. They gave speeches across the kingdom detailing how this "medicine" actually poisoned the bodies of the women so they could not have any more children. They stood up in the public squares preaching against this so-called "medicine" exposing how it was really a potion made by witches. Some people called them crazy for saying such things; others thought well perhaps these women are better off, at least they won't have to sacrifice more of their children. These courageous women did not mind this disdain and continued to preach the truth regardless, seeing many women caught in a cycle of addiction to these potions and returning repeatedly to offer their children as sacrifices when the "medicine" failed.

St. Michael's battalion, however, was small and their efforts seemed little in the face of the wide range of the dragon. Though they tracked where the dragon tended to look for its prey, they could not be in all places at all times. Many times the dragon attacked and left before the battalion could engage it. In addition, the King's agents often detained the battalion's rescue team and generally harassed them so that they could not intercept the mothers on their sorrowful march. It was disheartening to see that even when they could engage the dragon, the King stood aloof. Discouraged by George's failure, the King resolved no longer to dissuade his soldiers from persecuting the battalion, even though he knew his daughter supported them. The dragon had reigned for nearly three years now and many people had come to expect the beast would remain in the kingdom for good.

Yet, St. Michael's battalions did have their successes and souls in the kingdom started to take note that there was another force at work in their midst. The wizards became increasingly desperate and tried to create a lottery of all the infants in the kingdom, so they could get the number of sacrifices they wanted. However, some mothers forced to offer their children to these death merchants, rebelled and secretly passed them to the battalion. The wizards seeing many of their efforts frustrated by the battalion and its leader George, whispered rumors in the kings ear maligning them. They told him, "George is a fraud, a false prophet, who is only angering the dragon. Now the dragon will strike harder than ever."

In between battles, George continued training Sergius how to become a swordsman. They returned to the blacksmith to check on the progress of the sword. "Ah, see Sergius, John has just gotten to the tedious, but necessary, part of forming the sword."

The smith noticed them, but was busy hammering on a steel slab he had just pulled out of the fire. "Clank, clank, clank, splat." Black pieces cracked off and splattered away from the anvil.

George continued, "See, now he must heat up the pieces in a red hot fire to allow the dross to crust on the outside so that one can burn it away from the steel. Only in this way can he get pure steel. The hammering takes off the crust that is the unusable parts. He must keep at this for a while, hammering and firing the mixed ore until the steel is well tested. Pay close attention. You can learn from this process."

Sergius was curious. "What do you mean? I don't mean to take up the trade of a blacksmithing; I want to be a swordsman. What am I supposed to learn?"

"Remember the good words of Solomon, 'When you come to serve the Lord, prepare yourself for trials… Accept whatever befalls you, in crushing misfortune be patient; for in fire gold is tested, and worthy men in the crucible of humiliation.'[29] My dear Sergius, it is the patient heating and hammering that makes good steel for a sword. You can't avoid this process and if you try to avoid it, you end up with either a too bridle a blade or one too rigid that seems tough but shatters under pressure. The swordsman is like his sword. He too must be trained in fire and hammering. Does not the apostle James say, 'Count it all joy, my brethren, when you meet various trials, for you know that the testing of your faith produces steadfastness. And let steadfastness have its full effect, that you may be perfect and complete, lacking in nothing.'[30] This is the way we become perfect in the Lord. You will learn this in time."

Sergius walked away puzzling over what George meant, but he soon enough discovered what he meant. A few hours later Sergius was dashing to his usual hiding place near the cave when he noticed a gang of men shadowing him with clubs. He zigzagged back into one alley and out another. They split up, but finally two cornered Sergius. "Ah, we know you are working with that foreign knight, that trouble maker. We will show you what comes of those who oppose the King's work."

Sergius then thought, "If only I had a sword made even just of tin, but here I will stand, even without a weapon and fight them as I can."

He fought off the first thug with a hard blow to his arm, but the second one struck while he was landing the blow on his shoulder. As Sergius struggled to fight off the second foe, the first one knocked him on the head. Soon others thugs came and joined in the fray; they then beat Sergius from all sides. He fell to the ground bloodied and fearing for his life as he tried to crawl away. He prayed silently, "Lord, help me, I am trying to be your true servant. If I only had a sword, I would show them."

To his surprise, their chief stopped the beating and called out to Sergius as he tried to make his way out of the alley, "Yes, do crawl away. Like the animal you are, a pet to this foreign knight. We will let you live today, but send a message to this would be hero, George, and all who wish to follow him. Tell them, to stop opposing the work of his majesty and the wizards or more such beatings will come."

A few hours later one of the scouts came looking for Sergius, as he did not attend the regular meeting of the battalion. They found him lying, bleeding in the street and ran over to him as they called, "Are you okay? Who did this to you?"

"It was the King's agents. They wanted to send us a message to us so that we would stop opposing the King's work and hampering the wizards. Oh, I tried to fight them, I gave them everything I had, but they were too many."

"Let me get you home Sergius. You look terrible."

"No, no, just get me to George. I don't want him to think I was intimidated by this."

The two then struggled to the small cottage where George was staying. When George saw the blooded face of Sergius, he called out to some women close by, "Oh, hurry, our good fighter has been hurt in battle."

Sergius grabbed the shirt cuff of George, "Oh, I will be all right in a few days. They said they did this to give you and the battalion a message. Oh, if I only had a sword I would have showed them they did not intimidate me. I would have then given them a message."

George smiled, "I see you still have your fighting spirit. Thank God, though you did not have your sword."

"What do you mean by that?"

"Sergius, they did not kill you because it was not yet the Lord's time to take you, but if you had a sword you would have tried to rush ahead of the Lord. You are no swordsman yet; it is obvious they had orders not to kill you, but if you had a sword and it struck an unfortunate blow, I am not sure they would have spared you. I have seen such men as these, once they get started in their brutality it is hard for them to hold back. No, no, you would have only enraged them enough to kill you. Now you live to fight another day.

This is a lesson every swordsman must learn when to draw his sword and when to hold it firmly in its sheath. You are on your way to becoming a swordsman. You have earned your steel."

Sergius questioned George with a perplexed face, "How did I do that?"

"Just like the iron ore you have been hammered a bit today after going through the fire."

"Ah, that is what you meant. Did you know then that this would happen to me? Why did you not warn me? Isn't there an easier way to become a master swordsman?"

"I am sorry this happened to you. I am. No, I did not know that it would come in this way. Rather, I knew the Lord would allow you to be hammered a bit and go through fire, but I did not know what form it would take. The Lord has his ways. He uses different methods to burn off the dross of His chosen ones. Yet, we have help in this endeavor, which reminds me. I just got word that the package I was expecting came in. The local priest is holding it for me. Let us go gather this package."

"What does this package have to do with anything, George?"

"You will see, be patient?"

They made their way to the priest's residence where George greeted the pastor, "Hello Father. I heard that you received the package that I was waiting for. You are bringing a true grace to me."

The priest smiled, "Yes indeed, this is some of the finest incense one can find. I hear they use it for the most solemn liturgies in the free lands of the East. When Mesopotamia became Christian, the King ordered that this be used to worship Christ. It has a long tradition and is not so easy to get. You should thank our good God in His providence that I could get hold of a bit of it for you."

"Thank you, Father I will put it to good use for training our good warrior here."

"Okay, now you hurry off with my blessing. Train our good neophyte to be a warrior in the Lord. Go now."

"Thank you again, Father."

As they walked off, George with a big smile related to Sergius the significance of the incense, "See this Sergius, this is a special ingredient that they use to make the incense for divine worship in Arabia. I once heard a holy priest preach how we need to pray during our labors to make it like holy incense, a holy offering to the Lord. I then thought to myself, 'Well, how am I to do this as a soldier?' Then it came to me that I too could bath my sword in a holy pool. Inspired by this, I took some of the herbs used for incense and mixed them into a pale of water. Then I soaked the metal I wanted to use for my sword in this holy pool. After long experience, I found these elements gave the best results. This then is the fruit of my prayers.

I learned through experimenting that one could make the steel strong but not too bridle by gracing it with leaven of this holy mixture. What you have to do is to soak the steel in a pool mixed with this holy ingredient and let it sit for a while. The steel will then soak in the graces of the mixture, so that the metal gets just the right temperament for making a good sword."

They then popped their heads into the smith's shop, "John, my good man, I have brought the leaven that I was speaking about."

"Oh, you have, hmm. I am not used to adding anything to my steel. What do you mean by leaven? I am mean sir, no disrespect or nothing, but I am not a baker, am I?"

"Well, not a baker of bread, but baker of hearty steel. I will show you how to make this steel."

"Okay, now John, I want you to bring that basin full of water you use to harden the steel right after burning it."

"No problem. Now what?"

"Okay, place the slabs of steel into the water and just let them lay there."

"Yeh, okay. What next?"

"Okay, let me pour this holy mixture over the water and mix it up very well."

"Ah, yes, I see my good Lord. The mix is becoming a slight gold. Hmm, and how long will the steel soak like this?"

"Oh, my good John, we will leave it overnight. I think these pieces really need to soak up the graces of this holy mixture."

He then turned to Sergius and commented; "Now we must be off. We must pull together Gideon's army."

Then they left the blacksmith's shop. John, however, continued to ponder what it is that the knight had done to this steel. He had never seen such a marvel. He thought, "Hmm, soaking steel in some sort of holy elixir. To get, what did he call it, 'graces from the mixture.' Hmm, 'grace' is that not what God gives us? Humph, well if this works, I guess I will be graced by God also. Maybe I can use some of that holy mixture to help me with other projects?"

George understood that he could not bond together St. Michael's battalion by rigorous training alone, for steel fixed too stiffly will shatter under stress. As they celebrated the weekly Sunday festival, he gathered them together after the liturgy for a joyful communion in the Lord. They came together in the parlor of one of the richer patrons. There was a fine blue-sky with a slight wind that called forth the beginning of spring. George greeted other guests outside in the courtyard.

"Ah, a grand day to you all today, isn't the air so fresh today?"

Sergius was not much for social gatherings, but he was there at George's insistence. In typical fashion, as everyone else was enjoying the gathering, he was trying to work out the next day's schedule. Everything had to make sense to him and he saw no worth in light-hearted engagements; they only stirred up the emotions. With a stern face he looked back at George when he greeted him, "Yeh, I guess it is fine day."

"Oh come on Sergius, you must learn to be light sometimes, else you will become like a caged rat wanting to claw at everything that appears in front of your face."

Sergius frowned not knowing what to say. He did not like the comparison to a rat that seemed like a weak animal to him. "Humph" he said.

"Sergius take our good friend Bacchus here; he delights in passing on fine irony. It keeps his mind keen and the tension light."

"Why yes, my noble George. I believe humor is a sign of a true gentleman. A gentleman knows how to throw a good barb without insult and bend contours on faces chiseled to straightly. Come now, Sergius, don't always be so serious-minded."

Bacchus smiled keenly and commented, "So, I hear you want to be a swordsman like George here. Well, I would challenge you to face off first with our good Kathleen here in a sword match. I have special swords made for this duel, whoever strike his opponent three times first wins. Please if you could come here Lady Kathleen, I want to you to enter into a duel with our good Sergius."

"Oh, yes, Bacchus, I would love to take on Sergius, I have bested everyone else today."

"Hah, you humor me, Bacchus, bring me these swords. Surely, I can best this tiny little woman. I promise you I will try not to prick her with the blade."

"Now don't be so confident Sergius, she is the strong mother of six little ones and knows all the tricks. She may end up pricking you."

Bacchus then brought out his special swords to the delight of George and the other guests. To Sergius' surprise, they were not metal blades at all with a sharp edge but rather made of some sort of wood. He also noticed that the 'sword' was composed of several pieces and had buttons on what would be the hilt.

"What kind of swords are these Bacchus? Are these just training swords then?"

"My dear Sergius, they are the blades of humor. You shall see, but first I must explain to you the rules; for this is no ordinary dual. Note the 'blade' is protruding out from the end now. Okay, now I place the key in and turn it and see the 'blade' has folded in on itself all crumpled up."

"Yes, so what are all these buttons for?"

"Okay, wait a little. I will explain it in time. In this contest you must not only slash with the sword but you must give a good jab too with your wit."

"What do you mean, 'with your wit'?"

"Well, she will first level a humorous insult against you, and you must react with a pleasant rejoinder. She can slash with the sword while she jabs with her wit. While you can only react after you have given a good come back."

"Well, how do I fight back with this sword all folded in on itself?"

"You must press the right button for it to protrude."

"But, how do I know which one it is? Ah, that is part of the humor of the duel. You don't know which one it is."

Kathleen interrupted, "Okay, enough talk Sergius. Be on your guard for I wield my sword now. You men are all alike trying to figure things out before you act, like a mouse who studies a trap while the clamp is coming down upon it."

"Whack."

"Heh, what was that for."

"That was my first thrust. You did not respond.

"Okay, okay. Umm… You wear your pride like a lion prancing in full view."

"Wiz...Ah, but the pride of lion shows its glory, thud. Hah, I blocked your assault. Now hear this, 'The thrust of your sword is like bursts of a tadpole, out like a dart and finished like a frog.'"

"Wiz..... Umm, Watch this frog leap from danger. Whoosh, whack."

"Heh, I pressed the button and only confetti came out and she wacked me again. That's not fair, Bacchus."

"It is part of the game, my dear Sergius. Now fight on, she is about to strike again."

"You are certainly a frog dancing now in hot water, but thinking himself taking a bath. Wiz…Hah, but even hot water extinguishes the flame that heats it. Whack. Splash."

All laugh as they see the Sergius sword squirt water back into his face.

"Three thrusts hitting solidly. That means you lose Sergius."

"Heh, what is this so called sword?"

"What kind of game is this, Bacchus?"

"It is the sword of humility. It takes strategy, awareness, and wit. Something it looks like you need to work on, my good Sergius", said George.

"You all are making fun of Sergius. What fun is this? Everyone is beating up on the serious minded soldier, I see. It seems like everyone is after me."

George replied, "Calm down now Sergius. I tell you what. I will show you how to have a bit of fun. I will sing a song for everyone."

Kathleen, Bacchus, and the others were amazed. Kathleen delightfully exclaimed, "You, George? A great knight like you can sing? Oh how interesting. Do you play an instrument also?"

"Why, yes. I spotted that Kithara there. Pass it to me and I will sing a little tune I composed a while back."

He plucked a note and held it for a measure as he started into his tune…

"The glory of God is
man fully alive.
Those who see God
partake of life.

Those who see God then
are fully alive,
alive in Him
immortally.

God is the source of
all activity
in creation,
animating
being as good.

Through His Word all learn
of the one God
perfect being
source of all.

Creation's order
reveals beauty
a wide vision
of its Author.

The Word revealed
the truth of God
to men giving
men to God
deifying man. [31]

Sergius, who had sat spellbound during all of George's performance, now broke the silence, "I guess I see a bit of what you are getting at George. The swordsman needs to be able to bend a little bit, so he too is not so rigid or he will shatter under pressure. Is that the words you used? Teach me this virtue, master. Show me how to bend without breaking."

"In time, in time, with every good action we do and every good choice we make we conform ourselves to the One who is the maker of a metal, the designer of all swordsman. He it is that mints men if we let Him and He it is that implanted in our nature the need for recreation."

Here is your first lesson. We must always give thanks to the Lord for the means through which he chooses to give us graces, whether it is through persecution, humiliation, or through a woman. For he chose a woman, His mother, to be the glorious means through which he came into the world. Let us then give praise to the Lord Jesus for his mother Mary, who was the means through which we received all of our graces. Everyone now join with me as I sing her praises. George intoned a note and then many voices joined in singing:

Under your mercy
we take our refuge
Mother of God
Reject us not.

Hear us in our need
our supplications
we send to you.
Deliver us.

Protect from danger
all who call on you.
You who alone
are the chaste one,
the blessed one.[32]

# Chapter 12

## *A Sordid gathering*

S ergius was not the only one who felt uncomfortable observing the merriment of the battalion. Spirits also that roamed the sky observed the doings of the battalion and looked on it with hatred. These spirits never rest but delighted in the destructive force of the dragon, for it was the pride of their offspring. *They also had a chief who inspired merriment*, but their festivities were of a different sort. Their party drew some of the most celebrated luminaries in the Kingdom of Terrasindei.

The wizards arranged the gathering to press their influence upon the King. The King entered his great ballroom through the door leading out of his private living quarters. He knew that his court officials had planned a party, but he was surprised to see it was a costume party. Some guests seemed to be dressed up as various gods; others wore masks depicting great figures. Janus walked up to him, as he headed down the stairs to greet the people. The King grabbed hold of him and pulled him close to him saying, "I did not know that this was to be a costume party. What is the occasion?"

"Ah, it was my idea, Your Highness. It gives us an occasion to show forth the splendor of the kingdom to those of importance. The people trust you now, because of our work; we want to help build a renewed confidence in your leadership through this party. Many nobles and wealthy merchants have been clamoring to meet our core of wizards. This event allows us to meet them in a friendly atmosphere."

The King was ruminating over how a costume party could help him win over the confidence of the people when he encountered his first guest. "Well, hello, Hercules right? You look like that Greek figure?"

"Your Highness, how wonderful to see you. Oh, I wanted very much to pose as Hercules. He was so strong, a real giant in his time. From what I've heard, no mortal was faster than he was, or had beaten him in a wrestling match, or had more brute strength than he had. Oh, how awesome he must have been, muscle bound and sculpted. How the women must have ran after him. Do you like the fake muscles? My wife made them. She thinks it really brings out my manliness."

"Oh, yes, I have never seen such a display before, ah, Hercules."

"Don't you recognize my voice, Your Highness? I am really Dom Ricoli, the Sicilian merchant who owns the shipyard."

"Oh, yes, I recognize your voice now," The King said lying.

To his left an alluring sight caught the King's attention. He could see a young woman dressed only in a loose white linen strip. The white linen tied at the waist, wrapped around her midsection leaving her midriff exposed, then flowed around her back and across her chest, as if a painter just brushed a white swath across her body.

The King was a bit abashed at the sight of her but also intrigued. "And who might you be my dear?"

"I am Venus, the goddess of love."

"Indeed, you seem to embody her. You are a sight that would bring many a man to worship you."

"But, I do not recognize your face. Who are you really my dear?"

"Oh, I am, "Venus" that is who I wished to be called by. Am I not elegant? I want all the men to know me from now on as, 'Venus.' Why should I be anyone else?"

The King rather confused by this response nervously takes this as jesting, "Ah, indeed, you are right. No need for another name, the men will run after you in that stunning attire. Okay, 'Venus' is what we shall call you then."

The King then greeted the next guest, "Ah, it is Julius Caesar. Are we rejoining the Roman Empire then?" the King said jokingly to his aide Celsius who was standing nearby.

"Of course not, Your Highness. Caesar was a figure that we all admire for his leadership, boldness and willingness to sacrifice for his kingdom. I see some of those traits in you, Your Highness. You lead us and show us how to make the sacrifices necessary for our kingdom just as he did. You have demonstrated these traits dealing with that difficult situation with the dragon."

The King ignored this last statement as he laughed nervously. "Ah yes, I did what I had to do. Oh, look, there is a genie. I always thought they would bring good luck."

Janus recognized the King's nervousness. He thus kept the conversation on other subjects saying, "Oh yes, there are many genies here. This genie here is really the head of the carpenter's guild. That genie is your governor in Miacum. I do not think anyone would have recognized him. Notice his wife is also dressed up as a female genie. I really like the way they have matching hairstyles. Oh, and over there that genie is one of your court officials. Can you guess who it is?"

The King squinted with his eyes as he peered at the figure. "No, I can't say who that might be."

"Oh, that is your finance minister. Don't worry. I think he put your money to good use paying for that costume."

The King wandered around taking the whole scene in for a while. After greeting several more people, he noticed the wizards mixing among the costumed characters. He had no problem recognizing them because they were not wearing any masks or special costumes. The King upon noticing this inquired of Janus, "Why is it that your fellow wizards are not dressed up for this occasion?"

"Oh my dear King, they are acting as our ambassadors. You see our wizards' council organized this event. Everyone who is important wanted to meet the, "mysterious and intriguing figures" as they say who are advising the King. We staged this party so that the people could meet us, and you could show your regard for us. It would not be fitting if they could not recognize us, for they all wanted to meet the 'grey-cloaked figures.' It was essential then that we wear the garb of our trade."

The King replied sheeply, "Oh yes, I guess you already have costumes."

At that moment, it dawned on the King that the whole party centered on the wizards. As he was pondering over this fact, a woman behind him drew his attention away as she shrieked out, "Look someone is dressed as a crocodile. Oh, how hideous. That person just has no taste. Oh, it reminds us of that terrible dragon vexing us now."

The King turned his head abruptly to see the crocodile, not out of curiosity, but rather because his peace was disturbed by the talk of the dragon. He tried to change the subject, "Oh, I think the costume is original, maybe a bit over the top, but not out keeping with the party at all."

Janus, however, jumped in seeing it was now an opportune time to reply, "Oh, yes it is a good representation of a monster. Our good council knows how to deal with them just as we are working to tame that dragon."

Venus, hearing this interjects, "You think then that in time you will be able to tame the beast?"

Janus replied, "Oh yes, my dear, as soon as we get rid of the forces opposing our work we will tame the beast. We know our art well. It only takes time."

Venus replied giddily, "Oh, how wonderful are these hooded men. They have brought real class to our kingdom. Aren't we so lucky to have these wizards to defend us?"

Janus smiled back at her in a modest way. "Ah, my dear Lady, we are only trying to give the fruits of art to mankind. We saw a kingdom in need and we rushed here."

Dom Ricoli, with his herculean figure, then chimed in, "Indeed, you wizards are the real muscle behind the kingdom. I only appear to have it with this costume. In fact, I would be terrified to confront the dragon. You are the ones with real power."

The King felt a little taken back by this statement, as if the merchant were belittling him for not have the strength of the wizards himself. Janus noticing this, tried to soften the compliment. "Ah, we would never be here battling this social scourge at all if it were not for the King. He has supported the many sacrifices required to carry on this long campaign against the beast."

Hercules replied, "Quite right my good sir. Yeh, I guess it would not have been so easy to convince people to offer their little ones, but in the end, I guess the little ones were better off. I know so many children that grow up in filth, a burden to our kingdom. Sacrificing them to this beast helps our kingdom in the end. Oops, did I say that, so bluntly. I must be drinking a few too many. Anyway, sacrifices were needed."

Caesar replied, "Oh yes, the drink does not blind you. A good leader must make these hard decisions. I salute the King for making these hard decisions. Who will join me?"

All raised their goblets saying, "Cheers to our good King."

The people then continued conversing to each other about the great work of the wizards and the King for offering the horrid, but necessary sacrifices to keep the kingdom going.

As the people carried on, a curious character slipped through the crowd grabbing the attention of the King. It was actually two characters, one a finely dressed young man and another, which seemed to be a mirror, reflecting back the image of the young man. The King looked with amazement at the costumed figure of a young man. "My, my, who are you?"

"Oh, Your Highness, I am just so proud of my costume. I am sure it is the most original. I am Narcissist, the young man in love with his own image. See here, this is my slave playing the mirror. He is a perfectly obedient slave. This costume just fits me perfectly. Oh, how splendid a costume, oh, how splendid indeed, don't you think?"

The King nodded timidly while secretly thinking, "Indeed a perfect costume for him. Oh, what a pity that slave has to put up with that."

Just then, Janus called all the people together for a special presentation. "My fellow characters, legendary heroes, gods and all, I ask you now to come down from your immortal spheres for a little while to give acclaim to our great King. He is no fiction of our imagination but the true leader amongst us. He is the one who knows how to make the tough sacrifices, which the people do not always appreciate but are necessary for the well-being of our kingdom. He is the one who surrounds himself with the great luminaries you have met tonight. You all know he is in the midst of a difficult campaign against the dragon, which has become more difficult because of the opposition of some in the kingdom. I hope no one here could be numbered amongst this number."

A loud cry then rang out, "No, no, no! All hail to our good King."

Janus replied, "Very good. I knew you are all very honorable. In honor of our good King, I prepared some special performance by one of the best Persian dancers. She came in from the Arabian desert just for this performance."

A Persian flute then started to play and a tambourine soon joined in. The King smiled nervously as a young Persian girl peeked her head out from behind a curtain. At first, she seemed to be just teasing the crowd by bopping her head out, then just her naked legs. Then she twirled the whole curtain up around her and slowly unrolled it as she whirled out before the delighted crowd. She was dressed in the scantily manner of Persian belly dancers. She slithered around the floor in a lascivious dance like a snake curling up and then striking, at once appearing threatening and then the next moment appearing coy.

The King smiled nervously as if he were delighted. His Christian upbringing told him this was wrong, but his desire to appease his host muffled his sentiments. The girl made a point of curling up close to the King, as if she were tempting him to eat from her hand. He was somewhat abashed by the temptress turning away out of shyness, but as she pulled his head back around, he did not resist for he was also curious to behold the scene. As a finale, she did a series of six large twirls and then suddenly fell into a curled position as the music stopped. There she posed all balled up with her midsection displayed as the centerpiece. The crowd clapped a hearty approval.

After the applause dissipated, Hercules turned to Venus, "Wow. I neveeer saw no Persian dancer before. Them are reaaal good. Can't beat that."

Venus smiled slightly, while she tried to move away discreetly from his reach, then he commented to another guest, "She was fabulous. I have seen many other Persian dancers, but she is one of the best. It is a real art, you see. One must be very athletic to do this type of dance. This dancer really showed how to use her body to display the movements in the dance. I am going to run off to see if I can meet her."

The crowd continued for a while to speak about the marvelous dance. Finally, as the crowd was dispersing, the King noticed Mortepulchra; she was not wearing any special costume. "Ah, my dear Mortepulchra, you did not wear any special costume. You came simply as yourself."

She stared back at the King with a cold confidence, as if she were commanding the King and he was her servant. "Indeed, Your Highness, this is true. I have no need of a costume; I have no need to mask my identity. We masters of nature have power enough through our will power. All people of intelligence recognize this and they come to us in droves. Pardon me now, Your Highness, I have an appointment that I cannot miss."

Breaking then all royal protocol, Mortepulchra turned her back on the King and left without his leave. The incident left the King speechless for a moment as he felt dismissed, yet, for some reason he felt as if it were his fault. Speaking to himself he said, "She is right. I must give greater heed to her kind, if I wish to have power over people like this. That is where the real power is, my dear Felix. You must teach yourself of this reality."

Later that night Mortepulchra joined her coven for a special gathering. They gathered around a circle of fire, as witches do, all taking their place in a mystical formation. She smiled in an inviting way as several other women filed in around her. "Come now, my dear female masters. Circle around me as we light the sacred fire to our true mother, Divas. She is the one who shows us where our true power lies. She is the one who makes us equal to any man who walks the face of the earth. She is the one who makes us divine greater than any man on earth. Let us enter into the divinity so that the divinity may become great in us."

Then one among them came forth with something wrapped in a blanket. "See good Lord and mother, Mortepulchra, I bring my offering to you the fruit of my flesh."

Mortepulchra then placed the poor little creature in the circle of fire. Then all started their unholy chant as they swayed slowly together. "All is holy, so holy. All is sacred, so sacred. All is one."[33]

Out of the dark sky then descended the dragon, but not one among their midst was terrified, nor did any break the rhythm of their swaying bodies. The dragon alighted right in the middle of the circle of fire with its mighty jaws looking down at the poor creature in the center."

Mortepulchra stepped forward and reached out to pet the dragon. "Ah, my poor little one, how the people of this land have persecuted you. How they have mistreated you, but see, you have a good friend in me. See now, we have brought you a flesh offering."

After a few moments, Mortepulchra continued, "Now eat, partake of our flesh which is given up for you. Take and drink of its blood."

The dragon tore into the flesh of the poor little child on that unholy altar while the priestesses looked on. Then a seeming contentment came over the dragon, as if it were purring like a cat, pleased with Mortepulchra's caress. One could perceive what looked like a smile come across the face of the dragon. This horrible feast continued deep into the night.

That night the people of Terrasindei felt a coldness sweep through the kingdom. It seemed like the warmth of some comforting presence had left the land. All at once, the climate changed from being mild and comfortable to a terrible cold, as if a storm suddenly blew in. The air seemed heavy with coldness, yet when people stepped out into the dark, they noticed no wind. It became so cold that quite a few homes lit their winter fires that night even as spring was upon them. The members of St. Michael's battalion felt this coldness also and wondered what it meant.

Over the next few days, a surge of persecutions descended upon the battalion. The wizards started to spread various rumors among the peoples about them. One said, "Members of the battalion were withholding taxes from the King."

Another rumor claimed, "This battalion wishes to overthrow the King. They have entered into a treasonous pack."

Another said, "They employ a foreign knight so that he can help to usher in a foreign power."

Still another rumor said, "They are trying to cause civil disturbances so that the government will collapse. Thus, they rile up the dragon by preventing sacrifices so that the beast will attack more fiercely later. It is all part of their plan."

The King's agents also carried out a plan to destroy the material support of the battalion. One agent walked into a tavern which he knew a member of St. Michael's battalions owned and called out, "You there, do you own this tavern? We are looking for a Max."

"Yes, I am Max. Why?"

"Well, we have heard that you have been keeping a brood of rats on your land and that you have been mixing their meat into your dishes to keep the costs down. Therefore, we are shutting down your tavern for the sake of public health."

"Well, that is absurd. I run a clean tavern here. I would never do such a thing."

As he was saying this, another agent came out of the back room holding a gutted rat, "I found this in his kitchen Sir."

One could see a cook running after the agent who was just exiting the kitchen. He called out, "I tried to stop them, Max, but they rushed in before I could do anything."

The first agent upon seeing the rat exclaimed, "So, we have proof here."

The cook tried to explain the true story, "No, no you put...", but the second agent grabbed him and pulled him back into the kitchen before he could finish his explanation.

The first agent then quickly called upon several soldiers waiting outside, "Okay board up this establishment. This tavern will not be serving anything for a while."

As Max's customers fled, he sat dejected and asked himself, "What am I to do now? How am I to survive? Is this what I get for working against the dragon? I don't know if I can take this?"

A few days later, the King's agents burst into Domus Spiritus. The members of the battalion that were present scattered when they saw the soldiers breaking into the door. A widow, who lived in a small cottage next door, was the caretaker of the meeting hall. She was friendly to the battalion and offered to do this as service for no charge. The agents now targeted her because of this. They crashed through her door and announced to her as she was cleaning the floor, "We have heard that this is a place where those plotting against the King meet. I am here by order of the King to cease any evidence of a plot against him. All are to remain here while we search."

They scoured through the widow's little cottage looking for any evidence of the battalion's marks, but the members had learned to hold the meetings in various locations. The soldiers found little evidence of the battalion's presence and nothing to show they were conspiring against the King. However, one agent, when he noticed that there were a few more dishes than normal in Domus Spiritum, announced, "I see there have been a number of people here. Look at all these extra dishes. Certainly, my dear widow you could not be using them all. Therefore, I declare this house confiscated by the King. An agent will come by tomorrow with the papers. Then we shall post a guard here making sure this house is no longer used for treasonous purposes. You are lucky we don't throw you in prison for this offense."

After the soldiers, left, the widow burst into tears, turning toward the one member of the battalion present, her nephew. She exclaimed, "Oh, I can't let them take this place. This is all that I have. I know you are doing worthy work, but it would ruin me to lose this place, and I can't be thrown in prison as they almost did today. If they had seen more of the members here and how I was involved with the battalion, I don't know what would have happened to me."

Later others tried to calm her down saying, "Don't worry. You are okay now. The Lord is watching over you. We will move our meetings elsewhere for a while. We will talk to our contact in the court for you. We will make sure that you can keep the house."

However, fear and stress took hold of her. She now would always peek around the corner every time she opened the door. Later, when the members felt she was no longer in danger, they came back to her seeking a donation of food. However, she called out to them, "Oh, go away from here. Don't you see I can't deal with it anymore. I helped you in the name of the Lord and look what it has brought me."

This constant verbal and material persecution caused some in the battalion to lose heart. They complained to George, "Is not the Lord on our side?"

The faithful in St. Michael's battalion continued in their efforts to counter the dragon. However, they noticed the dragon was becoming more aggressive as the persecutions increased. He was now attacking more places and going to sights they had never seen attacked before. It now sought to take the fight directly to the battalion, despite the blessed missiles. That night the dragon ranged the sky looking for George and his battalion. Someone had given the dragon a signal as to where the battalion was meeting. The dragon circled patiently until it recognized some of the members trying to make their way to an altar of sacrifice. This time, however, the dragon did not first go after the prey on the altar of sacrifice, but sought to engage the battalion before devouring the sacrifice. The dragon dove down upon the house where they met and scorched the whole edifice with fire. The owner of the house was just able to escape the burning flames that encompassed it while everyone raced outside. He sat dejected by its side as it burnt to the ground.

The next few nights, similar events took place. It seemed that the King's agents had determined where many of the members lived and signaled to the dragon to attack their residence. This shook the resolve of some members in the battalion so that many started to slip away from active duty. Many who had lost material wealth slipped away from the battalion, and some even stayed away from the Church for fear that they would be associated with the battalion.

During all this, the King remained passive allowing these outrages to continue. Whenever the King's agents came to him with plans to block the efforts of the battalion, he would not even hear them through but simply replied, "Do, what you may. Do what you may. Only do not trouble me with the details."

# Chapter 13

## *Battling phantoms of the soul*

T he harassment of the battalion brought anxiety to George, disturbing his normally optimistic demeanor. He could tell that the pressure of the fight was getting to everyone. He saw now that the battalion seemed to be slipping away from him. As he looked around him, he saw that Sergius, Bacchus, and a few others remained steadfast, but many others started to grumble and would avoid him when he came by. He felt as if the weight of the whole battle was on him and he just could not bear it anymore.

As he struggled with these feelings, he found the daily routine becoming increasingly a drag on him; everything seemed frustrated. A scout gave him a report that they had spotted the dragon. He showed him the lamp directing them to the northeastern quadrant and told him that some other members of the battalion were on their way. George's heart, trained as a soldier, started to race at the expectation of another battle, but he still had some trepidation, as nothing seemed to be going as he planned. He spoke to himself saying, "Come now, you are a soldier. Pull yourself together. You should always be ready for battle. It is on you; now charge out now."

Holding onto some hope, he then rushed to the quadrant where they had seen the dragon. As he drew close, however, he unexpectedly ran into a packed street. It seemed there was some gathering of men sitting around drinking and smoking on the main street. It struck him oddly, "Hmm, this is unusual for this time of night."

He tried to detour through side streets, but now a cart blocked off the whole throughway obstructing him. He tried another path; however, there seemed to be a new construction project clogging up the way. These obstacles seemed to him not to be a coincidence. Just then, he noticed out of the corner of his eye some of the King's agents. One agent was directing workmen to start the construction project on the street that happened to be obstructing George. He said to himself, "Ah, I see there is a conspiracy at hand."

In frustration, he tried to make his way around the blockage by sneaking through a tavern door and popping out the other side. Finally, he made his way to the location of the sighting. He noticed the other members of the team were also just making it there. When they took a measure of the scene, their hearts plummeted, recognizing they were too late. They saw before them a burnt out shell of a cottage and the scorched remains of a man, woman, and two children. It was a terrible sight to see. The woman seemed in the act of trying to protect the children, while the man was face down with a bottle of alcohol close by his side. George, in a last act of mercy, folded the arms of their charred remains and signed them on the foreheads with a cross. He whispered a prayer, "Hold not their sins against them, Lord and may their souls rest in peace."

One of members of the battalion broke down in frustration at the sight. He tugged on the arm of George and pulled him away from the scene, as the neighbors finally peeked out from the protection of their locked doors. The frustrated battalion member's face was blanched white and he seemed to be both anxious and angry as he exclaimed, "I just can't do this anymore, George. This is the third time this week we were too late. I can't stand to see the sight of the dragon's work. Those charred remains don't even look human. I can't take it anymore."

George recognized that he had broken from his normal custom of calling him, "sir" or "captain," but instead just spoke what he felt without any deference to titles.

The distraught member then walked away from the scene throwing down his shield and tearing off the insignia of membership pinned to his shirt, saying , "I am finished George. No more, no more."

Before George could process this, a neighbor of the victims poked him from behind. He turned about seeking who it was. "Are you George, that so called 'knight' who people say has been opposing the dragon?"

George astonished at the question replied simply, "Yes, I am George."

The old woman replied, "Well, this is your fault. Yes, indeed it is. I saw those wizards milling around before this here beast attacked. They knew it was coming. They knew you were coming also. They told us to hide in our cottages. They said they knew the patterns of the dragon and were trying to limit the damage of its attacks.

When I asked them, 'Why could they not stop the beast all together?' They said, 'Because you and your ragged group were enraging it.' The way I see it this dragon would not be here threatening us, unless you were agitating it. It is your fault."

After this encounter, George walked away in a lull from the scene. It was getting on winter, and he could feel the cold biting into his skin as he walked away. George knew the wizards had really planned the attack. They were choosing their victims now, to keep the dragon away from the homes of their rich merchant friends. Their strategy was to discredit George and the battalion in the minds of the people and discourage its members. It seemed to be working.

As George was pondering the plight of the battalion, Sergius came running up to him asking, "How is the sword coming? Is it ready yet? I am so eager to start to use it?"

George, in his fatigue over the distress of the battalion, had forgotten about the sword they commissioned. Thus, he responded simply, "Oh, yes, I will look into it and let you know."

After this encounter, George realized he had been impatience with Sergius and repented. He decided to meander down to the blacksmith's shop to see how the sword was coming. He took his time making his way there, as he now had little to do because of the disarray in the battalion. He thought as he walked along, "At least I can do some good today by making sure the sword is coming along well."

He greeted John, "Hello, good sir. Say how is the sword coming along?"

"Well, my Lord, I have to admit in the last few days, I have not been able to get much work done on it recently. I am sorry, but I had many pressing projects given to me by order of the King's agents."

"Thanks. I will check back in a few days."

This disappointed George and dejected him further. Though he did not express it to John, he sensed a smell of conspiracy. Not that he mistrusted the good blacksmith, but the timing of the King's pressing projects seemed too much of a coincidence.

Exhausted, George then sought the Lord with a greater outpouring of prayer. He determined to spent the next day fasting as he sought to humble his heart. In his depressed state, he looked intently at the Lord reserved in the Church and whispered a lowly prayer, "Lord, I am not worthy to be in your presence. I try to do your will, but I do not always know how to do it correctly. My sins and my pride get in the way. I set out to oppose the dragon using every means I knew. We tracked the beast; we made a meticulous plan to oppose its attacks; we fought the rhetoric of the wizards; we used the talent of every soul that cooperated with us. I realize now, Lord, that the battalion cannot defeat the dragon through our measly human efforts. What more, Lord, are we missing? What have I not done that I should do? This battle is beyond me, Lord. Send me help. Give me insight that I may know what to do."

That night George meandered slowly through the streets as he tried to make sense of his failures. He asked himself repeatedly, "Why must this happen? What could I have done?'

He called out to the Lord in prayer, but his heart seemed empty of affections, so that he could not hear God speaking. He called out in the night, "Is He there? Is He listening?"

Then he caught himself, "Yes, He is. I know You are listening, but I just can't grab hold of you Lord. Show me the way."

He tried to go over again the battles in his mind, as he went through a checklist in his mind, "Well, the strategy seems good. I set up a good battle formation. I had a well laid out plan for battle. I trained my scouts well. I designed the means of communication well. Yet, I see Lord I could not overcome the obstructions that stopped us from even making it to the battleground. Could I have prevented this persecution? Was there some method of rhetoric that I overlooked that could have influenced sentiment in the kingdom?

I see now, I have not led them as I should have; they became disheartened when they faced failure; they were weak under persecution. Yes, that is it. I trained them in good techniques, but I did not train them how to be good soldiers. Yet, they are not soldiers; they are simple people whom I tried to make into soldiers. Why then did I try to train them like soldiers?

George unsheathed his sword and peered down at the blade as if studying its contours. He noticed his own reflection in the blade, which he studied for a bit. He thought, "How mature looking I have become. Yet, I did not always look this way."

He looked more intently again at the sword and his eyes fixed on the word engraved on this hilt of the sword, "spiritus." He commented to himself, "Hmm, 'Spirit.' But what spirit is it that leads me?"

Thoughts of his youth then flooded into his consciousness. He recalled the first sword he held when he was only twelve. He noticed how the light reflected off this sword so different from the one he had when he was twelve, which was rusty and old. His first sword was only a plaything really, not a sword for battle. He reminisced about how he used to fool around with other boys his age making as if he were fighting a battle.

He looked down again at the sword and recalled himself as a teenager learning for the first time how properly to wield a sword. "Ah, how heavy it felt."

He pictured himself again as a youth dueling with another young opponent a few years older with wooden swords. He remembered, "I was the best among that group when we used wooden swords. Ah, but when the real swords came out, I could not keep the blade up. Oh what a lashing I got from just about anyone who came against me in those first few months of training."

He thought, "And how awkward I was. I felt so out of place among the true men of arms then. I felt like a pretender who had to prove himself and *really*, I needed to prove I belonged. Oh and when I tried to lead other boys, I was really like a mouse directing other mice, running back and forth by instinct, but I had no real sense of how to lead. Yet, I had to *feel* like I was leading them. It made me *feel* important like I was an adult. Why was I so concerned about my reputation?"

He held the sword aloft over his head as if imitating his boyish ways of past. He said to himself, "Now too, I see I am just a pigmy of a tribune trying to lead this battalion. Am I better than that boy who wanted to prove himself? Have I just remained a juvenile who is trying to show he can lead? Why is it that I have failed to lead this crew? Am I not really a toy soldier leading a make believe army into battle? Am I not treating them as if I was playing one of my childhood games all over again?

Did I not rush when forming this battalion following childish fervor? Was it that I acted like a boy again imagining an adventure in which I was the hero? Am I not a looking to fulfill a boy's fairy tale? Ah, when I rushed in after that dragon I was seeking to live in those tales again, looking for a monster to defeat just as I did when I was a boy. Yet, this was a real monster now, and I did not win. Was it because I was running after it like a boy chasing a fantasy? Lord, was I really just playing a boy's game? Show me the way."

George found himself walking around befuddled while lightly tapping the sword against his open palm. He walked back and forth with a constrained face. He looked up to heaven every few moments as if looking for a response. Then he continued his pace back and forth. He looked down at the earth as if a thought just struck him, but then he shook his head realizing it was just a fantasy. He raised his hands at last and wrenched out a prayer from the depth of his soul, "Lord, show me the truth. Show me what I am to do. Before you I am always a child."

He buried his hands into his head as he sank deeply into prayer. As he lowered his arms, he turned the sword over exposing the other side of the blade. He noticed the light again reflecting off this side of the blade and his eyes were fixed again on the engraved word, "veritas." He thought translating it, "'truth.' Lord, show me the 'truth.'"

He caught sight again of his image reflected on the blade and now new memories flooded into his mind. He saw himself praying before each battle for fortitude then charging out courageously. In these memories, he was no longer an awkward boy, but a confident man who knew his mission and dashed forth to do his duty. He saw himself at the edge of a barricade peering out at an enemy in dreadful anticipation of the charge to come. He remembered his fear and the struggle to overcome the feeling of terror welling up in his innards, giving him a sick feeling. He recalled himself calling to the Lord in this terror for courage and then all at once seeing his feet running forward as he charged into battle. Lastly, he recalled the charge he led through that haunted forest, not fearing any supposed demon or dragon.

Reflecting, he said to himself as if talking in the third person, "Ah Lord, I see in these memories a man led by you, a courageous man, willing to charge into battle under your protection. You drove this man forward and he followed your inspiration. I see that others followed because of his courageous example. I see others imitating his prayers before battle recognizing it gave this man fortitude. Ah, indeed Lord, this man was a leader like Gideon of old; who heard your voice and led by your command."

"Yet, Lord, which one am I? Am I the boy soldier, awkward still looking for respect or the courageous commander leading the charge into battle? My crew is slipping away from me Lord. I try to lead, but they do not follow. Is it that I am too pushy, too childish? Is it that I am doing things too much my way and not letting you work through me?"

He then buried his head in his arms again as he poured out his heart in prayer, "Show me the way Lord. Show me the way…"

That afternoon, during the time for rest, he hears a thud, thud, thud, on the door of the cottage at which he was staying. He thought, "Who can it be, venturing out at this time of day and thumping that way?"

He opened the door and peered out. To his surprise, he saw an old woman who seemed like she could barely stand, bent over and holding up her whole weight with a rickety old cane. "Hello, my good young man. My name is Maria. I have heard much about you. Yes, I have. I have been following your doings ever since I heard there was a devout young foreign knight in our midst. I see now the reports are true."

"If I may ask good mother, what it is that was reported to you about me?"

"That you were a stout young man, willing to stand up in the Lord. Oh, this is true indeed. You look stout, strong, and of good character. I am sure you are of good worth."

"My dear Madame, how can you be so sure of me on sight? Have you not heard the reports that my battalion is falling apart? Don't you know that we have not succeeded in driving out the dragon?"

"No, no, no, I see the truth. You are a man of good worth. Oh, you may have had your troubles. This is the Lord's way. Yet, I can see you have a prayerful spirit. You give your heart to the Lord. Ah yes, this is the form of you. Yes, yes, these 'failures,' as you call them, do not blur the brightness of your spirit, you are a bright spirit indeed."

"Madame, you seem like a good grandmother with perception. Why do you say my soul is bright?"

"Ah, my good son, yes, yes, we never see everything in our own reflections. It takes another to point it out to you. I see, yes, I do. I have seen this many times. Oh, I know souls; I have studied them for years, old ones, young ones, wild ones, shy ones, ones who called themselves great, and ones who called themselves humble. Your spirit shines bright. This is the truth of your reflection. Now trust me, son, don't doubt. You keep going, don't stop because you skinned your knee a few times. Now my boy, you are called to be a great warrior. Yes, indeed that is the truth. No more doubt. No more doubt. This is the truth. Now I have said what I came to say. I must go now. Yes, I must go."

George watched curiously, as the old grandmother turned about and pulled herself along with the cane, seeming to dig into the ground with every step. It looked as if she was spending the very last of her energy with every step, yet she never seemed to slow down or rest. George stared for a few minutes with admiration as she continued to drag herself along. Not once did she halter, not once did she seem to slow down.

He thought as he saw this spectacle, "Certainly, that is something to admire. She just keeps going; nothing will stop her. She must have seen so much through the years. There is a bundle of wisdom tied up in that old body. Yes, Lord, I see you spoke to me through her. She showed me the truth of who I am. I am called to be your warrior. You have been leading me through these trials, training me, and now I see you are teaching me how to lead a battalion through tribulations. Direct me now to what I should do next."

George then with a peaceful continent turned again to prayer waiting for the Lord's direction. A priest happened upon George as he was pouring his heart out in the local Church. He stopped and asked, "What ails you that you are so pensive today?"

"Father, I am trying. I am real trying to do the Lord's will and fight the dragon, but I am not sure I am really doing it in the manner He wants me to. I organized a battalion to fight the dragon as I thought He directed me to. I did my best to train them in the virtues and lead them in prayer, but now I find they are turning away from me when persecution comes our way. I believe I am called to this path, to be a great warrior, to be a leader. The Lord has confirmed this for me. But I know not how I am to do it."

The priest replied smiling, "I see. Now the Lord can really use you."

"Really use me! What do you mean, Father?"

"Now you must live in faith. It is when you learn to let go of control and let the grace of God lead. That is when He can really use you."

"So, how am to get this grace to lead and to do my way of thinking?

"You must raise up an army of faith?"

"What do you mean, 'an army of faith'?

"This is not your battle alone or just the battalion's battle. No, you must call on the entire mystical body of Christ. You need an army of intercessors to pray for you. This kingdom has become infested not by just one beast, but by thousands, maybe millions. Don't you see? These can be driven out only by the conversion of millions of hearts.

You must make an army of intercessors to bring this kingdom to conversion, and you will defeat whatever beast you encounter. I will help you get a start. I will send word out to my whole parish seeking three days of adoration with the intention of bringing the kingdom to repentance. The good hearty souls will show up; the simple ones that the world seems to forget, I find are the best. They will be the start of your army. Once we get it planted here, I am sure the Spirit will help it spread throughout all the parishes in the kingdom. Then you will have a real powerhouse behind you.

George jumped up excitedly, "Yes, yes, Father, that is the key. We need an army of intercessors, adorers, and souls seeking penance. Ah yes, the pure simple hearted souls, the suffering, and the forgotten elderly, the lame, and dumb. They will make up my army."

# Chapter 14

# *Passing on the art of spiritual warfare*

G eorge now knew where the strength of the battalion must reside, not in technical training, not in the molding of battle expertise, but in the persevering prayers of faithful souls. The battalion must win the battle for grace to defeat the dragon; to win the battle, only an army of prayer warriors would do. He saw now that this dragon came upon Terrasindei because of the people's sinfulness, and only through their sincere repentance would they overcome it.

George whispered to himself, "Prayer, prayer, this is the key. This will win the battle for grace and nothing else. I must find for myself prayer warriors who will call down grace from heaven in a torrential rain. Let it drench everything, let it pour, let it flood this kingdom!"

He then rushed off excitedly with a huge smile on his face, confident that he knew the Lord's will. It was a cold December day but George felt spring coming upon him, enlivening his heart. He rushed from church to church seeking pious souls to be his rear guard. He peeked into churches at midday looking for old women bent over with prayers. Finding one, he knelt down beside and tapped her on the shoulder saying, "Excuse me, good Mother." He used the respectful title, common at the time for older women. "I see you are very devoted to prayer. I am in great need of your help."

Being a hearty soul the woman was keen to respond to this call for help, but was a bit perplexed, asking, "Yes, what do you need young man that a woman like me can do?"

"Well, you see, I tried to form what I called a 'battalion,' a military core of volunteers to fight the dragon that is attacking Terrasindei. I tried to form them in holiness and to do their job well, but I neglected their supply line. I see now, they need great prayer warriors to support them in battle."

"Oh, I can do that young man. What intentions exactly do you want me to prayer for?"

George enumerated their needs. "Please prayer for their perseverance, for wisdom in following the Lord's will and courage in the face of hostility. Please pray that souls in Terrasindei come to repentance. Only in this way can we defeat the dragon.

He made similar little speeches in churches here and there, seeking prayer support from similar frail humble figures all over the kingdom. He went to the far corners of the kingdom, seeking the prayers of consecrated virgins and holy veiled women. He even directed Sergius and the remaining faithful members of the battalion to stop their active work for a while. Then they were to focus on recruiting members for their prayer core. Sergius at first was perplexed at this change; he was eager to get at the dragon in direct battle. He even questioned George, "Why can't we just continue opposing the beast with our swords and arrows?"

George replied with patience saying, "Ah, my good Sergius, I know your instinct is to charge at the dragon with all your muscle. Yet, I tell you we cannot defeat the beast with might alone. Now is the time we must pull back, like a good battalion regrouping, and then we wait to strike again with greater force. This is an important part of the spiritual life, knowing when to retreat in a particular battle, wait for reinforcements and then strike with a greater, renewed force later. Only in this way can you win wars. I tell you Sergius, it is the same with all temptations. There is a time one must flee, a time to stand strong and a time to seek reinforcements. Did not our Lord say, 'a general who has ten thousand men will measure whether he can attack an army with twenty thousand?'[34] I tell you, one should know their personal strengths and weaknesses and judge whether they can win a particular battle. There are many battles in a war. In some battles, one recognizes that he can stand strong facing the onslaught of the enemy, so he stays put when the attack comes. In other battles, he recognizes that the enemy is too fierce for him so he retreats, until he can reengage the enemy under better conditions. Finally, there are some battles that humiliate us, driving us back, which reveal to us our need to seek reinforcements. Now is the time to seek reinforcements, Sergius.

"We want to win the war Sergius, and I tell you one man alone cannot win a war. You must learn how to be a good member in a battalion, but we need a grand army supporting our little battalion to win this war. This is why we go out to recruit our true *reserves*."

Sergius, upon hearing this softened, and started to meditate on what George said. He walked around for a few minutes as if trying to work something out in his mind then responded, "I see, yes, I see you are right. I know too what we can do to get more reinforcements."

"And what do you propose my good Sergius?"

"We should create St. Michael prayer guilds all over the kingdom, souls that offer up special prayers for us. They can meet together asking the intercession of the heavenly court, our good Queen Mother Mary and the angels. They can offer sacrifices and keep vigil for us. During Lent, they can offer special prayers of fasting and sacrifice for us for the whole of the forty days. They will be the reserves that support our battalion, as you say."

"Yes, this is a great idea Sergius. Put your enthusiasm for battle to use now organizing such guilds. Yes, yes, go off we are in urgent need of reserves. Go to the ends of the kingdom."

Soon they established guilds all over the kingdom and people started to notice the efforts of St. Michael's battalion. Before the kingdom had seemed like a dead carcass waiting for some bird of prey to come and devour it. Now, new life came into the kingdom. It was, as if, a light were lit in many churches that seemed dark for many years. The remnant of devout souls started to take notice of the battalion and even a few not so devout were drawn into the battle being inspired to support the battalion with the simple gesture of prayers.

The new Archbishop Petrus Romanus noticed the work of the St. Michael guilds that were appearing all across the kingdom. Jocundus, the former archbishop, had been called to another see. Archbishop Romanus was his own man, not beholden to the King, as was the former archbishop; rather he was a praying soul who sought the Lord's will in all things. Upon hearing about the guilds, he gave a homily at the start of Lent in the Cathedral on their work.

"We are now entering into that time of year again when the season of prayer and fasting is upon us. In this time, we recall how our Lord spent forty days in the desert to enter into our temptations and do battle with our eternal foe. I tell you, the foe that he fought is among us now in the form of a beast that rages in our souls. You hear of the beast that ranges in the skies above, but I tell you, there is a worst beast that lives in the hearts of too many in this kingdom. It tempts us to sin through lust, desires and false images of ourselves. I tell you *now* is the time to enter into the desert with our Lord to overcome that beast. Let Him conquer the beast in you, as He conquered that eternal foe in the desert years ago."

"We cannot defeat the beast that ranges in the sky, until we defeat the beast that ranges in our souls. We have been blessed with a few courageous souls who have taken it upon themselves to battle this dragon, but I tell you now they need our help. They need us to pray and fast entering into battle with the beast that lives in the hearts of too many. Let us together enter into a spirit of repentance and reparation. Like Moses who prostrated himself on Mount Sinai turning away the wrath of God, let us likewise put our faces to the ground and do penance for those who do not repent so the Lord may have mercy on our kingdom."

"The Spirit has raised a core of prayer warriors called St. Michael's prayer guilds. These support the work of the brave battalion through their prayers. Such groups can bring our kingdom out of the desert of sin, which we now find ourselves, into the promised land of peace and virtue. I encourage you all then to take hold of this opportunity, join the guild, and fight the beast that plagues the interior of our hearts. Then we will win the battle with the beast that attacks from above…."

After this inspiring homily St. Michael's battalion had no problem forming guilds. One thing, however, still worried George,how would they bring repentance to the royal palace? The King's agents were still working to frustrate the work of the battalion. He knew prayer was the key, but he also knew that prayer relied on the power of intercession. It then struck him, "Lord, I see now is the time to call on the good princess to plead for our cause. She is the only who can help us."

George thus sent word to her through Procuvera's faithful maiden. He gave her the following message:

"Oh please, good princess, intercede for us as Esther of old. The King's men are sorely trying us. Without your help, all the work of our battalion will be frustrated. Trust in the Lord and you will have the courage of Esther and the wisdom of Daniel. Please act quickly; we are gravely in need of your help."

When Procuvera heard the words of the note read by her maid, she responded, "Thank you. I will do everything I can to intercede for them."

This plea greatly moved her and she kept turning it over in her thoughts. She called out to the Lord in prayer, "What am I do Lord? Yes, I hear you calling me. Yet, it is not so easy to oppose my father the King? Yet, how can I let down this battalion who are the only ones standing up for the little ones?"

After pausing for a moment, she ended her internal debate saying, "I must act. I can't stand by and let this continue. I will appeal to him as a loving daughter. Yes, yes, that is it."

Procuvera, then no longer a girl, took hold of her womanhood that night and slipped into her father's chamber. The king welcomed her with a smile, "Oh my good dear, what can I do for you?"

"Father, remember some time ago, when I spoke to you about the good Christians opposing the dragon and the knight who was leading them?"

"Yes, I remember. That knight disappointed me greatly."

"Father, I really think you should change your mind. I know George and the battalion have had their failures. But, father putting your trust in the wizards is to make a pact with demons. They are doing more harm than help. Think about it.

I have seen how they work. They keep asking for more sacrifices; they keep pressuring you. I fear, sometimes, they are saying spells against you. I can just feel it. Aren't we Christian, father? Why should you trust in wizards and witches and not in the true God? I tell you they are evil. Do not trust them."

"Oh, I had hoped you would not hear about the sacrifices and the doings of wizards and witches. A King must make difficult choices, in tough times. I don't like sacrificing innocent little ones to stop this beast, but this seems the only way possible."

"Father, the Christians battalion is fighting the dragon in a different way. Can't you accept that God might have a plan different from the prudent path of politics? Does political strategy rule everything? I mean, did you and mom decide to have me because of politics? Does a father love a child because of politics? Are these farces also?"

"No, no, my child, it was not that way between your mother and me. I learned to love her. It is true our marriage was arranged because of politics, but I came to truly love her. And now, well now that your mother is gone, you are the love of my life. I tell you this is truth. Don't you know I love you?"

"Oh father, I know you love me. But, but, father can't you show this same love to these poor innocent little ones, by helping the brave souls defending them?"

"You remind me so much of your beloved mother when you stand up to me like this. She used to stand up to me, not afraid to proclaim the truth just as you are doing now. This was part of what made her seem so beautiful to me."

"I miss her too, father. I think the best way to remember her is to do what is right."

"Yes, you are right. I will tell my agents to call off this persecution."

Soon after, the King called his agents into his presence saying, "I want you to slow down the persecutions of St. Michael's battalion."

"But, Sir, they are opposing the sacrifices we give to the dragon. Won't the wizards revolt? Then what will we do?"

"I know there will be problems, but you can call it off for a bit without much harm, right?"

"Well..."

"Yes, I will it. You can do it. But do this quietly and don't advertise this command. I know the wizards will be anxious, but I must, I must stop this. I mean what they are doing. I mean I have to at least slow it down. Just be discreet and they won't react strongly."

After this decision, the battalion enjoyed a period of peace, which gave George a chance to think through how he was to train the active members of the battalion. He brought his strategy to the Lord in prayer saying, "Ah yes, Lord, I see I have been charging forward just as I did in that cave during the first encounter with the dragon. Yet, we need hearty souls who fast on your word and trust in you, not just brave souls who may be fool hearty. I see, Lord, I must take stock of the talents of those whom you have entrusted to me and lead them to holiness. It is only in this refining that we can be effective in our fight against the dragon."

George then remembered it was time to see how Sergius' sword was coming along. He was sure the Lord was making a way for him and was excited to see the progress on the sword. George knocked on the door of Sergius' cottage calling out, "Ah Sergius, it is time we check again on your sword. I bet the iron is being forged now."

"Oh, yeh, in the turmoil and the excitement of organizing these guilds, I almost forgot. Let's go."

They made their way to the blacksmith's shop. Just as George expected, he saw John busy forging the blade of the sword they had commissioned. They heard a "clank, clank" and watched black metal shards flake off.

John noticed them and called out, "Oh, hello my good Lord and worthy sir. I must tell you this is good metal, which we have here. It is the finest, I think, I have ever worked with. The leaven or mix, or whatever you call it, made this a real good metal, a very good quality for a blade."

George replied, "Very good, my dear man. Can you please explain what you are doing? I want Sergius to study all the details to teach him a lesson."

"Indeed sir, I would be proud to explain my art. I just finished tempering the metal. For this, I had to heat repeatedly the metal until it was nice bright and glowing. Oh, it was a long process. You see, with each strike I broke off the last remnants of the mixed ore.

Now I am getting to the part where I normalize it. You can watch me. As soon as I pull it out of the furnace, I have to plunge it real quick like into water."

They hear "clank, clank" again. "Okay, now comes the sharpening. I will flatten and curve the end repeatedly, until it comes out with a nice edge. Then I will clash steel against steel. I will dash the edge of the metal against this other rough blade I use for sharpening it. Lastly, I will put on the hilt. Then it will be all yours, Sergius."

After this little explanation, George gave a commentary about the actions to Sergius saying, "Note the details in this. You can see in this process the same manner in which a great warrior is made. To wield properly the sword the warrior must also be formed. He too must go through the fire. This is why we had to go through the persecution by the King's agents. Then after the heat of the battle, there is often a lull. During this time a good warrior learns to be refreshed in the bath of reflection. After this bath, the soldier is hammered again when the battle restarts. This repeated hammering, allows all the dross to be knocked off the warrior in training. Now you can try to shortcut this process, but it will not make for a fine sword or a true warrior. No, a blade worthy of warfare must endure this process. So too a good soldier must go through his forging to make a fine warrior.

"Thank you, John, when do expect to finish the blade? I would like to show it to a few others."

"Oh, I should finish the blade today, but the hilt I still have to make."

"I want to show off the blade even without the hilt."

"Good. I will come back later for it."

Sergius and George then went their separate ways, as they had errands to run in different locations. As Sergius made his way through the streets, he noticed Princess Procuvera's carriage meandering through the streets some fifty feet off or so. He could just make out her continence through the carriage window. This passing vision of her delighted him. He had always thought her beautiful, but something struck him this day. He thought to himself, "Yes, she is pretty, but her purity and courage makes her more beautiful, a refreshing sight. Yes, that is it. Like there is something worthy in this world to defend. Oh, if I could be as courageous and disciplined a swordsman as she is graced with beauty, than I would be a great swordsman indeed."

He walked off slowly, contemplating this thought.

Meanwhile George assembled the remnants of his fighting battalion and made an effort to call back those who had drifted away. He spoke to them saying, "I realize that many of you have become disheartened because of our failures in the face of persecution. It is not easy to continue the battle when it seems our efforts come to nothing. Yet, I tell you they were not for nothing. I too have experienced failure both in this campaign and in past battles. Trust me; I have failed many times, often because I made mistakes. Only through the grace of God have I gotten this far."

"Yet, I tell you there is meaning in these failures, but one can only find this through the cross. For the apostles the death of Jesus seemed like a failure when they first witnessed it; however, in time, they came to see it was really like the death of a seed which brings new life. Likewise, our failings and trials, when we join them to the cross of our Lord, can become seeds sprouting into fruitful plants."

"This germ of life starts in us. If we allow it, grace will change us making us virtuous so that we become like Christ, even conforming to his suffering and death. Yet, I know this is hard. I am still working on this process of dying to myself and I must continue to die if we are to defeat this beast. For, as the good Archbishop Romanus said, 'The beast reigns within all our souls.' Only by dying to our self, we will be able to kill the beast that afflicts us."

"I tell you the beast still has a foothold in my soul. I see this now. I wanted to be the glorious hero, picked by our Lord, and acclaimed by a kingdom, just like a boy in a fairy tale. No, this is not the Lord's way. The Lord had to humble me, to remind me that we are one body in Christ. I could not triumph alone, nor can we as a battalion hope to defeat this dragon just through our human efforts."

"This is why we started St. Michael's guilds. We need an army of prayer warriors to call grace down upon us in abundance. They will enter into the spiritual warfare, while we enter into the physical warfare. We have let the stench of vice suffocate the air too long, only the breath of grace can drive it out. Let us plant these guilds in our hearts, and then we will have the power to conquer anything that comes our way."

"Now I have something to show you." George then uncovered the unfinished sword he fetched from the blacksmith. "Come closer everyone, I want to show you this sword we commissioned. I picked this up from the blacksmith this afternoon. I was advising Sergius here how to commission a fine sword for warfare. While we were watching it being made, I explained to him the virtue that goes into sword making. There is a lesson in this sword for everyone, not just the swordsman who wields it."

Then using a blanket to hold it up he lifted it aloft for all to see. "You see this sword is not finished. It is only yet a blade with no hilt. I tell you even unfinished it has already acquired much virtue. Sergius and I intervened often during its forging to make sure it was made in the right way. We made sure the raw material received a good hammering, through the hands of a good blacksmith, to make sure all dross chaffed off. Likewise, our little battalion had to be hammered so all our dross would be knocked off. The Lord allowed this then to remove the dross from our souls.

As it is not yet finished, so too our task is not yet completed. This sword still needs a hilt with a good grip and a guard. Of course, without a hilt, the blade would cut the one holding it and it would be cumbersome, no good for fighting. The guard additionally, protects the hand of the one who wields the sword. This I consider the "grace" of the sword, for just as the guard protects the swordsman's body likewise grace protects his soul. A good grip also is important for it allows the swordsman to have a good handle on the sword. Without a good grip, the swordsman becomes vulnerable and distracted, concerned with holding onto the sword. Likewise, a good swordsman will always have a good grip on the reality of the situation. Our Lord gave us an intellect to perceive reality around us, if we do not use this we are our demeaning our Creator.

Finally, we must not forget about the pommel. This end piece gives the sword balance. Good balance is an absolute necessity. The swordsman too, must have good balance. If he is lacking in balance, it does not matter how good the sword is. Our festivities remind us that we need to take time to recreate in the Lord. There is a time for fun and a time to be serious; if either is lacking, the swordsman will be too on edge, ready to attack anything, or a flighty wimp who shrinks from any battle.

Thus, you see before you the unfinished sword. Let us finish this sword together. Let us keep up the fight against this dragon. Who is with me?"

Upon hearing this oration, those assembled were silent for a moment, and then Sergius came forward. "My true Captain, I will take that sword and have it finished. Who is with me?"

Others in the assembly followed with subdued affirmations, nodding their heads in agreement as they said, "Yes, I will."

Another, "We have been through much, but I see now it was the Lord's will. I will rejoin the battle."

Another, "Yes, you were right we need to be formed through hammering like this sword. I will see it through."

One by one almost all those assembled agreed to continue the campaign. It was not an exuberant acclamation like the one George first heard when he formed the battalion, but there was a sense that this was a more mature affirmation. In this "yes," they showed a more serene acceptance of the fatigue of the battle. In this "yes," they accepted that they had to endure more. In this "yes," they took up their cross and followed Christ.

Thereafter, the battalion grew closer together in communion. The respite from persecution allowed them to hone the strategy of their combat and rescue units. With their new outlook, they felt a sense of peace flow over them. They prayed together each day and prepared themselves with short bursts of prayer before they rushed off into the fray. They could also sense a cloud of prayers helping them along the way. They knew St. Michael's guilds were fighting the spiritual battle for them. The battalion entered into the Lenten season, with a day of fasting, to help them to prepare for their daily battle with the beast. From then on, George focused them on battling the beast roaring in their own souls, and consequently they found that the battle with the dragon became less difficult.

From then on, they found that each battle now helped St. Michael's battalion to grow more integrated. Over time, the members came to recognize their weaknesses and sought now the grace of the Lord to help them overcome them. They no longer saw their weaknesses as just failures that tempted them to walk away from the battle, but a forging of their own souls. The battalion thus was training their souls into a strongly forged instrument that the Lord could put to use. They learned to be a cohesive unit, battling their weaknesses and reaching beyond what they thought they could do.

George helped them in this forging, guiding the members as he could to be at once tough, but also capable of flexibility, like a fine sword ready for battle. Seeing their hard work, he wanted to bring a bit of relief to their struggles and thus invited them to a celebration for the Feast of the Annunciation. He arranged for them to gather at Kathleen's country church to celebrate the great feast day, which recalled the Angel Gabriel's greeting to Mary, when Mary conceived by the Holy Spirit and the Word of God became incarnate.

Kathleen's church had celebrated this day with great solemnity for many years. The Lord gave them a splendid spring day, colored with the sight of newly blooming flowers and a gentle breeze that refreshed everyone. Walking into the church, one was struck by the garlands of assorted colors flooding the church. Kathleen explained how each family in the parish had lovingly made their own garland to decorate the church with a wonderful plethora of diversity, all in honor of Our Lady. The mosaic of the Annunciation framed the whole spectacular sight like an image of a lady magically presiding over an enchanted garden. Many candles illuminated the mosaic causing its splendid colors to sparkle as the flames flickered. Not too far from the mosaic, there was another beautiful statue of the Virgin with a blue veil and a white dress. The whole church looked magnificent as the afternoon sun peeked through the windows.

Then the great liturgy started with a deacon leading the way, swinging the incense, followed by six acolytes proudly bearing candles, visiting clergy, vicars, and finally the pastor. The congregation joined in the chant that started when the procession began. As the priest came to the altar, he donned an ornate vestment and began the liturgy. The catechumens sat in front, listening closely as the Word of God was proclaimed. As  Christians in training, they left before the great mystery started processing out of the Church for special instruction in the ways of the Lord. The glory of the Lord was on the Church that day, as it came time for the great Mystery of the Lord's presence to be unveiled. The people introduced the Mystery, as they recalled the chant of the Angels, "Holy, holy, holy…"[35]

After the liturgy, the congregation waited attentively in the church. Kathleen poked the members of the battalion. "Wait here. Don't leave the church yet. What you see next is so beautiful. The young ladies of our parish will make a presentation to the Virgin now."

Then several young girls came out dressed in colorful garb, beautiful in their modesty, which called one to glorify the Lord who could inspire such a sight. Each girls dress was original, showing how much pride her mother put into making them. They wore a light veil, as was the custom of young ladies, on top of which was a garland of flowers. George seeing this, commented to Kathleen, "You were right. How beautiful all the girls look today; they are like little images of the Blessed Virgin Mary, pure and bright. If all the girls in Terrasindei were like these little ones, the whole kingdom would glow."

Kathleen responded, "Oh yes, they are the pride of our parish. On this great feast, the mothers vie to make her girl look the prettiest. The pastor though is keen to keep them focused on the meaning of the feast. Listen now, he is calling each girl by name to come forward and make an offering to the Blessed Virgin Mary."

They could hear the priest announce from the lectern, "Pearl, come forward and place your flower in the garland. Blancus, come forward to place your flower in the garland…"

Kathleen commented, "See how beautiful it is. Each is placing a flower in the garland that will crown the Blessed Virgin Mary. The pastor made sure he has catechized all the girls about the significance of this garland. It represents the purity they must keep their entire lives. They are all dressed like little images of the Virgin Mary, while they bring a flower to her statue signifying to them whom they must imitate. It is a powerful and moving symbol that really touches the girls in our parish. I tell you the dragon has no foothold here."

Bacchus, seeing this commented, "Ah, it is beautiful indeed. Look now the pastor is placing the garland they made on the statue of Our Lady. A fitting crown, made with such purity."

After the crowning, all the girls came together in rows. Then Kathleen jumped up saying, "Oh pardon me, it is time to sing to Our Lady. The whole parish joins in this tradition."

Wonderful singing then swept through the Church as they sang the song of Our Lady:

Magnificat anima mea Dominum,
et exsultavit spiritus meus in Deo salvatore meo,
quia respexit humilitatem ancillae suae.
Ecce enim ex hoc beatam me dicent omnes generationes,
quia fecit mihi magna,
qui potens est,
et sanctum nomen eius,
et misericordia eius in progenies et progenies
timentibus eum.
Fecit potentiam in brachio suo,
dispersit superbos mente cordis sui;
deposuit potentes de sede
et exaltavit humiles;
esurientes implevit bonis
et divites dimisit inanes.
Suscepit Israel puerum suum,
recordatus misericordiae,
sicut locutus est ad patres nostros,
Abraham et semini eius in saecula

# Chapter 15

# *The Second great battle with the dragon*

*I*n his mind, George now felt a vision pressing upon his mind. He saw himself boldly attacking the dragon like a daydream that he could not put away. George tried to dismiss the thought of attacking the beast as a phantom for he did not trust his past imaginings. However, the thought kept pressing upon him. It had been nearly three and a half years since George had started on his pilgrimage and a year since he first engaged the dragon. He had had many doubts during that time. Thus, he thought, "Is this you speaking Lord? I am not sure, for I see now I cannot defeat this dragon through my own power. Why then does my heart beat so urgently, now pushing me to charge again into the realm of the beast?"

He brought his concerns to the Lord in prayer as he prepared for the holy Mass. The first reading in the Mass was from the book of Revelation. It spoke about the angels who stood constantly before the altar of God adoring him and giving him praise. The angels were worshiping the Lord in the heavenly realms with incense representing the prayers of the faithful rising up to Him. In the midst of the heavenly scene, there was a strange creature, a lamb that lived although it looked like it was slain.[36] The priest explained in his homily, "The Lord Jesus was the true Lamb, slain for our sins, and now he appears in his glory as a slain lamb who reigns in heaven with angels who offer him worship."

As he heard the heavenly scene described, George's mind wandered from earthly realities to the worship in heaven. He noticed the smell of incense pervading the church as the deacon swung the thurible, processing around the altar. "Hmm," he thought as he inhaled a bit of the incense and beheld the smoke rising to heaven. "Lord, I recognize in this sweet smell my prayers rising up to you. Lord, listen to my pleading. I seek light Lord, show me the way."

George and the whole assembly then looked toward the East waiting for the coming of the Lord as the great Mystery unfolded. As the priest started into the Eucharistic anaphora, some words of the liturgy struck George in a way like never before.

"O God the Father of our Lord Jesus Christ, the Father of mercies and God of all comfort, who sittest above the cherubim and art glorified by the seraphim, before whom stand a thousand-thousand archangels, ten-thousand-times-ten thousand angels, hosts rational and heavenly, who hast vouchsafed to sanctify and perfect the offerings and gifts and perfection of fruits which are offered to thee for a sweet smelling savour by the grace of thine only-begotten Son and by the descent of thine Holy Spirit."

"Sanctify, O Lord, our souls and bodies, that with a pure heart and with soul enlightened and with face unashamed we may make bold to call upon thee, O God, heavenly Father, almighty, holy."[37]

Later that night, George was contemplating the work of these angels who take our prayers up to the heavenly throne. His mind turned to the mystical symbols he heard described in the Book of Revelation and recalled the image depicted on the mosaic that first led him on this quest to battle this dragon. He thought, "A woman fighting a dragon it was. Ah yes, this too is from the Book of Revelation."

He scrambled to find a copy of the Holy Scriptures to look up the passage.

"Here it is. It says, 'The heavens in the sky opened up. Then John, the beloved, saw the ark of the covenant and then a woman appears clothed with the Sun with the Moon under her feet.'[38] Now how does this all involve me, Lord? Why, Lord, do these images press on my heart?"

George continued deep in meditation as he tried to picture in his mind the heavenly woman described in the scriptures. He became lost in the meanderings of his thoughts, and he started to lose track of everything around him, fixated as he was on these mystical symbols. He mumbled to himself, "Who is the woman? Who is this that beckons me?"

The wind blew through quietly as he remained transfixed delving into these images. He was content to let his mind just ride along with the slightly blowing breeze. To his surprise, he heard the small wisp of a voice in the quiet little wind. He listened more attentively and heard the word, "Come."

He thought, "Am I imagining this?"

Then it came again more clearly, "Come now, I am the one who calls you."

He was not sure what it meant, but he instinctively went toward the direction of the voice. He craned his ear, knowing from experience that the Lord often speaks this way in the concentrated voice of silence. He heard it again, "Come."

He could now make out that it was the voice of a woman beckoning him outside. He saw nothing, but it was as if her quiet gentle voice was being carried by the wind. He followed the flow of the wind to see its source. Again, he heard, "Come up hither."

He followed the lovely voice up the hillside to the place from which it seemed to originate. There before him, a light appeared as if coming from the hill itself. Though bright beyond anything he had ever seen, the light did not hurt his eyes and his vision could easily penetrate it. From the midst of the light, he noticed a small glowing globe emerging that encircled a woman. Light emanated from the woman as if it was her very clothing, and she seemed to be riding something that looked like the crescent of the moon.

He knelt and murmured under his breath, "It is the woman of the Apocalypse, the Virgin that I saw in the mosaic. How beautiful she is."

He was in rapture as he knelt before the sight. The motherly figure then slipped through the globe of light and appeared right in front of him. She smiled in a way that brightened George's very soul, and her whole continence seemed to betoken kindness. Then she started to speak with the most gentle and inviting tone of voice saying, "My little one, do not be anxious. The Lord has heard your pleading and has seen your humility. I am the mother of your Divine Savior. I have done battle with the dragon before you were even born. I have obtained from my Son, Jesus, a gift to help you in your battle with the dragon. I give you a shield. It will protect you from the fire of the dragon. It will be a shelter for you when the darkness seems to envelope you, and the only light you see is the fiery flame of the dragon seeking to devour you. The dragon's breath will not reach you as long as you hold this shield close to you, nor will you feel the heat of the flames. Trust in its worth and it will never fail you. This is a gift for you to grow strong in faith and a sign for you that the Lord will triumph over this dragon through you. My Son has already triumphed over this dragon in times past. He will triumph through you and end the reign of the dragon. Trust in this word."

Then the queenly figure reached into her mantle that somehow seemed to be hiding an object larger than the volume of her dress. It was a finely engraved shield appearing out of the mist passing in and out of the folds of the mantle. The shield had a figure of a pierced lamb emblazoned on it and the word, "Fidelus" engraved above the figure. George took hold of it wondering if this was all real. His mind turned toward the tales he had heard of knights receiving great favors from a queen, and thus he sheepishly tried to imitate how they acted in these tales. "Thank you my Queen and Mother. Do pray for me that I may be worthy of this gift."

"Always my good child, always I pray for you."

Then the heavenly vision receded back away from George's eyes, slipping back out of this reality leaving him alone. George, stunned at what he just saw, looked down at his hands to confirm that he really did receive the gift that he saw in the vision. It was truly there in his hands.

He stared down in amazement at the heavenly gift he had received and spontaneously exclaimed, "Oh sweet Virgin, my Queen and Mother. Thank you for this gift; it is magnificent, so beautiful. Thank you. Thank you. Thank you."

He studied its marks and emblem; it pictured a lamb posing as if it were slain with a crown showing its authority. He thought, "Aha, I see humility conquers all Lord. Help me always to have the faith that it is You who are leading me."

Now George took up the shield and prepared a new plan to engage the dragon, trusting his new gift would help him. He prayed, fasted, then waited for the word of the Lord. The thought filled his mind, "Now is the time to act. Now is the time to engage the dragon."

Then he saw again the waking vision of himself boldly attacking the dragon. No matter what he did, he could not put it out of his thoughts. He did not doubt this imaginative vision was from the Lord now, because it gave him great peace whenever he thought about. Everything in his being told him it was from the Holy Spirit, for he was filled with courage and fearlessness like never before. He had proof of his faith in his hands as he held the shield close to him. He knew the dragon could do him no harm behind this shield. He concluded, "It must be the Lord's inspiration."

Therefore, he started to plan in his mind a strategy to assault the dragon in its lair. He pictured himself creeping through the crevices. He knew this time he could be bolder in attacking the dragon then the last time, for he had the assurance that his shield would protect him. He pictured in his mind each step as he spoke to himself, "I will approach it stealthily close to where it sleeps then charge out in front of it and pierce its eye first. Yes, this is where I should strike it. For the dragon counts on its fiery breath to annihilate anything that comes near its head. I have an advantage now with this shield, of which the dragon is not aware."

Enflamed now with enthusiasm, George ventured forth into the cave of the dragon right in the middle of the day. He knew the dragon slept during the day, but it would not sleep today. He wound his way through the dark caverns and passageways leading to the heart of the mountain where the dragon resided. He thought, "The bowels of earth can no longer hide this beast."

As he went deeper into the cave, he noticed remains of victims the dragon had devoured. He could see crushed skulls and little limbs still visible, at first sight one might not believe they were even human remains, but he knew better. He turned away from this sight, enraged that men could allow such evil to take hold in their midst. He said a small prayer for the souls of these little ones so brutally killed. Finally, he knew he was almost upon the dragon for he recognized the air growing colder and thicker, and smelled the same terrible scent as before. "That terrible smell of evil," he thought, "I must be close."

Finally, he reached the very place where the dragon slumbered. He carefully drew near, knowing that even with a shield like his he could not presume that it would protect him in every way. He positioned himself to strike first the eye so to blind the dragon. He stealthily drew close, raised his sword above his head and drove mightily down at the eye of the dragon, but just as the sword's edge touched the eye, the beast woke up and the sword glanced off, only cutting a slash in the eyelid, while the rest of the eye remained unharmed.

The blow disoriented the dragon for a moment as it flailed at its scraped eye, causing it to draw back, but this lasted only for a few seconds, for then it recognized there was a battle at hand. In a flash, the dragon regained its composure extending its legs and mighty wings in an effort to push George far enough back so it could engulf him in flames. As the dragon drove George away, he thrust at it. With sufficient space now the dragon spewed out a mighty burst of fire at George. He, however, remained firm in his position hiding behind his shield that protected him, just as the heavenly Lady had told him it would. The flame lapped off the sides of his shield and the metal frame remained cool to the touch.

As the dragon caught its breath, George lunged again at the beast, but it was too fast for him. The dragon reared back again to spew forth another blast of its fiery breath at George. The flames again simply lapped harmlessly off the sides of George's shield. George drove again at the dragon. Yet again, the dragon was too quick, moving rapidly to the side as it threw another breath of fire at George. Five times the dragon and George struck at each other in similar matter. Each time George hid himself behind the shield, which remained cool to the touch, but George realized he could not take much more of this close combat, for the air in the cave had become suffocating due to the fiery breath of the beast. Thus, George fled the immediate vicinity of the beast, perspiring profusely as he tried to grasp his breath. The dragon too was exhausted, after throwing forth its flame repeatedly, and took a respite to catch its breath.

George, seeing the dragon tired, drove back into the suffocating chamber despite his short breath. George thrust at the dragon, but the beast was ready after all and turned about quickly, whipping George with its mighty tale throwing him against the wall. Dazed, but unharmed he turned back to the battle. However, the dragon started a new strategy. It snapped at George with its fierce teeth seeking to devour him with its terrible jaw; only the shield prevented the dragon from carrying out its design as the teeth of the beast slid off the shield's edge. George struggled to fight back striking the dragon repeatedly in the head, but he could not pierce through its scales. The dragon finally regained its breath and unleashed a long fiery stream right at George. The stream lasted for a good ten seconds pulling all the air from the room. George at last had to flee the chamber which was now completely without air. He could no longer breath anywhere close to the dragon; thus, he fled back through the passageway.

The dragon pursued him and continued its long streams of flames, seeing that George must flee further back when he drove all the air from the passageways. In this manner, the dragon drove George all the way back to the entrance. Finally, George exited out into the light of the day. As the dragon came close to the open sunlight it turned away feeling the light burning into its flesh. As the dragon retreated, it pulled rocks down in front of itself, blocking George from pursuing.

George knew the battle was over for the day. He left the scene of the battle exhausted and a bit confused. Although the dragon still lived, he knew he had rattled it. Yet, this did not seem enough. He wondered, "Why did not I defeat it? Surely, God was leading me this time?"

Remembering the lessons the Lord had taught him, he turned to the Lord saying, "I see now Lord, there is still much suffering for me to endure. In my pride, I still want to run before you Lord. Yet, I see I must wait on you Lord. What do you ask of me now?"

For a few days, there was a peace in the town and the people rejoiced after hearing how George engaged the beast. The King, seeing the enthusiasm of the people, organized a parade in honor of George as he came for the Sunday liturgy, marking the beginning of Passion Week. Many people came out of their homes and businesses to wave at George as he walked through the main thorough way. The people gave a real enthusiastic display for their mighty hero. George smiled accordingly, even as he thought, "It is a bit early to be congratulating me, but I guess it shows the tide is turning against the wizards. Maybe this heralds a conversion of hearts."

George, however, did not let the accolades take hold of him. He entered into Passion Week with much prayer and fasting, for he recognized that the battle was right at hand and prepared himself for further combat. Meanwhile, the dragon barricaded itself in its cave, seeming to sense that there was a force upon it, which it should fear. It blocked off all the entrances to the cave, except one high up the mountain, protruding from a vertical face that it was sure no man could climb. Now the dragon had an impregnable fortress, or so it seemed in the mind of the beast.

The public parade showed that the King was becoming a follower of George. The King's heart was starting to turn away from evil, as he beheld the virtuous example of his daughter, Procuvera. Still yet, the King's heart was waffling. The wizards were unsettled and troubled at this new turn of events. The wizards recognized that the King had lost trust in them. Therefore, they started conspiring to wrestle control of the kingdom from him. Janus arranged a meeting with Mortepulchra. There he explained the situation to her, "My dear we are in great need of your help. If we let George go on like this, everyone will believe in him.[39] We need you to contact the dragon and direct it to pour its rage upon the populace, not sparing anyone. We want them to see the wrath of the dragon. Let it loose; teach the populace that George is not in control of the dragon, and give a message to the King that he still needs our assistance."

Late Monday night, Mortepulchra went to the foot of the mountain where the dragon resided. She called out a mystical prayer, "Soul of me, companion to me, come now to your true mother."

The dragon, upon hearing the soothing words of the prayer peeked out of its enclosed shelter and came to meet Mortepulchra. She greeted the dragon with a smile and caressed its backside softly as it bent over to feel her touch. She pulled a dead lamb from a sack that she was carrying; she knew it was one of the dragon's favorite snacks. The dragon devoured the sacrifice happily. She then whispered to the dragon, "There, there, I know your suffering. I know the vile knight has intruded on your space. Now is the time to take vengeance. Now is the time to show your domination over the kingdom. Spare no one; tear apart the confidence of those who hunt you. Fill your belly with sacrifices of your own desire. You are free now. Be who nature called you to be. Be free."

Later that night, after hearing the consoling words of Mortepulchra, the dragon reemerged from its fortified stronghold. It roamed out and struck randomly at the innocent as it pleased. It attacked a few young men making their way back from a night out, and then a little later it attacked a few children left out to wander not far from their house. After that, it dove down upon the business district and set it ablaze. Then it headed for the docks and set all the docks in the bay on fire, pausing to pick off a sailor, snoozing after a late night drink. Even the wizards who had unleashed the dragon were astonished at its ferocity that night.

The battalion tried to counter the dragon when they heard word of its attacks, but they were just not quick enough. It seemed now the dragon was not so much interested in entirely devouring its victims or burning the houses to ashes, but sought quick attacks, just long enough to provide lethal blows, or to start fires on as many housetops as it could. There seemed little pattern in the attack, making it too hard for the battalion to predict where the next one might be.

George seeing the fury of the dragon entered into prayer, seeking light for how to engage the beast. He besought the Lord with prayer and fasting seeking an answer. His prayers, however, were cold and dry. As his soul was confused the tremendous onslaught of the dragon continued, which he could not counter. The same pattern of attacks continued the next night, and George prayed and fasted more intensely trying to understand why he could not overcome the dragon. He knew prayer was the only thing now that could counter the dragon, so he turned to it with his whole heart.

Meanwhile, the wizards could see the agitation on the face of the King. They made sure the King's agents stood aloof as the dragon reigned down its fury upon the kingdom. This latest rampage of the dragon, coming right after the King had thrown a parade in honor of George, made the King look comical to some in the kingdom. The King, embarrassed, turned to his aides, "I see perhaps, I made a mistake in giving support to this figure George. Oh, why did I have to honor him publicly? How stupid was that? I am not sure what I should do now. I must think over this for a bit. Yes, I must think."

The King's chamberlain had been for a while now under the influence of the wizards. He thought they "cut a fine form" in his estimate, so he jumped on the opportunity to make a suggestion. "Oh, Your Highness, you are quite worn out. You need your rest. Why don't you go off to your country estate for a few days and forget all about the concerns of the kingdom?"

The King looked back at him with a weary look, "Why yes, yes, that is what I should do. Just get out of here. I need a time of retreat, a time to reflect on things and put things right before I make any more poor decisions. I will go to that estate out on the eastern edge and enjoy the sunrise for a few days, as I stroll far away from the worries here. Yes, that is it."

While the King made his way to his country retreat, the wizards seized the opportunity. As soon as they heard from the chamberlain that the King was departing, they sent out word to their various cohorts, "Now is the time to act. Now is the time to disperse St. Michael's battalion, shut down all these guilds they started, and hunt down their leader, George, that we may get rid of this bothersome character."

# Chapter 16

# *The Week of passion and betrayal*

O n Tuesday night, the dragon continued to terrorize while the wizards made plans to overthrow the kingdom. The wizards even found help from a member of St. Michael's battalion, Van. He was one of the first to sign up for the battalion, for he admired George's charismatic personality. He was a member of the light brigade that ran to sites fending off the dragon with a blessed crossbow. He had accompanied George many times as they confronted the dragon. In time, his fervor for George faded as he came to see their activities as fruitless. He had tried to hint to George that he did not want be a part of the battalion at one point. Yet, he had gained renewed hope when they created the prayer guilds, and he beheld the enthusiasm of the people for George after his second venture into the cave.

Now, he thought the beast, in his estimation, was not contained at all. Thus, he thought, "I see now George can't help our kingdom. I will then go to the only force in the kingdom that can contain the dragon, the wizards. Yes, I will throw my lot in with them."

He put out a feeler to an old friend, Tumidus. "Hello, Tumidus. I understand that you have been keeping up with the changing scene in the palace?"

"Why yes, my old friend, I have managed to keep up with those who count in the kingdom. I heard that you got involved with that battalion opposing the wizards. Not a wise choice, you know."

"I see that now. This is part of why I want to talk to you."

"You know, I have not seen you for a while."

"Well, I got involved in the Church and got out of my old ways of running around with you guys. I guess I did not pay enough attention to you. I have not seen the other guys we used to drink with for a while either. I guess I did dismiss you guys without reason. I should have kept in contact with you."

"Hmm. So, what is it you want?"

"Well, as I guess you heard, I took up with that foreign knight, George. I thought he might be able to drive this beast far from me and the whole kingdom. Yet, I see now, I was mistaken. The beast is still here. I want to throw my lot in with those who can control it."

"I see Van. I have heard about this George. You are right to doubt him. Everybody important in the kingdom thinks poorly of him. All the King's agents deride him, and the King's new grey-hooded advisors are constantly complaining that he is interfering with their work."

"Ah yes, it is the grey-hooded men that I want to speak to you about. I want to meet them to get control over this beast again—I just have to meet them—these attacks of the beast are driving me crazy!"

"Okay, don't worry. I will arrange it. Wednesday night you can meet them."

The next evening the King's agents sent a message to Van telling him to meet them at the great hall. He made his way to the appointed location; where a slave greeted him in a cordial way and ushered him into the great hall. As he looked around, he noticed twenty grey-cloaked figures peering at him. They looked like mysterious mystical figures, with their arms folded under their cloaks, grey hoods over their heads and their faces just visible. This disturbed Van a little, but when the King's personal courtier greeted him, dressed in courtly attire, he calmed down. He thought, "Ah, they consider me important to have such a greeting."

Minicus, one of the King's agents, greeted him with a smile, "Ah, Van, I am glad to meet you. I am so very pleased you could come this night."

"Oh, I did not expect such a greeting in such a grand hall and with so many prominent people here to meet me."

"Oh, don't be shy; we are all very pleased that you came. When we heard that you had worked with that foreign knight, we hastily assembled this meeting."

"Oh, you mean George. Well, I thought he was a great knight, but I see now he is a false savior. How can I help you?"

"Well, we just want to do what is best for the kingdom. We recognize that George may have had the best of intentions, but his good intentions have been interfering with the work of these fine men behind me."

Van took a glance back at the wizards and shimmered a bit. Then hiding his trepidation he replied, "Oh yes, I see. Yes, I have come to see them too. Though, I do not follow their beliefs, I have come to see they are the only ones who have real control over the dragon. I just want this beast far away from me. How can I help you to do this?"

"Well, we want to bring George in for questioning, and then convince him to leave the kingdom. Therefore, we need to know where we can find him, what places he likes to frequent and when we can catch him alone. It would be best for the long term good of Terrasindei that he leave the kingdom."

"I see. Oh, this is just fine. I will tell you where he normally goes for meetings, training the battalion and where you can find him during his free time. I too want what is best for the kingdom."

Together then they made a plan to bring George in for questioning. The King's agents, however, had no real intention to question George. They just wanted him out of the way, exiled or dead, it did not matter. So they could then lay waste to his battalion. Thus, they pressed Van for details, not just about George's habits, but where each member of the battalion lived, where they all met, when they met, using the pretext of making sure they could capture George. After acquiring this information, they started a reign of terror on anyone associated with the battalion. The next day, they rushed into the cottages of those known to associate with George and without any pretense arrested them. They went to the far ends of the kingdom seeking out all those associated with the battalion that day. Their campaign continued throughout the night and even through the next day. Meanwhile, the dragon continued its rampage.

That day, George was spending a leisurely afternoon at one of the manors owned by Kathleen's family. She was hosting him this day as they relaxed in the countryside. He was contemplating the gospel accounts of Jesus' actions in the days leading up to his Passion, when a member of the battalion came running up to him, "George, George, you must flee! They are after you and the whole battalion."

"Who is after me?"

"The king's agents are here. The wizards have taken control and are persecuting the whole battalion. I hear they want to kill you. They are storming into our houses and tearing up the whole kingdom looking for you."

"But, why? For what?"

"No time to explain. I am not sure if they were tracking me here also. You must flee."

Just then, Kathleen rushed up, accompanied by her father. Kathleen announced, "He is right. There is no time. A whole division of soldiers were just spotted racing toward the manor."

Kathleen's father interjected, "Take one of the horses in the stall, the black one. He is the fastest. Go son, go. I have heard they are in a great frenzy. I am not sure they will even respect my nobility."

George then ran off to the stall but looked back at Kathleen asking, "What will happen to you?"

Kathleen yelled back at him, "It is you they want. We will delay them. Now go."

George rushed into the stall and saw that their servant had already prepared the horse. He jumped onto the already saddled horse and raced off while the King's soldiers were just making it to the manor. He thought, "Where shall I go?"

Then he remembered a broken down shack that Sergius had. He knew this was on the outskirts of the kingdom, not Sergius' main residence, but just a workshop for his agriculture tools where he sometimes spent the night during the planting season. He thought, "Sergius will certainly be around there now. We are right in the middle of the planting season."

He thus raced toward it, hoping that he could hide out there for a bit. After a long fast ride, he reached the broken down hut. He knocked timidly on the door. It swung open but Sergius was not there. He recognized it was not yet evening and Sergius must be still sowing the seeds. He thought, "Oh, he is a hard worker."

He chugged down several gulps of water from a canister then settled down in the hut and waited until evening. He was hungry and exhausted, but could find nothing to eat in the hut, and he knew he must keep an eye out, for they were still after him. As evening drew near, he strolled outside to take a stretch and scout the land. He noticed a little country church next to a small sloping hill. He started to complain to the Lord in his heart, "Lord, what have I done wrong? Why have you dispersed the battalion? I tried to humble myself; I built prayer guilds to bring conversion to the land, and I took hold of the shield of faith that you gave me. What more can I do?"

George continued to wander trying to work it all out in his mind. He recalled his many failures leading the battalion, the persecution by the King's agents, and now his hunger and exhaustion while he fled for his life. All of it together seemed to eat at him now. After scouting the area for a little while, he determined it was safe and sat down in front of church on the hillside looking toward the west. Still though the sum of the situation was eating at him, in frustration he impulsively grabbed his sword from his sheath and drove it into the ground in front of him, saying to God, "Here is your sword Lord. You gave me this weapon. To you I return it. Now you tell me, what am I to do with this weapon made by the hand of an angel? I plead with you, tell me Lord!"

He then knelt down and prayed for a few minutes as the sword laid thrust into the ground behind him, but no response seemed to come. He yelled out to the Lord, "Nothing, Lord, nothing. Is this the response you give me?"

He then started to walk away, leaving the sword thrust into the ground behind him in frustration. After a few steps, he noticed a shadow peaking over his shoulder. He could see the outline of the hilt and the blade which together formed a figure of a cross in the shadow. He turned off to the side and now could see the cross-shaped shadow with clarity. Then he heard a small whisper echoing in his head, "Take up your cross. Take up your cross."

He knew the Lord was speaking to him in this whisper and telling him that he must take up the sword again. George then slowly walked back to the sword thrust into the ground and knelt before it. He heard the whispering voice again saying, "This is the cross that you must bear."

He looked at the sword as if studying its dimension, knowing it was the measure of the cross he must take up. He measured its length, the sharpness of its blade, and the manner of its insignia. Then slowly he pulled it out of the ground, as he whispered to God, "Yes, Lord, I will take up this cross."

Then he meticulously and now with reverence slid the sword back into its sheath and slowly walked away.

As the night started to become darker, George remembered that it was the Thursday of the Holy Mysteries. He turned his gaze toward the small local church and made his way there. Soon a small group of the faithful joined him. He was not afraid while in the church, for he knew by experience that those who attended such liturgies were likely opposed to the dragon. That night the liturgy seemed to come alive to him moving his soul in a profound way as the mysteries were unveiled. He felt the very presence of God come into him, and his soul was nourished by a tremendous grace. He pondered the meaning of these Mysteries. "Lord, how could you show so much love in sacrificing yourself for us? How is it that you loved us so much as to give us your very body and blood? How can I, who am weak, take up my cross and follow you? Lord give me grace to continue the battle through the nourishment that you give me tonight."

Then the thought of the persecution flooded back into his mind and the seemingly never-ending battle with the dragon. His heart was flooded with a bit of anxiety and his pulse raced a bit while he thought about his frustrations. He turned to the Lord again asking, "Lord, will there be a time when I sip again of the fruit of the vine rejoicing in your presence?"

*That same night the King's heart was stirred while he enjoyed his country retreat.* He happened to look at the calendar and realized it was Holy Thursday. Memories of his youthful piety flooded into his mind. He thought, "Ah, how happy those times were, when I entered into the devotions of this night. Oh how I took it all in as a youth. Seeing the washing of the feet and pondering the gifts our Lord Jesus gave us. Oh, how happy I was. And why am I not there tonight?"

He felt a cool breeze blow across his neck refreshing him. He looked around but did not see any open window. All at once, he seemed to be struck with the notion that it was the Lord who had sent this breeze, and He was calling him now to renew his devotion. He looked about and saw the breeze blow through the whole countryside, somehow penetrating the walls of his country estate. He had a sense then that there was a hand upon his kingdom, a spirit moving in the midst of its boundaries. He rejoiced in that cool breeze and his soul seemed to rest peacefully, as if he were falling into a light trance. "Ah, yes Lord, I had forgotten the delight of your presence. I see Lord you are here tonight. Yet, how can I be so bold as to speak to you in this way? I am such a sinner. What must I do Lord? What must I do? I know, I must rush to the cathedral to experience again that which I knew as a child, the grace of this night."

He jumped up and exclaimed to his manservant. "Make ready my carriage. I wish to return to the capital right now."

The servant startled replied, "Your Highness, you want to return at this hour? We will be travelling in the darkness, Your Highness."

"Yes, yes, now. I want you to take me directly to the Cathedral, yes, the Cathedral. This is where I must be tonight."

"Okay, whatever you say, Your Highness."

As the faithful started to leave after the priest symbolically buried the great Mystery for the long vigil, George stepped outside. Just as he stepped out, Sergius came rushing up to him on a horse. Not far behind him, he recognized Van also making his way there on horseback. Something did not seem right. George had left his horse near the little hut, and now Sergius was racing to him saddled on that horse. As if suddenly awoken from a stupor, George recognized the peril of the situation. Van was leading a troop of the King's soldiers his way, and Sergius was only just ahead of them on horseback. Sergius quickly dismounted and yelled out to George, "Now quickly take the horse and flee."

George's eyes were wide open, and his heart pulsating with the alertness of a trained soldier, as his mind raced to take in the whole seen within the span of a few seconds. He hesitated a little though, as he saw Sergius had no way to escape. Sergius recognizing this told him, "I will not leave until I see you get on this horse and flee."

There was no choice then. George reluctantly mounted the horse quickly with his sword and shield by his side racing off just in front of the king's soldiers. He could just make out with his peripheral vision Sergius surrendering to the King's soldiers. George had no time to be sullen. He raced off into the darkness trying to hold back his emotions, as he knew the kings soldiers were in pursuit. He galloped toward the east away from the capital city. As he raced off into the night, he remembered the psalm the Lord quoted in seeming despair while hanging on the cross. He had it fixed in his memory, reciting it every Friday. He needed something to keep his mind calm. He recited it now with new meaning:

"My God, my God, why hast thou forsaken me? Why art thou so far from helping me, from the words of my groaning? O my God, I cry by day, but thou dost not answer; and by night, but find no rest…"

He interjected, "Yes, Lord, how is that you forsake me this night. My enemies pursue me, a traitor has turned against me Lord."

He turned back to the words of Psalm as the kings soldiers continued in pursuit,

"Be not far from me, for trouble is near and there is none to help. Many bulls encompass me, strong bulls of Bashan surround me; they open wide their mouths at me, like a ravening and roaring lion. I am poured out like water, and all my bones are out of joint; my heart is like wax, it is melted within my breast; my strength is dried up like a potsherd, and my tongue cleaves to my jaws; thou dost lay me in the dust of death. Yea, dogs are round about me; a company of evildoers encircle me..."

As he saw a few of the King's men starting to close upon him, he called out to the Lord, "Help me to find safety from those that would entrap me!"

He turned back to the Psalm recognizing its words were exactly the prayer he needed now:

"But thou, O Lord, be not far off! O thou my help, hasten to my aid! Deliver my soul from the sword, my life from the power of the dog! Save me from the mouth of the lion, my afflicted soul from the horns of the wild oxen!"

In a mad dash, he drove his horse over a small ridge charging down a hill. He looked back to see how his pursuers handled the ridge. With great relief, he saw them pull up. His horse was a mountain breed, used to the rough hills, but the soldiers horses were of a cultivated stock, not used to rough terrain. As he galloped away, he breathed more easily, and now he recalled the last part of the psalm:

"I will tell of thy name to my brethren; in the midst of the congregation, I will praise thee: You who fear the Lord, praise him! All you sons of Jacob, glorify him, and stand in awe of him, all you sons of Israel! For he has not despised or abhorred the affliction of the afflicted; and he has not hid his face from him, but has heard, when he cried to him..."

After several minutes, he pulled up to see if they found any way around the ridge. It seemed he had lost them. As he caught his breath, he recited the last verse,

...men shall tell of the Lord to the coming generation, and proclaim his deliverance to a people yet unborn, that he has wrought it."[40]

George continued in an easterly direction trying to get as far as he could away from Valde Venalicium, which lies at the center of the kingdom. The darkness of the night then started to grow thick upon him, as he went further into the wilderness. The horse stayed at a mild trot making its own way without George's prodding. The exhaustion of the pursuit now started to catch up with George; he knew he must continue, but the day's events had taken a lot out of him. He looked down out at his feet to see how his reflexes were holding up. To his surprise, he could barely make out the features of his feet, for it had grown very dark. He thought back to earlier in the night and vaguely remembered that he could clearly see the stars and the moon as he left the church, but now things seem to have grown much more obscure.

He stopped for short break to revive himself and get his bearings. He looked out at the night and said to himself, "Hmm, no more moonlight and I cannot see the stars. Yet, I do not see any clouds in the sky. What is that dims my vision? Lord, you know that I cannot mark my way in this darkness. Where are you leading me?"

He carried on further going by instinct in what he thought was the same direction, for he felt he must make more distance between himself and his pursuers despite his near total exhaustion. The darkness though seemed to be enclosing even more upon him now. Now he could barely even see his hand at the end of his arm. He started to feel some shivers, but the temperature still seemed mild. He thought, "This darkness is not natural. I must be hallucinating. It seems to be affecting my thinking."

He dismounted near a small creek that he only noticed because of the splashing of the horse's feet. He knelt down to drink and splashed himself with water in attempt to clear his senses. As he bent down, he felt something brush against him, as if a dark blanket was dragged over his left shoulder. He turned about quickly and called out,

"What was that?"

Then he felt the same sensation on his other side. He turned quickly to the side where he felt the presence while he held his shield at the ready in front of him. Then he felt it again, this time as if a sheet had slipped over his head, dimming his vision for a moment. He lifted up his sword trying to fight off whatever had just passed over him. He felt now there was some dark presence near him. Suddenly, it seemed as if the dark presence was passing all about him. His eyes darted back and forth and his limbs became rigid stuck in a defensive posture. He thought, "What is this darkness that creeps upon me? I can't drive it away. What is coming upon me and where I am heading?"

His mind then raced back to some childhood fears, which he thought he had long since forgotten. He remembered a nightmare he had while just a young boy. In his boyhood dream, he saw himself in a dark vast valley completely alone. He could see no living thing and only dim lights peaking over the mountaintops. As he looked out at the landscape and saw a dark volcanic ash covered the ground, making it so nothing could grow. He recalled how in the dream he was looking for his parents. Then he started to feel increasingly fearful because the terrain become more and more unfriendly and he had no idea where he was. Finally, he broke down in tears, as a feeling of despair and loneliness enveloped him. He remembered how when he woke up the nightmare ended.

He shook his head back and forth rapidly, as he suddenly realized he was lost in the childhood memory. He thought, "Why did I recall this dream now? Am I still that scared little boy? What is this loneliness that closes in upon me now?"

He looked around now at his limbs, but could see nothing at all, not even his shoulder. He called out to the Lord, "Lord show me yourself in this darkness, so that I can find myself again."

Reality then seemed to slip away from him as he fell into a deep sleep, but somehow his eyes remained wide open. It seemed to him he was returning to his early infancy in his mother's womb, being reformed in the obscurity of his dreams. Through the cloudy mist of his thoughts emerged a clear image, a lively dream. He saw a light approaching him as if through a tunnel. It drew closer then formed into a globe right next to him. Then Jesus appeared out the globe in glory, with light emitting from his wounded arms, legs and head. He appeared majestic and solemn, but it allayed George's fears as he greeted him kindly, "My child, I have heard your prayer presented to me by my dear Mother. Be not afraid! I am with you. I come tonight to be with you in your anxiety. I am sharing it with you this night. Do not despair. I know this dragon afflicts you and the people of this land, and it seems all help has abandoned you. Know that I have already overcome this dragon, and I will triumph over it in this land through your hand."

George then was completely at peace, as his arms now rested by his side and his eyes fixed on the glorious vision that appeared before him. George let his sword and shield fall to the ground as he dropped to his knees. Jesus continued to speak to him. "Our Father in heaven has anointed you, marked you on the forehead with his sign, and chosen you to overcome this dragon. Trust in this anointing and be my true soldier. Now listen closely to what I tell you. I give you words that will help you to overcome the dragon. Repeat them and sear them into your memory:

**When the darkness seems to encompass you and even hope seems to be lost,**

**so that even your faith is taken away from you; then is the time to leap into the darkness and strike at the neck of the dragon.**

Jesus then reached out toward George and touched him at which point he suddenly woke up.

The tremendous feeling of peace remained with George as he rubbed his eyes trying to adjust now to the bright sky. He noticed it was morning and he was in the middle of a field, but the surroundings were still somewhat obscure. Day was upon the small kingdom, yet the sun seemed strangely dimmed. The sense of peace then rushed from his soul as reality came upon him again. He tried to reconnect his thoughts to his situation saying to himself, "Ah yes, it is Friday. I was fleeing the King's agents and then…"

The vision then flooded back into his mind, "Ah yes, the dream or was it a dream? It was so vivid. So real and I see now suddenly it is day, even if it is still a bit obscure, when just a moment ago it was the darkest of nights."

He looked about; the sun was out and no cloud was in the sky, yet, the sky was a dark blue, not the bright hue of a normal sunny day. George studied the dim colored sky wondering what darkened it. He thought again about the vision, "Was this real? Yes, it must have been real. For the image is seared into my mind. Yet, it was a dream for I am awake, but I remember vividly the words Jesus gave me, as if they were burned into my eyelids."

He pondered this as he gathered himself to journey further to he knew not where. He simply knew the Lord seemed to be driving him into a rugged and rocky terrain. As he pondered the verses seared into his mind, he felt these words calling out to him, "Keep going, keep going, the Lord's destiny awaits you to the east, pursue it."

Without any more thought then he continued eastward. He reached the outskirts of the kingdom where he came upon a forgotten old house-church. This was a modest structure, but beautiful as a symbol of faith in a wide-open country, far away from places of importance. It reminded him of the church of his youth where he first learned to sign himself with the cross. The church he knew as a small boy was on the outer edge of the Roman Empire in an area not regarded by many. He thought, "How far I have come, Lord. I guess it is the forgotten little ones you choose for the great tasks, so as to confound the world."

He peeked inside the small church; there was no one there, but two candles burned brightly on either side of a large crucifix set in the middle of the church. George walked reverently into the church and knelt down to venerate the cross. A sense of peace took hold of him. Somehow, despite the King's men who hounded him, he felt safe here. He remained at the small church throughout the afternoon contemplating the cross…

*At the same time, others prayed across the kingdom.*

That day, Procuvera went to her father with a special cross she wanted to show him. Her father was just waking up. He had arrived back in the capital city just in time to enjoy part of the vigil at St. Michael the Archangel Cathedral, but he had not yet gone to the court to hear about the latest news. The Princess knocked lightly on the door, which was already slightly open. The king turned about and smiled when he saw his daughter. "Yes, what can I do for you, my love?"

"Oh father, I remembered this beautiful cross that the Lord gave me when I was a child. It is a fine remembrance of mother's love and has always called me to think of what our Lord did for us. I want to lend it to the bishop for display today, but I thought we could first venerate it privately."

"Oh my daughter it is quite large. How did you carry it here?"

"It was no bother father, my devotion made it feel light."

She then placed it on her father's desk. She bent over to kiss it, grasping it with both hands as she closed her eyes in act of sincere devotion. The King looked shyly upon it. Procuvera urged him on though, "Go ahead father. The Lord Jesus knows your sinfulness. Do not be afraid."

At this urging, the King bent over taking the cross with only one hand, while the other hand waved awkwardly to the side, as if he did not want fully to take hold of the cross. He kissed the cross with his eyes open and turned about quickly. Procuvera patted him on the back as she commented, "Very good father, very good."

The King stared at the cross for a few seconds, as if he was remembering an old fond thought. Then he announced to his daughter, "Oh my dear, by all means you should lend it to the bishop this day. We should not keep this treasure to ourselves."

That day St. Michael's battalion, scattered as it was with some members imprisoned, nevertheless, was unified in prayer. Kathleen opened up her house to members of the St. Michael's guild to pray for George and the conversion of the kingdom. They lit many candles in her home chapel on his behalf. Bacchus and Sergius prayed together in prison, not heeding their surroundings. They knelt on the stone tile of the prison cell offering psalms in chorus in the full sight of the other prisoners.

Archbishop Romanus, a wise man, with a prayerful soul, sensed there was a new spirit hovering over his kingdom. That day he gave himself over to prayer. He prostrated in the sanctuary before the crucifix imploring the Lord for his kingdom. He prayed earnestly that the Spirit would breathe down upon the people of Terrasindei and create them anew, alive in Christ their Lord. He prayed for those far away from the faith that they would return; he prayed for unbelievers; he prayed for those who denied the faith; he prayed for all the needs of faithful, and for all who are in need. He poured his heart out in a litany of supplication, seeking that the graces won by the Cross would bring salvation to his kingdom this day.

# Chapter 17

# *The Battle for the soul of Terrasindei*

That day, as it came upon the ninth hour, there was a strange silence in the kingdom. People across the kingdom felt a sudden angst in the souls, conversations came to a stop, a cold shiver seemed to run across everybody, even the dogs stopped howling and perked up their ears as if waiting for something momentous to happen. A small boy near the western border of the kingdom cried out, "Look there! What is that black cloud which is coming our way?"

The boy's father, a shop owner, looked out from his window and froze as he watched the approaching cloud. A maid, making her way hastily on an errand, noticed the boy and his father peering off behind her. She wondered what drew their attention so intently, then she noticed a dark shadow starting to cover everything in front of her. She turned around then dropped her basket exclaiming, "Oh my, what is that?"

As the darkness made its way further east, everyone in the kingdom stopped what they were doing and stared in awe. They watched as what seemed like inverted black tide of darkness rolled through the skies encompassing all light in its path. Soon the darkness obscured everything even descending down to the ground, making a fog thicker than anyone had ever seen. Souls looked around and could see nothing, not even their arms and legs. The blackness engulfed the whole kingdom, as if a giant hand erased the whole sky.

All stood in wonder and fear at the strange phenomenon. Even the wizards who hailed themselves as masters of nature and their cohorts the witches, peeked outside in amazement. Janus suddenly felt a great shiver coming upon him even as he stood close to a fire. He noticed even the light coming from his window dimmed and his fire started mysteriously withering. He went outside to see it more closely as he said, "What is this? What is the power that can produce this?"

Mortepulchra, who had been in conference with Janus, also peeked outside. She had been feeling uncomfortable all day for she knew it was the day of the enemies' triumph. Her eyes became transfixed as she too now stared at the approaching cloud. Both stood together in silence watching it for over a minute. A young wizard rushed up to them and was astonished to see that the great masters of his art even seemed surprised at the sight of this wonder. He thought, "What power can do this? Even they do not know not what this is."

Finally, Mortepulchra broke the silence, "Ah, this is a terrible omen. I have always hated this day when the enemy gave his life. This darkness signals our end, I tell you. We have no power over this blackness; soon it will envelop us; soon it will suffocate us."

She then cowered back into the house looking like an animal struck by its master. Janus' face turned a slight blue, cold with fear, as he watched Mortepulchra leave. He then became very distressed as horrid fears started to flood his mind. "It is our end she said. She is right. We must flee. I must hide. I must run from the darkness. I must get out of here." Yet, his body stayed motionless in a seizure of fear and depression. He remained frozen in his distress, like a statue just carved of man who once was.

In St. Michael the Archangel Cathedral, the bishop rose breaking off his supplication, as he too noticed the strange darkness blotting out the sunlight coming through the windows. He stood for a few minutes at the door of the cathedral watching with wonder this phenomenon coming upon the land. Soon he was joined by the other priests of the cathedral, and they stare together silently watching this black fog enveloping the kingdom. When all light had been eclipsed, the bishop turned to his priests, "Now is the time to pray and seek repentance for the kingdom. My prayer has been answered."

After the initial shock, people started to become acclimated to the darkness, and they peeked out to see if there were any signs of light; mysteriously, a few dim lights pierced the darkness. The people squinted with their eyes to make out from where the light came and recognized it was coming from the churches. The churches seemed to emit a light, somehow visible from a distance even through the darkness. All across the kingdom, the blessed candles from the Church shined brightly in the midst of the night.

George, meanwhile, was unaware of the darkness rolling in from the west. He was content simply to sit gazing upon the cross. No one bothered him, only a breeze blew gentle through on occasion; it was a secure and peaceful sanctuary. He seemed to be lost in an oasis of peace while the kingdom around him was in turmoil; however, this peace was soon to be disturbed. Just after the ninth hour, George noticed a shadow start to creep over his shoulder. He looked to the west, from where the darkness was emerging, and stared in wonder at the sight of the dark cloud that seems to be rolling in at a rapid speed.

Soon the darkness encompassed everything around George. His horse, seeing the dark cloud rolling in, became skittish and galloped off out of sight. He was now completely alone. He looked around, but could see almost nothing as if the landscape was erased right before his eyes. He could only make out the figure of the small church, not a few feet from him. Noticing that the church remained visible, he stared in wonder at how it could shine brightly even though lit by only two candles that adorned the cross. Mysteriously, the candles seemed brighter now, highlighting more strongly the outline of the cross in contrast to the darkness surrounding it. George peered intently at this sight wondering what it could mean. He took it as a sign of consolation that the cross was shining so brightly in the darkness and whispered to the Lord, "Yes, Lord, I see the light in the darkness."

From the midst of the dark fog, George seemed to hear a voice whispering to him, "You must journey out into the darkness."

His recent experiences had made him attuned to this whispering, but still he doubted his senses. Then he heard it again, "Go into the darkness."

He knew this voice now. He looked back at the cross and the two lights that flickered by its side. Summoning up his courage, he picked up an old torch close to the door and lit it from one of the candles. He looked again at the cross for a moment saying a quick prayer, "Lord, give me courage in this battle."

He then slipped out into the darkness with only the torch to light his way. As he walked away, he noticed that the darkness seemed to become thicker the further he travelled from the Church. He recalled the darkness from the previous night, but this darkness seemed much denser than what he felt the night before. He even thought he could taste the darkness in his mouth now, nevertheless, he journeyed farther into its midst. He told himself as he ventured out, "I must pray and wait on the Lord in the face of this darkness. There is nothing more that I can do. I must trust in the Lord and he will see me through."

As people noticed that the candles in the churches still shined brightly in the midst of the darkness, they carefully made their way to the doorsteps of the sanctuaries. The priests generously passed on to souls the flame that pierced the darkness, thus many lit torches and candles from the blessed candles shone in the churches. The bishop, seeing people flock to the churches to kindle their flames, sent out emissaries to all the homes and businesses to bring the sacred flames to them. So it was that the dim light of the blessed candles were seen bobbing up and down slightly as their emissaries carried the holy fire to the ends of the kingdom.

Far off at the western edge of the kingdom the day before the darkness rolled in, the dragon was having a restless sleep. During that day, the dragon could not sleep well for its slumber kept being disturbed as it tossed this way and that. When the darkness started to creep over the kingdom, it woke up with a jolt, as if a terrifying coldness had just rolled over it. The dragon, which seemed not to fear anything, suddenly began to cower. Its instinct took over; the dragon crept out of its abode feeling that some force was suffocating the air in the cave. The darkness encroached into its abode, causing the dragon to creep along as now even its keen sight was useless through the thick fog.

Finally, the dragon cleared the cave and drove out into the open air with a mighty thrust of its wings. Fearing the strange darkness that encompassed it, the dragon speed deep into the sky as fast as it could, seeking to escape the dark abyss. However, even at the limits of its range the dragon could find no relief from the suffocating darkness. Quickly then it sped east in the direction following the rolling black mass in hopes of finding the edge of the darkness.

As the long night set in, Archbishop Romanus prepared a special vigil recognizing that many souls felt drawn to remain in the church, after having their lights kindled by the blessed candles. Many who had not seen the inside of the church for years found their way there that night. Souls felt at peace in the church for the darkness seemed to choke the very light from the sky, even dimming torches that people carried. The people prayed earnestly to God to save them from the dread which came from they knew not where. Archbishop Romanus remained in vigil before the cross, keeping the hours in its presence, even as the darkness seemed to hover over the kingdom. The Archbishop reached up to heaven to call down the prayers of the saints and angels as he began a litany,

"Lord, have mercy."

The people responded, "Lord, have mercy."

"Christ, have mercy."

They responded again, "Christ, have mercy."

Back and forth it went, in keeping with the sacred tradition. The bishop would call out and the people would respond. One could hear the chorus echoing in the Cathedral:

"Lord, have mercy."          "Lord, have mercy."

"Christ, hear us."          "Christ, graciously hear us."

"God the Father of Heaven,"    "Have mercy on us."

"God the Son, Redeemer of the world,"

                           "Have mercy on us."

"God the Holy Ghost,"       "Have mercy on us."

"Holy Trinity, One God,"     "Have mercy on us."

"Holy Mary, Queen of Angels," "Pray for us."

"Holy Mother of God,"        "Pray for us."

"Holy Virgin of virgins,"      "Pray for us."

"Saint Michael, who wast ever the defender of the people of God,"

                           "Pray for us"…

Deep in the night, the dragon reached the center of the kingdom and noticed the light from the blessed candles in St. Michael's Cathedral piercing straight through the darkness, right up into the heavens. Seeing this, the dragon halted its flight and started to circle just in front of these strange lights. Even in complete darkness this light seemed abrasive to the dragon's eyes even more so than the noonday sun. The dragon flew back and forth trying to shade its eyes as it looked for a way around it, but it seemed the light went out from the church in all directions.

Finally, the dragon frustrated decided to dive down upon the source of the light and destroy it as its root. The dragon thus dove down in full attack mode, seeking to throw a tremendous fiery breath at the structure that emitted the light, so to rid itself of this annoyance. Just as it started to approach within striking distance of the Cathedral, the dragon was suddenly thrust backward, as if a lance had struck it smartly in the chest. The dragon stunned fell for a few hundred feet, before it regained control and started to fly free again.

The dragon peered around with its eyes wide open looking for that which lanced at it. Suddenly from its backside, it felt another lancing strike. The dragon drew back from the thrust, trying to flee the unseen foe. Then again, it felt a lance thrusting at its back causing the beast to coil in pain. Then a few more quick lances came upon the dragon driving the beast, in its horror, right through the light emanating from the Cathedral burning its flesh as it passed through. The thrusts continued and drove the dragon further away from the cathedral. The dragon tried to turn about quickly in the air and snap at the foe anticipating its next blow. It was no use though; the unseen foe timed the blows perfectly and drove the beast with each lancing shot in an eastward direction. Repeatedly, this unseen foe drove at the dragon and the best efforts of the beast had no power to stop the harassment. Every few miles the dragon fell to the ground to catch its breath, but its foe would not give up and kept driving the dragon into the darkness by his unrelenting attacks. Deep into the night then the dragon was driven further and further to the east.

George meanwhile had his own struggles as he tried to make his way in the darkness.

He turned about to mark his distance from the church, but in horror recognized that he has lost sight of the church and could no longer recognize the cross illuminated in the darkness. Then a quick breeze came that extinguished his torch despite his vain attempt to protect it. He now was completely blind so he struggled forward just on instinct. He mumbled a pray to the Lord, "Okay, Lord, I trust you even though I can no longer see any signs of your presence."

In complete darkness, he continued moving about, feeling it was better to keep on moving than to sit still and give into the darkness. He tried to keep his mind occupied as there was nothing for his eyes to set on. He turned to prayer running over in his mind the penitential psalms. However, the darkness came to wear on him during the hours. It seemed as if the strange fog started physically to weigh him down; each step became more and more difficult. He was tempted to stop, but felt he would become completely immobilized if he were to remain still, so he continued. He called out to the Lord in the darkness, "Are you there? Do you see my struggles?"

He heard no response, but went on anyway as he continued to recite the penitential psalms.

"O Lord, do not reprove me in Thy wrath, nor in Thy anger chastise me. Have mercy on me, Lord, for I am weak, heal me, Lord, for my body is in torment. And my soul is greatly troubled, but Thou, O Lord, how long? Turn to me, O Lord, and deliver my soul; save me on account of Thy mercy."[41]

As the night reached its peak, the dragon's unseen foe finally let up on it. Unbeknownst to the dragon, its foe had driven it right to the field where George was doing his vigil. The dragon took a moment to regain its strength and stopped in midair circling around, as it inspected the health of its wings that had suffered torture from the unknown assailant. It circled slowly about as it could now make out the moonlight starting to peek through the fog. It followed the light down to the earth below. At the same time, George peered up at the moonlight, which was the first thing in the sky he had seen break through the darkness. Right then the dragon's eyes met George's and the beast became fixed on him. The dragon recognized George from its many battles with the battalion and his attack in its lair. Driven by instinct, it now equated George with the unknown foe that had been harassing it and dove quickly down on him.

The dragon threw out a long flame of fire while it drove straight down on George like a falcon seeking its prey. Seeing his peril George quickly drew his sword and shield, and took up a defensive position crouching low to the ground. The dragon crashed into his shield attempting to crush George with its weight. The attack knocked George to the ground, but he withstood the blow unharmed. The dragon then clawed at George with its legs but George drove the beast back with his sword.

Right before the dragon was about to drive the claws of its hind legs into his shield, George leaped to the side hiding in the darkness. The dragon shot out a long flame in the same direction. George, however, had already dashed to another spot. The dragon turned about in that direction as the brief light from its flame illuminated the area showing it where its prey was dashing. It threw another flame at George. However, he had receded more deeply into the darkness, so the dragon could not locate him. In a rage, the dragon whipped its head in a full circle throwing a long flame in all directions. However, the beast did not hit its mark as George was now well out of its range.

The dragon took again to the air and roamed around trying to track its prey. George dashed back and forth in a zigzag motion so the dragon could not follow its path. The dragon remained circling intently squinting into the darkness, waiting for the moonlight to break through and illuminate its sight. George started again to recite the penitential psalms:

"Out of the depths have I cried unto Thee, O Lord: Lord hear my voice. Let Thine ears be attentive to the voice of my supplication."[42]

The dragon finally spotted George and drove like a bird of prey straight for him spewing a river of fire. George raised his shield above him protecting himself from the fire and the claws of the beast, but the weight of the beast again knocked him over. Once more, the dragon circled around until it spotted George and dove upon him with the same result. Deep into the night, George and the beast battled, but none could get the better. At times George was able to catch his breath by hiding in the darkness, but after a while, the dragon would find him by the moonlight or the short illumination from its fiery breath. Repeatedly they clashed until both were exhausted. Finally, George found a crevice in a rock under which he could hide, and the dragon gave up searching for a while so it to could rest and recuperate. George slumped over there exhausted and uncertain. He called out to the Lord, "When will this end? Will you not give me some relief from the beast?"

After a long respite, the dragon finally spotted George hiding under the rock and the battle continued. George felt almost desperate as he realized there was no way he could take the offensive against the dragon. He could not reach into the sky and pull the beast down to the earth, engaging it as he did in the cave. All he could do now was to shield himself and flee into the darkness like a prairie dog chased by a ferocious predator. Right up until dawn the exhausting match between hunter and prey continued. Finally, the moon faded away as the day came and the dark fog set in again providing cover for George. To protect himself from an accidental encounter he found the cleft of a rock and lay down to sleep for a while.

Elsewhere in the kingdom on that Saturday night, the people were turning their hearts to prayer, out of fear of the blackness they turned to repent of their sins. In homes all across the kingdom, mothers held their children tightly as they saw the darkness remain over their land. Fearing the sight one child called out, "What can we do mother?"

The mother replied, "Honey, in the face of this darkness all we can do is pray."

Meanwhile, she turned her eyes longingly toward her husband, as if he could provide the family some security. The husband noticed the glance, but was busy scanning the horizon through the window. As he realized he could see nothing, he then embraced both mother and child saying, "Yes, today all we can do is pray and repent for our sins. This is a work of God, only He can help us now."

In far the eastern edge of the kingdom, George woke up trying to remember where he was and somehow determine what time it was. The darkness made this task nearly impossible. However, as his senses came back to him, he realized that the dragon must be near. He prayed for strength and the help of God. As if an answer to his prayer, he saw a small pool not far off reflecting light from an unknown source. He crept silently to the pool feeling as if he was almost dying from thirst and exhaustion. He plunged into the pool and came out feeling life rush back into him. This mysteriously satisfied him completely, causing him to recall Elijah in the desert fed by the angel with bread and drink after which he walked for forty days on that food alone. Reflecting on this he thought, "I see, Lord, thank you for sending me your angel tonight. Certainly he has refreshed me as Elijah was nourished in the desert."

George now strengthened for the battle, moved away from the rock formation during what should be the daylights hours of Saturday. He had to creep along in the darkness for he could barely see beyond his hands, so dark was it. In the darkness, he prayed and waited, asking God, "What do want me to do now, Lord?"

Yet, all seemed silent—George lived in the silence for a while—then he whispered another prayer pleading for God's assistance, but there was only stillness and darkness. Fantasies floated into George's thoughts. Dark and oppressive images seemed to press against him. It was if they touched his very soul. His soul seemed to be enclosed by the darkness, his intellect became clouded and unclear, his will alone seemed to be untouched allowing him to drive himself forward. He spoke to himself, "Keep going forward, keep moving; keep trusting in the Lord."

Dark images continued to creep about him and they seemed to tear courage right from his soul. He felt a deep sense of despair, and started to doubt his faith in God. However, he pressed his hand against his chest and repeated to himself, "I believe. I believe. I believe!" The doubts persisted and he was not sure whether these were within his soul or coming from the outside. All was dark.

He pondered these images asking, "Are these demons? Can demons twist ones souls from the interior as this darkness does? How is it that my soul can be affected by this darkness, it is not made of matter like this fog? Is this darkness real, or just inside of me? I can see nothing; I sense nothing; all is dark. This is what I know, but I believe in you Lord through the darkness."

George then poured though his memories trying to grab onto to something that could make sense of his present reality. He looked through his past actions seeing them now, as if from afar, like eyeing an old chronicle of tales that one found on a bookshelf. He searched through this bookshelf for what might be causing his current malaise. He felt like a doctor examining a patient before him, as it were disconnected from himself. He thus examined himself, "Who is this person that I ponder? Is it I? I can feel this person's arms and legs. Yet, why does my mind seem so disconnected from this body in the midst of this darkness?"

He flexed his arms and legs, but his confusion continued. He heard voices in his head asking, "Did you really see an angel? Is God really leading you? Is God not really a mist like that which passes before your eyes now?"

With all his strength of will, he drove off these thoughts saying to himself, "No they were real. I will follow you whatever you ask, Lord." Yet fear and uncertainty pressed upon him. When he tried to recall the visions he had of St. Michael and the Blessed Virgin Mary, the face of demons appeared in their place. He tried to dismiss these images and recall the face of Jesus, yet this seemed obscured in a fog. He asked himself then, "Am I going mad?"

Meanwhile, homes and business across the kingdom remained alit kindled by the sacred flame from the blessed candles that broke through the darkness. In the Cathedral likewise, all was dark, save the flickering of the blessed flames; the bishop seeing this brought out the great candle to give people a more prominent sign of hope. He had the deacon hold it up before all and proclaim, "This is the Light of Christ. Come let us worship."

Right at that moment, the dark fog upon the kingdom started to dissipate and souls looked up with hope as they could sense the darkness lifting. Souls then streamed into the cathedral recognizing that the mysterious light that dissipated the darkness was emanating from this location. As the light from the great candle was mysteriously magnified it even reached the corridors of the palace. A little while later, the peasants who faithfully filled the cathedral were surprised to see Princess Procuvera making her way there, for she normally only worshiped in the palace chapel.

The crowds parted, making way for the noble princess to enter. However, Procuvera halted before entering when she noticed Maria; the old woman slowly making her away through the masses into the cathedral. The good princess stopped, struck by the simple dignity and inner radiance of this old woman struggling along. She put out her arm saying, "Please, madam, let me help you to your seat. Take my arm and we will walk together."

Maria looked sidewise at who it was that offered her help as if taking in the soul of the princess. She seemed to recognize in that gaze not only Procuvera's royal dignity, but her true virtue and kindliness. She replied with the most pleasant of voices, "Yes, true princess, you can help me in. Let us together pray for the kingdom tonight."

As Maria entered the cathedral holding the arm of Procuvera, a change came over the continence of Maria. To the onlookers it seemed as if her face grew younger, her simple clothes seemed to sparkle, her back straightened up, and she unloosed her arm from the hold of the princess. Now both walked together with a quiet dignity that drew the attention of others in the cathedral.

Together they made their way in a slow procession of beauty and virtue, a true princess and true wisdom. A simple peasant, looking on the scene thought, "Ah, how they look alike. I have never before noticed the hidden beauty of this Maria, which seemed lost in the wrinkles of her face. Yet, today she looks as magnificent as Procuvera, as if Maria were of the same noble blood."

A little later, without anyone noticing, the King also slipped into the cathedral to pray and seek repentance for his sins. Though escorted by two servants, no one recognized his royal person as he chose to dress like one of his servants. He borrowed this garb from one of his humble servants so to give himself more over to penance. He had come to recognize that the coming of the dragon was his fault. Now he knew he must do penance to make up for his poor stewardship of the kingdom; he knew he must do penance for allowing this beast to reign under his rule.

The King quietly took a seat amongst the faithful and turned his heart over to prayer. A peasant next to him was struck by wonder at the figure kneeling before him, as he heard the King start into the Lamentations of Jeremiah, "How lonely sits the city that was full of people! How like a widow has she become, she that was great among the nations! ...."

Meanwhile, George was still struggling in the darkness. He fought to get out a few words welling up from his oppressed heart, but something seemed to stifle his attempt. Then with a tremendous effort, he wrenched a sound from the depths of his soul exclaiming, "Mother Mary, help me!" Immediately, afterward he felt his soul clear a bit and poured forth a desperate plea to the Virgin's Son, "Jesus, my Lord and God, have mercy on me a sinner."

At the very same moment, the archbishop was bringing his prayers to a high point and intoning the "Gloria in Excelesis Deo..." When the heavens responded with a large thunderclap and the skies were lit up above the kingdom.

Hearing the thunder, a few souls peeked out to see what made the noise as it sounded like thunder. They could see the lightning flickering off to the east...

At the same time, George felt the heaviness lifting from him as he too heard the sound of a thunderclap. He smiled as he looked up into the heavens exclaiming, "Oh good Mother, thank you for bringing my prayer to your Son. Good, Holy Spirit, I hear your voice roaring in the sound of the heavens above!"

He then took courage recognizing that the thunderclap marked the end of the darkness. Soon, he saw the fog lift entirely from the area, as he heard more thunderclaps and saw lightning streak through the air. His senses became completely alert as he beheld this heavenly chorus. He rejoiced in this chorus and admired it with awe. The dragon though was not in awe. The thunderclaps awoke the beast, jolting it to attention.

Archbishop Romanus recognizing the Spirit at work in the heavens, called out to the assembly, "Look to the East!"

The archbishop then directed the people to intercede for the kingdom as he called down the presence of the Lord. As the deacon billowed out incense before the Altar of the Lord, the archbishop called out,

"O merciful Lord, have mercy on us and help us. My Lord, pardon, purify, forget and blot out our faults and be not mindful of them; by thine infinite mercy, put away our terrible sins which are innumerable, and the sins of thy faithful people. Look kindly upon us."

"Have mercy upon us, our fathers, brothers, masters, superiors. Pardon, our dead and all the faithful departed, sons of the holy and glorious Church."

"Give rest, O Lord God, to their souls and bodies that the dew of thy mercies may refresh their members. Pardon us, O Christ, our King and our God, Lord full of glory, hear us and hasten to succor and deliver us."

"Accept our prayers, keep from us, O God, cruel punishments; do not retaliate upon us, make us worthy of eternal happiness."

"O God, Lord of all things, who didst receive the sacrifice of thanksgiving from all those who call upon thee with all their hearts, accept this incense which is offered to thee by the hands of thy miserable servants."[43]

The people felt the presence of God come into their midst in a powerful way. All bent their heads in reverence at the coming of the Lord. Some even prostrated face down before the glory of the Lord, as they felt the Almighty coming down upon them in a way greater than the holy Shekinah that hovered over the Jewish temple of old.

After the presence of the Lord came in full, the archbishop gave thanks to the Lord. Then inspired by the Holy Spirit, he entered into the fight with dragon from afar calling out to the infernal beast,

"See the cross of the Lord, oh dragon; be gone, you hostile power! In the name and by the power of our Lord Jesus Christ, We, by the power of our office, command you, be gone, and fly far from the Church of God, fly away from the souls made by God in His image and redeemed by the precious blood of the divine Lamb."

"No longer, dare, cunning serpent, to deceive us, to persecute God's Church. Therefore, accursed dragon and every diabolical legion, we adjure you by the living God, by the true God, by the holy God, by God, who so loved the world that He gave His only-begotten Son, that whoever believes in Him might not perish but have everlasting life. Cease deluding human creatures and filling them with the poison of everlasting damnation; desist from harming the Church and hampering her freedom."

"Be gone, Satan, who appears to us in the form of a dragon, father and master of lies, enemy of man's welfare. Give place to Christ, in whom you found none of your works. Give way to the one, holy, catholic, and apostolic Church, which Christ Himself purchased with His blood."

"Bow down, oh dragon, before God's mighty hand, tremble and flee as we call on the holy and awesome name of Jesus before whom the denizens of hell cower, to whom the heavenly Virtues and Powers, and Dominations are subject, whom the Cherubim and Seraphim praise with unending cries as they sing: 'Holy, holy, holy, Lord God of Sabaoth.'"[44]

After this impassioned prayer, Archbishop Romanus arose and called out, "Let us go forth in the name of the Lord! I feel the Lord calling us to the East to the place of the rising sun. This is where we will encounter the victory of our Lord, the true Easter of our salvation."

Then taking hold of the great candle, he led the people in a procession out the doors toward the East; the people followed along in a great procession carrying their candles enkindled by the blessed flame. It was a glorious sight to see the people exiting through the magnificent gilded golden doors, off to the side of the altar. The gilded door shimmered beautifully as the light from the candles reflected off it.

# Chapter 18

# *The Day of the Lord confronts the dragon*

B ack on the battlefield, the dragon was very agitated, for it had not slept much being constantly afflicted by a foreboding sense. The darkness was its home, but the dark fog had pressed upon it and now the lightning greatly disturbed it, inserting notes of light into the dark background. When the fog finally lifted after several hours, the beast now remembered its prey and sought George again with intensity. For the dragon, it seemed now this search was the only reason for its existence, so intent was it on destroying George. The dragon thus raced into the air as its eyes surveyed the area for the slightest movement.

George saw the battle was on again as he recognized the eyes of the dragon searching intently from the skies above. He knew now he was vulnerable to the dragon's attacks because it had perfect night vision and George still could do nothing but defend himself. George hid anxiously under the rock cleft, hoping it would protect him from the searching eyes of the beast. He turned to the Lord in his anxiety, "Lord, I cannot defeat this beast alone. You must help me."

Soon though, George's eyes met the dragon's eyes as it spotted George hiding under the cleft from a distance. George thus sprinted out from his hiding place trying to zigzag back and forth to throw off vision of the dragon. As he raced in the darkness of the night, he repeated a prayer out of desperation, "Lord Jesus, Son of God, have mercy on me a sinner. Lord Jesus, Son of God, have mercy on me a sinner."

The dragon, however, was not thrown off by George's zigzagging and followed him along. As it drew close, it started its familiar dive down upon him, but just as it was in range to spew out its fiery breath, lightning bolted from the sky and struck the beast's wing causing it to crash to the ground. George seeing this raced off a distance from the crash site. He then looked back and rejoiced saying to the Lord, "Thank you Lord, I see you are fighting for me now."

Slowly the beast revived itself after the terrible crash. After a little while the dragon rose up, checked its wings and seeing them still in intact, started to ascend to continue its pursuit. Before it got a few feet off the ground, however, huge ice balls started to fall from the sky; one stuck the dragon squarely on the head driving it back to the ground. George looked up and could see massive hail heading his way. He raced to try to get out of the path of the hail toward a close by that barn that seemed to offer some protection. Meanwhile, the beast tried again to ascend but felt the hail driving it back to the ground with every attempt. It seemed to the beast that this was no normal hail but rather like fireballs crashing into it, for each hit burned its skin. Flailing and howling the beast struggled to the only shelter in the area, the same barn in which George was hiding.

George, who was peering outside at the storm, noticed the dragon likewise struggling to make it to the barn. Recognized an opportunity, he positioned himself for an ambush and prayed that the Lord will guide his sword. The dragon dragged itself up to the threshold of the barn door where George waited hidden around the corner. As the dragon puts its head through the door, George struck it; however, just as in the cave, he did not pierce through the skin of the beast, but only managed to knock off a few scales without piercing the body. George, disappointed drew back, while the dragon now aware of George spewed forth a torrent of fire at him. Quickly, George put up his shield blocking the fireball from consuming him.

The dragon then drove into the barn, destroying the side of the barn as it burst through the doorway. Immediately it began to snap at George's shield with its mighty jaw to get at its prey. George, seeing the tactic of the dragon, backed further into the barn. The dragon in a rage spewed a flood of flames in all directions seeking to destroy everything in sight, thus causing most of the barn to catch flame. The dragon now had George cornered; for, he could not flee through the door as the dragon was blocking it, and he could not maneuver as the barn was all alit around him. He looked in desperation for a way out and spotted a loft still accessibly by a ladder; quickly he ascended it. Right at this moment, the hailstorm started to dissipate.

The dragon seeing George cornered in the loft spewed forth another mighty flame in all directions, so that now everything in the barn was alit save the far small corner where George was taking refuge. In a last bold move, George tried to charge right at the beast and through to the exit, but he saw now that a wall of flames blocked his way. George called out from the flames, "Lord Jesus, help me."

George looked around for a way out and spotted a shaft door that he saw was now his only hope to escape the flames encompassing him on all sides. As he struggled to open the shaft door, he noticed that the whole barn was creaking as if about to collapse in on itself. The dragon, seeing George cornered and feeling the flames now encompassing it, likewise retreated to the exit. With its last glance at George, it saw him racing toward the shaft door. The beast following its instincts then raced out of the barn to meet George on the other side of the shaft door.

As George opened the shaft door, he noticed that he could not see the ground through the darkness of the night; the thought ran through his mind, "It must be twenty feet or more down there and I would surely break a leg or other bones if I jumped, but I have no other choice."

Just as he was summing up the courage to jump, the beast's face appeared right in front of him. Right at that moment, the dawn was just starting to peek over the horizon, as the two stood confronting each other face-to-face, not more than a few feet away. The dragon immediately spewed out a fiery breath at George. The heroic warrior, quick as lightning, turned his shield in front of him to protect him from the flame. Again, the beast spewed its fiery breath and again George protected himself behind his shield. He knew, however, he had but precious few seconds to carry on this fight for the barn was teetering as if ready to collapse. The dragon frustrated that George remained unharmed behind his shield became enraged and the beast snapped at it with its jaw. To George's horror, the dragon managed to rip his shield, Fidelus, right from his hands.

For a moment, George lost hope, for he knew he could not retreat and now it seemed Fidelus, his faithful shield, had failed him. Then in a flash, it all came together as he saw the dragon struggling to free the shield from its jaw. He thought, 'Fidelus' of course means 'faith' and he remembered the verse that Jesus had given him:

**"When the darkness seems to encompass you and even hope seems to be lost, so that even your faith is taken away from you; then is the time to leap into the darkness and strike at the neck of the dragon."**

He knew now what the words meant and raised his sword high above his head to strike at the neck of the beast. *He leapt into the darkness* thrusting at the soft fold in the neck of the dragon, just as the beast bent its head back trying to dislodge the shield from its jaw. He knew he must land the blow squarely or die, for either the fall would kill him or the fiery breath of the dragon would consume him when the beast finally dislodged the shield. George's faith did not fail him, as the sword drove deeply into the dragon's neck. Feeling the pain of the blade piercing into its neck, the dragon flailed back and forth trying to throw George from the sword handle. He, however, hung on with all his might as the dragon struggled mightily, driving the sword deeper into the beast's throat as it fought him.

The dragon, which was standing on its hind legs, finally succumbed and fell straight back allowing George to drive his sword completely through the beast's throat and clean into the ground. The edge then set firmly into the earth as the dragon landed with a thud, while the shield remained lodged in its jaw. Thus, the dragon died with the shield, Fidelus, stuck in its jaw, the sword driven through its neck and George lying on its chest.

As George stood over the carcass of the beast, he saw the sun peeking over the crest of the eastern horizon. It was a beautiful Sunday morning with no cloud in the sky. Just then, he noticed a vast crowd coming toward him in a prayerful procession led by Archbishop Romanus. He noticed some familiar faces right behind the archbishop, the good Princess Procuvera with Maria and the King, dressed in the garb of a humble servant. As the King approached, he removed his hat and bowed acknowledging the true champion in his kingdom. George then smiled as he recognized Sergius, standing proudly with his new sword at his side. Right beside him were Bacchus and Kathleen who smiled back at George when he saw them. Unbeknownst to George, the King had decreed on Saturday the release of all those imprisoned by the wizards and that they and all their cohorts be driven from the kingdom.

As the crowd approached, George could hear them singing a song of joy for the risen Lord who had conquered:

> Glory to God! The morn appointed breaks,
> And earth awakes from all the woeful past;
> For, with the morn, the Lord of Life awakes,
> And sin and death into the grave are cast.

> Glory to God! The cross, with all its shame,
> Now sheds its glory o'er a ransomed world;
> For He who bore the burden of our blame,
> With pierced hands the foe to hell hath hurled.

> Glory to God! Sing ransomed souls again,
> And let your songs our glorious Victor laud,
> Who by His might hath snapped the tyrant's chain,
> And set us free to rise with Him to God.

> Darkness and night, farewell! The morn is here;

Welcome! The light that ushers in the day;
Visions of joy before our sight appear,
And like the clouds, our sorrows melt away.

Great Son of God, Immortal and renowned!
Brighter than morn the glory on Thy brow;
Crowns must be won, and Thou art nobly crowned,
For death is dead, and the beast is vanquished now. [45]

The sword lay thus stuck in the dragon's throat as a small breeze blew through the area refreshing everyone present. The whole crowd then stared at the cross-shaped sword thrust through the neck of the dragon as it swayed slightly in the cool breeze. The sword shined brightly as the first notes of daylight reflected off it. All was calm and the heavens were rejoicing for Christ had conquered.

# *Epilogue*

For a whole week after the defeat of the dragon, the kingdom celebrated with a feast, the likes of which the kingdom had never seen before. The people celebrated with a childlike joy, for they now recognized what God had given to them. Every day, for a whole week, they had parties more joyful than any of the pagan festivals they were known to organize for tourists, for their joy came from within, planted there by the Holy Spirit. They had no need for drunkenness, debauchery or the selling of fine wares for their experience of God satisfied all their desires so that they did not need anything else. They decorated the streets with fine works of chalk art and paper figurines to show their appreciation for Christ overcoming the beast. Many a household contributed making their own decorations, and businesses vied with one another to sponsor floats for great parades.

The sword stayed where George planted it, stuck right through the dragon's throat and set firmly in the ground. That Sunday, George had given a little oration saying, "This sword was meant for this battle and thus here it will remain. Let the sword stay here as a reminder of what came upon this kingdom, because the people of this land gave themselves over to sinful debauchery, and sacrificed even their innocent little ones to protect their hedonistic lifestyle. Let it stand here driven through the carcass of this dead dragon as a monument to how hard the struggle was to overcome such a beast once you allowed it to enter into your land.

Tell your children why it is here and command them to tell their grandchildren and likewise to tell their children after them. Never let this plague come upon your land again, but if you lose memory of this battle and another such dragon comes upon your land, let some hero take up this sword again to fight the dragon with the help of

Christ. This shield, however, I will take for myself. For I have many more battles to fight and I need this shield of faith to watch over me."

Thus, it was that the people left the sword stuck in the ground thrust through the neck of the beast. The carcass they left in place also to rot as it lay. Days went by, then weeks, months and the sword was left there in the now bare bones of the beast. Following George's advice, parents would come on pilgrimage to the sight to explain to their children the battle that took place there and told them about the great knight who, trusting in Christ, defeated the dragon.

Thereafter, the people lived in joy and peace for they made the worship of God the center of their kingdom, giving him their whole heart and soul. They were devoted in all they did to following Christ and protecting the innocent little ones of their society. They now looked with great care after the elderly, the little babies, and gave help to any woman who found herself pregnant out of wedlock because of the monsters that raged around her.

Years passed, and then decades, generation after generation in the kingdom of Terrasindei repeated the story of George and the dragon, fathers told their children and grandfathers their grandchildren. Thus, the kingdom remained in peace free from the affliction of any wild beasts; parents hearkened after their children and young people to their elders.

In time, George went off and fought many other great battles for the Lord. The Lord gave him new swords to fight these battles, while he held onto to the precious shield of faith given to him during the battle with the dragon, which protected him through everything. He fought bravely in all these battles, always seeking to know the spirit of the Lord and live the way of Christ in truth. After many years, he fought his last battle winning the greatest of contests; an evil King imprisoned him, tortured and killed him, through it all, he remained faithful to Christ. Thus, he was crowned a martyr for the faith and now he enjoys the great feast of heaven as an honored guest at the banquet. Sergius as well as Bacchus became great warriors for Christ winning the same crown as George.

Centuries past and the memory of George's battle with the dragon slipped into tales; fewer and fewer came to the sight to tell their children of the great battle and in time, the place was given over to the wilderness. Thus, the story of George and the dragon passed from history into legend. The sword, still stuck through the skeleton of the dragon, slowly disappeared from sight hidden due to the tall grass growing around it as did the bones of the beast, which dirt covered over blown by the wind.

Thus, we now come to our day and they say St. George never existed, and he certainly never fought a dragon *for beasts like this do not exist, nor ever did.* Therefore, the innocent little ones are sacrificed again to the dragon of our times that is much more ferocious then the one George fought. I tell you though, St. George was real, as was his sword, and so was his fight with a dragon. For, if one were to look hard enough, they could find that forgotten field where the sword still sways stuck into ground through the bones of an old beast. I tell you too, this sword remains unsullied and sharp just as on the day it pierced the head of the dragon by George's hand. It is ready now to be wielded again if only a new hero could be found.

## Invocation of St. George

O FAITHFUL servant of God and invincible Martyr, St. George; favored by God with the gift of faith, and inflamed with an ardent love of Christ, thou didst fight valiantly against the dragon of pride, falsehood, and deceit. Neither pain, nor torture, sword, nor death, could part thee from the love of Christ. I fervently implore thee for the sake of this love to help me by thy intercession to overcome the temptations that surround me, and to bear bravely the trials that oppress me, so that I may patiently carry the cross which is placed upon me; and let neither distress nor difficulties separate me from the love of Our Lord Jesus Christ. Valiant champion of the Faith, assist me in the combat against evil, that I may win the crown promised to them that persevere unto the end.

Imprimatur, Imprimi Potest and Nihil Obstat.

This prayer is an excerpted from "Novena in honor of St. George" in Hammer, Bonaventure. *The Fourteen Holy Helpers: Early Christian Saints Who Are Powerful with God : Including Novena Prayers.* Rockford, Ill: Tan Books and Publishers, 1995.

## Endnotes

[1] See the legendary tale *Beowulf.* The demon in the tale was named 'Grendel' and his mother in old English was named 'Aglæca.'

[2] Wisdom 13:3. The bible quotes are from The New American Bible (NAB) translation unless otherwise noted. Confraternity of Christian Doctrine, Catholic Church, and United States Catholic Conference. *The New American Bible.* Nashville: Catholic Bible Press, a division of Thomas Nelson Publishers, 1987.

[3] 1 Peter 5:8-9.

[4] See St. John Chrysostom, "Homily XXIV" on Romans. In this paragraph, he is condemning contraception. Contraceptives were known in the ancient world. See Dioscorides, *De Materia Medica,* Galen in *De simplicium medicamentorum* 6.3 to 9.18. *Soranus' Gynecology*, Bk. 1, 63. He speaks of methods of herbal contraceptives taken orally.

[5] Genesis 4:7.

[6] Jeremiah 6:16.

[7] St. Peter Chrysologus, *Saint Peter Chrysologus Selected Sermons and Saint Valerian Homilies*, Volume 1, sermon 155, trans. George E. Gans S.J. Washington D.C.: Catholic University Press, 1953, 264.

[8] Jeremiah 6:16.

[9] Job 1:7.

[10] Jeremiah 6:17.

[11] Colossians 1:24.

[12] Proverbs 1:7.

[13] Psalm 95:39-40.

[14] Jeremiah 6:15, 26.

[15] Derived from the prayer "Oblation of love" by St. Ignatius of Loyola, see his *Spiritual Exercises.*

[16] This description comes from some who claim mystical visions of the Life of St. Philomena. While recognition of her cult as a saint was approved by many popes and promoted by St. John Vianney, these visions were not the subject of official investigation.

[17] Archaeologists found these ornaments on the tomb of "Filomena" with indications that she was a martyr and venerated for her heroic witness. For more information about what we know about her and the papal

pronouncements          about          her          see          the          website
www.philomena.org/patroness.asp.

[18] See Hebrews 4:12-13.

[19] See Daniel 13:23-30. "Bel and the Dragon."

[20] Wisdom 18:5.

[21] *"Non est infans. Tua optio est. Recte facis fetu interficiendo. Solum pars matris ipsius est. Matri ipsi licet abortum parare. Fetus non est humanus."* (letters reversed in each word)

[22] *Solvo feminae. Servo suum vox electrum. Solvo vox ut parvulum abortum.*

[23] *"Libera feminas. Serva ius eorum optandi. Fetum feminis per tu interficere liceat."*

[24] 1 Kings 22:19-23.

[25] Isaiah 53:2.

[26] Proverbs, 25:4-5.

[27] 1 Peter 5:8-9.

[28] 1 Peter 4:10-11, Revised Standard Translation (RSV) Catholic Biblical Association (Great Britain). *The Holy Bible: Revised Standard Version, Catholic Edition,* San Francisco: Ignatius Press, 1994.

[29] Sirach 2:1-3;5-6.

[30] James 1:2.

[31] From St. Irenaeus *Against Heresies,* The text in italics is the basis for the song. *"The glory of God gives life; those who see God receive life...Men will therefore see God if they are to live; through the vision of God they become immortal and attain to God himself... God is the source of all activity throughout creation. He cannot be seen or described in his own nature and in all his greatness by any of his creatures. Yet he is certainly not unknown.* Through his Word the whole creation learns that there is one God the Father, who holds all things together and gives them their being. As it is written in the Gospel, No man has ever seen God, except the only-begotten Son, who is in the bosom of the Father; he has revealed him. From the beginning the Son is the one who teaches us about the Father; he is with the Father from the beginning. He was to reveal to the human race visions of prophecy, the diversity of spiritual gifts, his own ways of ministry, the glorification of the Father, all in due order and harmony, at the appointed time and for our instruction. Where there is order, there is also harmony; where there is harmony, there is also correct timing; where there is correct timing, there is also advantage.

The Word became the steward of the Father's grace for the advantage of men, for whose benefit he made such wonderful arrangements. He revealed

God to men and presented men to God. He safeguarded the invisibility of the Father to prevent man from treating God with contempt and to set before him a constant goal toward which to make progress. On the other hand, he revealed God to men and made him visible in many ways to prevent man from being totally separated from God and so cease to be. Life in man is the glory of God; the life of man is the vision of God. If the revelation of God through creation gives life to all who live upon the earth, much more does the manifestation of the Father through the Word give life to those who see God."

From *Against the Heresies* Bk. 4, 20-5-7. Saint Irenaeus. This quote is from. *The Liturgy of the Hours: According to the Roman Rite. 3, Ordinary Time, Weeks 1 - 17*. New York, NY: Catholic Book Publ, 2009.

[32] From Sub Tuum Praesidium prayer said to date from the 3rd century. "Under your mercy we take refuge, Mother of God, do not reject our supplications in necessity. But deliver us from danger. Alone chaste, alone blessed."

[33] In "Our Pantheistic Sisters," Anne Barbeau Gardiner, Review of *Green Sisters: A Spiritual Ecology* by Sarah McFarland Taylor, *New Oxford Review*, Volume LXXV, Number 2, February 2008. Downloaded from http://www.newoxfordreview.org/ January 2013.

[34] See Luke 14:31.

[35] From the triple sanctus before the Eucharistic prayer of the Mass. Inspired by Revelation 4:8.

[36] See Revelation Chapter 4 and 5.

[37] *The Anaphora of St. James*, cf. *Praeceptis salutaribus moniti* of the Roman rite. I Quoted in chapter II the "Syrian Rite" of *The Rites of Eastern Christendom*, vol. 1, by Archdale King, (Gorgias Press, Piscataway, NJ: 2007), 185. I changed the phrase in the original translation "[of] the seraphim" to "[by] the seraphim." This is ancient Eucharistic prayer still in use by some Eastern Rite Churches.

[38] See Revelation chapter 12.

[39] John 11:47.

[40] Psalm 22 RSV translation.

[41] Psalm 6.

[42] Psalm 129.

[43] Excerpt from the, *The Liturgy of St. James*, Quoted in chapter II the "Syrian Rite" of *The Rites of Eastern Christendom*, vol. 1, by Archdale King, Piscataway,

NJ: Gorgias Press, 2007, 154. This is an excerpt from one the most ancient anaphora or "Eucharistic Prayers" as we call them in the west.

[44] Excerpt from the "Exorcism of Place" in Chapter III "Exorcism of Satan and the Fallen Angels" in the Catholic Church, and Philip T. Weller. *The Roman Ritual.* Milwaukee: Bruce Pub. Co, 1964, 659-662. The author modified the prayer somewhat for dramatic effect. This prayer should only be used by priests who have authorization from their bishop.

[45] John Brownlie "Easter" 10,10,10,10, in Brownlie, John. *Hymns of the Early Church, Translated from Greek and Latin Sources; Together with Translations from a Later Period; Centos and Suggestions from the Greek; and Several Original Pieces.* London: Morgan & Scott, ld, 1913. I changed the original language in the last line from "sin" to "beast."